THE PRIMACY OF VISION IN VIRGIL'S *Aeneid*

THE PRIMACY OF VISION IN VIRGIL's *Aeneid*

Riggs Alden Smith

UNIVERSITY OF TEXAS PRESS

AUSTIN

Requests for permission to reproduce material from this work
should be sent to Permissions, University of Texas Press,
P.O. Box 7819, Austin, TX 78713–7819.

∞ The paper used in this book meets the minimum requirements of
ANSI/NISO Z39.48–1992 (R1997) (Permanence of Paper).

LIBRARY OF CONGRESS CATALOGING-IN-PUBLICATION DATA
Smith, Alden.
The primacy of vision in Virgil's *Aeneid* / Riggs Alden Smith.— 1st ed.
p.   cm.
Includes bibliographical references and index.
ISBN: 978-0-292-72622-2
1. Virgil. Aeneis.   2. Aeneas (Legendary character) in literature.
3. Epic poetry, Latin—History and criticism.   4. Visual perception in
literature.   5. Art and literature—Rome.   6. Visions in literature.
7. Rome—In literature.   8. Vision in literature.   I. Title.
PA6825.S63 2005
873'.01—dc22
2004028381

❦

Dianae,

meae uitae,

forsan et haec olim meminisse iuuabit.

Contents

✵

Preface and Acknowledgments

❦

My desire to consider vision in the *Aeneid* is in part derived from an interest in ancient art that I first cultivated at the Intercollegiate Center for Classical Studies in Rome, a program that I attended as an undergraduate under Mary Sturgeon and Fred Albertson. My own research about ecphrasis, which I considered in my first book, also influenced my consideration of the topic of vision in the *Aeneid*. Based on my preliminary studies, I gave papers at Princeton, Yale, Wesleyan, Columbia, Notre Dame of Maryland, Austin College, Texas Tech, Monmouth College, the University of Texas at Austin, the University of Vermont, and later, at Penn and Colorado. While only a little of the specific content of any of these lectures has come into this book, the development of my methodology is owed to them, and I wish to thank each of those departments for a warm reception and lively discussion. To Denis Feeney, David Quint, Jim O'Hara, Gareth Williams, Sister Thérèse Dougherty, Robert Cape, Edward George, Karl Galinsky, Tom Sienkewicz, Phil Ambrose, Joe Farrell, and Peter Knox, and all their colleagues, I express my gratitude here.

I wish to thank the committees for research grants and sabbaticals at Baylor University, for without a respite from my duties at Baylor and without adequate financial support I could not have undertaken this project; special thanks to Wallace Daniel, Thomas Hibbs, David Jeffrey, Donald Schmeltekopf, and Robert Sloan for support, encouragement, and vision. I would also like to thank Tommye Lou Davis for taking over as acting chair of the department in my absence.

I wrote this book in Philadelphia, where I used the resources of the University of Pennsylvania's Van Pelt Library. I wish to thank the kind librarians there, as well as those of Moody Library at Baylor and of the Classics Library at the University of Texas at Austin (particularly Bonnie) for timely assistance throughout this project. I thank my mother, too, for allowing me to stay with her in New Hope, Pennsylvania, so that I could take advantage of her home's proximity to the Penn campus. My own gentle colleagues at Baylor have been of great support and have offered numerous editorial insights. I acknowledge all of them for encouragement, among whom are Tommye Lou Davis, Daniel Eady, Chris Flood, Kevin Hawthorne, Carol King, John Nordling, and Amy Vail. Those who read and edited sizeable portions of the manuscript include Antony Augoustakis, Julia Dyson, Jeff Fish, Brent Froberg, Aaron Johnson, and John Thorburn. Megan Mauldin, my assistant in the University Scholars Program, was of great help in the final stages of this project. I also thank Richard Duran for insightful suggestions and Paulette Edwards for logistical support. My colleagues' observations have much improved this project.

My former students, too, have offered comments, suggestions, and encouragement. Among many I would like to thank Angeline Chiu, Jason Gajderowicz, Dan Hanchey, Dustin Heinen, Jeff Hunt, Leslie Hutton, Sean Mathis, Amanda Seamans-Mathis, and Michael Sloan. My current students, some of whom have studied Virgil with me and have read a previous version of this book, offered several insights. These students are Katie Calloway, Rosalyn Chan, Jonathan Dunbar, Lesley-Anne Dyer, Cory Elliott, Erik Ellis, Lindsay Fuller, Martin Gallagher, Karen Kelly, Christin Laroche, Rachel Miller, Emily Nicholson, Dionne Peniston, Katie Smith, Candace Spain, and Becky Tompkins.

I want also to thank other colleagues and friends who have assisted me in various different ways on this project: Michael Appleby, David Armstrong, Olof Brandt, Fred Crosson, Roald Docter, Carlo Gasparri, Timothy Johnson, Eric Kyllo, Paolo Liverani, Paul McCoy, Jan Stubbe Østergaard, Piergiacomo Petrioli, Steve and Brenda Ramer, David White, Orley Lindgren and Katriona Munthe-Lindgren (for a salutary retreat in Leksand amidst the chaos), and la familia Scariglia, for a similar retreat in Cumae. At Leksand I had the pleasure to meet Pia and Jan Thunholm. I wish to express my appreciation to Jan, whose beautiful linocut adorns this book's cover. Professor Bettina Bergmann of Mt. Holyoke was especially helpful in securing for me the photograph of Helen from the House of the Tragic Poet. I thank her for allowing me to use her copy of this photograph. To Philip Lockhart, Professor Emeritus, Dickinson College, I can barely begin to express my deepest gratitude. Phil's constant advice and encouragement and gentleness have shaped and guided me throughout my career.

As my work developed, I corresponded several times with Martin Jay,

Sidney Hellman Ehrman Professor of History at the University of California at Berkeley, whom I had the opportunity to meet when he was a fellow at the Institute for Advanced Studies at Princeton; he read an early draft of the first chapter and offered valuable insights. I also discussed the methodological aspects of this book with Lowell Edmunds, Professor of Classics at Rutgers, whose feedback on the first chapter was also helpful. I would especially like to acknowledge William S. Anderson, Graduate Professor of Classics at Berkeley. Bill read an early draft of the complete manuscript, causing me to reshape and clarify my arguments. I thank him much for his honest and constructive criticism and warm encouragement.

I would also like to thank the anonymous readers of University of Texas Press. I now know who these kind individuals are and I owe them much for their valuable comments. I also offer grateful acknowledgment to Jim Burr, Classics and History Editor; Nancy Moore; and the editorial staff of the University of Texas Press. It has been a true pleasure to work with all of them.

Finally, I want to thank some very special people. I thank first Thelma Mathews, my wonderful assistant in the Classics Department at Baylor, who facilitated many aspects of the production of this manuscript, from photocopying to mailings. To Jenny Cook, my assistant in the University Scholars Program and stalwart fellow laborer on this project, I owe more than I can possibly say here. She put in many late hours reading and rereading my work, offering numerous good suggestions and insightful comments. She is a superior editor, a remarkable proofreader, and a true friend. I thank my children, Katie, Harry, Ben, and Rachel, for their patience and encouragement throughout this project. Finally, to Diane, my wife and hero, for whom I am truly thankful and without whom not only this project but every aspect of my life would not be possible, I wish to express eternal, heartfelt gratitude. I dedicate this book to her.

Text and Art Acknowledgments

❧

The following was provided by Jan Thunholm: Cover illustration, *Aeneas and Turnus: The Final Duel.*

The following was provided by the Vatican Museum, with special thanks to Paolo Liverani, Director of the Vatican Museum, and to Padre Raffaele Farina, Prefetto della Biblioteca Apostolica Vaticana:

Figure 1.1: *Aeneas amidst the Storm.* From the fifth-century Codex Vergilianus Romanus. Vatican Museum.

The following were provided by Art Resource, in cooperation with the Museo Nazionale, Naples:

Figure 4.1: *Medea Meditating on Killing Her Children.* Pompeian Fresco. Museo Archeologico Nazionale, Naples.
Figure 4.2: *Phaedra and Maid Servant.* Pompeian Fresco. Museo Archeologico Nazionale, Naples.
Figure 5.1: *Theseus Having Slain the Minotaur.* Pompeian Fresco. Museo Archeologico Nazionale, Naples.

The following was provided by Dr. Bettina Bergmann from her personal collection:

Figure 4.3: *Helen Embarking.* Fresco from the House of the Tragic Poet. Museo Archeologico Nazionale, Naples.

The following was provided by Art Resource, in cooperation with the Berlin Staatlandes Museum:

Figure 4.4: *Helen in Her Boudoir.* Red-figured Attic drinking cup (kylix) from Nola, 450–440 BC. Side B. Berlin Staatlandes Museum. Photo: Johannes Laurentius.

All Latin citations of Virgil are taken from the edition of R. A. B. Mynors, ed., *P. Vergili Maronis Opera* (Oxford, 1969). Used by permission of Oxford University Press.

All English translations of Virgil are those of Allen Mandelbaum, tr., *The Aeneid of Virgil* (New York, 1971; rpt. 1981). Used by permission of Bantam Books, a division of Random House, Inc.

Abytbreviations

※

ACS	*American Classical Studies*
Acta Ant. Hung	*Acta Historica Academiae Scientiarum Hungaricae*
Aen.	*Aeneid*
AFL Nice	*Annales de la Faculté de Lettres et Sciences Humaines de Nice*
AHB	*Ancient History Bulletin*
AJA	*American Journal of Archaeology*
AJP	*American Journal of Philology*
Anth. Pal.	*Anthologia Palatina*
Appian *Bell Civ.*	Appian *Bellum Civile*
ARCA	*Classical and Medieval Texts, Papers and Monographs*
Arg	*Argonautica*
BMCR	*Bryn Mawr Classical Review*
CA	*Classical Antiquity*
Cass. Dio	Cassius Dio
Cat	*In Catilinam*
CJ	*Classical Journal*
Conf.	*Confessiones*
CQ	*Classical Quarterly*
CR	*Classical Review*
CW	*Classical Weekly*
Dial. Mort.	*Dialogi Mortuorum*
DK	*Diels-Kranz*
DRN	*De Rerum Natura*
Enc. Virg.	*Enciclopedia Virgiliana*
G.	*Georgics*

G&R	Greece and Rome
HSCP	*Harvard Studies in Classical Philology*
ICS	*Illinois Classical Studies*
Il.	*Iliad*
Inst.	*Institutio Oratoria*, Quintilian
JRA	*Journal of Roman Archaeology*
JRS	*Journal of Roman Studies*
Lewis and Short	Lewis and Short, *A Latin Dictionary*
LIMC	*Lexicon Iconographicum Mythologiae Classicae*
M.	Mandelbaum
Od.	*Odyssey*
OED	*Oxford English Dictionary*
OLD	*Oxford Latin Dictionary*
PCPhS	*Proceedings of the Cambridge Philological Society*
Pliny *NH*	Pliny *Naturalis Historia*
PVS	*Proceedings of the Virgil Society*
REL	*Revue des Études Latin*
RG	*Res Gestae*
RhM	*Rheinisches Museum*
TAPA	*Transactions of the American Philological Association*
TLL	*Thesaurus Linguae Latinae*
WS	*Wiener Studien*
YCS	*Yale Classical Studies*

Virgilian commentaries will be referred to by the editor's last name. If the editor has written more than one commentary, the last name and year of publication will be given.

THE PRIMACY OF VISION IN VIRGIL'S *Aeneid*

CHAPTER I

Prophaenomena ad Vergilium

Much have I travell'd in the realms of gold,
  And many goodly states and kingdoms seen;
  Round many western islands have I been
Which bards in fealty to Apollo hold.
Oft of one wide expanse had I been told
  That deep-brow'd Homer ruled as his demesne;
  Yet did I never breathe its pure serene
Till I heard Chapman speak out loud and bold:
Then felt I like some watcher of the skies
  When a new planet swims into his ken;
Or like stout Cortez when with eagle eyes
  He star'd at the Pacific—and all his men
Look'd at each other with a wild surmise—
  Silent, upon a peak in Darien.

JOHN KEATS[1]

"Eagle eyes" is an expression often applied to people of uncommon perception and piercing vision, those able to see things hard to perceive. Throughout "On First Looking into Chapman's Homer," Keats' manipulation of vision does more than create lingering images; it offers a kind of theoretical point of access for the poem. The sightless Homer now becomes tactile: his realm visible, its aura breathable, and his voice, through Chapman, finally audible. Chapman's translation of Homer gives the reader a new vision of the poet, allowing Keats to extol and describe through a strikingly visual simile. Keats' poem celebrates vision, emphasizing both acquisition of knowledge and the response of wonder. Homer's blindness contrasts with Cortez and his men, who marvel at the spectacular sight before them. These different perspectives converge to create for the reader a rich literary vista.

Keats' use of vision, therefore, is not a mere matter of perspective but a subjective experience informed by the intertextual resonance with Chapman's Homer. This subjectivity is not defined simply as a character's subjective posture, that is, the relative point of view of a character, but rather as the poet's ability to exploit his characters' vantage points, as Keats does with Cortez. Vantage point is thus linked to the notion of subjectivity.

Richard Heinze[2] and William Anderson[3] have both addressed subjectivity in Virgil, and Brooks Otis[4] has devoted an entire chapter to Virgil's subjective style, explaining that Virgil narrates through his characters, identifying with their perspective: "Virgil is constantly conscious of himself inside his characters. He thinks through them and for them."[5] While this aspect of Virgil's style offers an interesting line of inquiry and will generally inform my discussion, the overall scope of this study is broader.

"Focalization," a component of the theoretical framework of the late Don Fowler, has offered Virgilian scholarship a point of departure for the study of issues related to point of view.[6] This mode of interpretation, formulated by the French narratologist Gérard Genette,[7] has been profitably applied to Polybius,[8] Lucan,[9] Livy,[10] and Ovid[11] in recent Latin studies. Behind Genette's theory of narratology lies the question "Who sees?" In this book, I wish to ascertain how vision functions within the Virgilian narrative by asking not only the question "Who sees?" but also "What is seen?" and "How does Virgil employ vision and visual perspectives to suggest the thoughts and motives of his characters?"

The importance of vision in the *Aeneid* increases as the poem approaches its telos. That telos is ultimately Rome's foundation, which begins, symbolically, with Aeneas' killing of Turnus. I will seek to connect vision to that telos, considering how information gathered visually differs from that gathered aurally. Thus I will contrast visual and verbal modes of communication and perception that anticipate the poem's telos.

A quarter of a century ago, Michael Putnam made the powerful observation that throughout the *Aeneid*, "words are replaced more regularly by deeds."[12] Virgil's poem obviously includes a number of speeches, a necessary form of presenting and garnering information in epic narrative. In the *Aeneid*, however, speeches are also used to counter another method of information gathering that emerges within the text, namely, vision.[13] In the final analysis, Virgil contrasts oratory with vision in such a way that, after continuous tension between rhetoric and vision throughout the poem, vision ultimately triumphs as the dominant means of communication and perception.[14]

This tension between sight and speech reflects the time when Virgil composed the *Aeneid*, a period situated between the waning influence of the art of rhetoric in the Roman Republic and the waxing influence of images in the new empire.[15] Paul Zanker and Karl Galinsky have shown that visual messages played a major role in shaping Augustan culture. Zanker notes that images primarily serve the creation of a new mythology of Rome.[16] Galinsky furthers this discussion by showing how the use of images during the Augustan "renaissance" of art and literature reflected the unique environment of the *pax Augusta*. Yet as Galinsky has convincingly shown, these images were not mere propaganda.[17] The Forum Augustum served as a cultural center, the approximate equivalent of the Athenian acropolis.[18] Shortly after Virgil's death, the Ara Pacis would proclaim the Augustan peace while also suggesting a reformulation of the *concordia ordinum*.[19] Augustus' completion of the Theater of Marcellus did not merely continue Julius Caesar's building program, but it also gave tangible evidence of the first emperor's interaction with the populace.

In Virgil's day, Augustan architecture and other artistic expression redefined the Roman world.[20] This development is also reflected in poetry. For example, Karl Galinsky and Michael Putnam have each fruitfully compared the content of Horace's *Odes* 4 to that of the Ara Pacis.[21] Tibullus' topographical poem, too, reveals how a poet can overlay geographical and historical details to suggest the importance of the *urbs* as the setting of a love affair (2.5).[22] Such examples demonstrate the Augustan texts' heightened emphasis on visual themes, particularly those tied to a new understanding of the world as reflected in imperial building. Structures such as the Palatine temple of Apollo[23] and art objects such as the Augustus of Prima Porta[24] acted as bearers of messages that reflected the highly visual aspects of Augustan society. Virgil's use of vision, therefore, ultimately signals a communication shift that the social climate of Augustan Rome had already begun to embrace.

Based on these observations, for the current undertaking I will establish two ideas as operating premises:

1. Within the context of the decline of Republican rhetoric, the Augustan age was peculiarly rife with and indebted to visual conveyance of ideas (Zanker's and Galinsky's overarching contribution).
2. For characters in Virgil's *Aeneid*, vision emerges as the most

3

prominent way of constructing and interpreting reality. This is particularly true of Aeneas, who reacts to visual stimuli more efficiently than he does to verbal requests.

On the basis of these premises, I will argue that Virgil's poem encompasses a subtle shift from rhetoric to vision as the primary means of conveying and gathering information. This shift is important because it informs Aeneas' decisions in the epic, from leaving Dido to killing Turnus. To support and explicate this thesis, I will apply the philosophical formulations of the twentieth-century French philosopher Maurice Merleau-Ponty to Virgil's principal character, Aeneas.[25] My use of Merleau-Ponty is not meant to introduce a tight phenomenological approach to reading. Others such as Gadamer and Ingarden[26] have done this successfully, within the contexts of their hermeneutic and structuralist systems.

Ingarden's analysis of the literary work of art's anatomy, its essential structure, is derived from his essential commitment to phenomenological analysis. Ingarden looks back to ancient models such as Aristotle to assist in this regard, and to important early modern work such as Lessing's *Laocoon*.[27] Gadamer, whose hermeneutic approach to ancient text was applied successfully to Horace's *Ode* 1.19 by Lowell Edmunds, also takes an approach essentially indebted to phenomenology, though with more emphasis on the aesthetic value of a literary work. Both of these theorists—Ingarden and Gadamer—demonstrate the essential validity of phenomenological consideration of a text. Beyond them, in interpretations of medieval and Renaissance literatures one finds rich and provocative applications of phenomenological theory.[28] In classical studies, recent contributions such as those found in *The Roman Gaze*, edited by David Fredrick,[29] have called attention to the importance of vision in Roman art and architecture. Sharrock's discussion of the Portland vase[30] stands out as particularly exemplary of how important the visual culture was in the Augustan period. Images were not merely in the service of the state but were also part and parcel of domestic and public life.

My application of Merleau-Ponty's phenomenology is not the sole basis of my methodological approach to this book, but rather a strategy or compass within the context of the methodological premises derived from the contributions of Zanker and Galinsky. Specifically, I will use aspects of Merleau-Ponty's phenomenological theory to reformulate point of view as a kind of active and participatory vision of the world on the part of characters within the narrative. Inasmuch as some of Virgil's characters are well aware of their own world through what they see and the way they are seen, I have adopted for them the term *voyant-visible*, which Merleau-Ponty uses to describe the human being who embraces life's challenges visually and visibly. The *voyant-visible* is the centerpiece of Merleau-Ponty's philosophy and is particularly applicable to the central figure of Virgil's narrative, Aeneas.

THEORY

Merleau-Ponty developed his theories about phenomenology in response to a tradition of phenomenological debate that had already been advanced in Germany. Thus, to a certain extent, in forming his philosophy, Merleau-Ponty was reacting to such thinkers as Nietzsche, who questioned the still widely prevalent divide between the human and divine viewpoint in Cartesian dualism.[31] Later, Merleau-Ponty's contemporary, Jean-Paul Sartre, tendered a well-known distrust of vision[32] that would ultimately bleed into Lacan's psychoanalytical vilification of the ego, Irigaray's gender-sensitive anti-ocularcentrism, Derrida's anti-heliocentrism,[33] and Lyotard's discursive figurality.[34] In his seminal study of the history of vision, Martin Jay points out that, in modern and postmodern western philosophical discourse, Merleau-Ponty resists the trend toward the denigration of vision and instead affirms its role in a proper understanding of the world. Such an affirmation of a visual relationship to one's environment is well suited to my consideration of vision in the *Aeneid*.[35]

Although Merleau-Ponty died before he could fully develop his theories about phenomenology, his work reveals that he had begun to consider meaningfully the ontological divide between word and sight.[36] The Merleau-Pontian concept of vision begins with physical sight but extends to the notion of metaphysical gaze. Despite the limitations of empiricism in the context of a philosophical study of nature,[37] Merleau-Ponty believed that physical sight undergirds the search for truth. To some extent, Merleau-Ponty unites the Cartesian *cogito* with the person "in the world," whose vantage point is not a "God's-eye view" but worldly in a human and humane sense. In bringing together the two Cartesian visions, "the vision upon which I reflect" (i.e., the *cogito*) and the "vision that really takes place,"[38] Merleau-Ponty fleshes out his concept of the one who sees and is seen.

As I noted above, I am particularly indebted to his formulation of the visually motivated protagonist, the *voyant-visible*; this is the person who, almost instinctively, makes decisions based on what he sees. This perception is not based on social convention, as conveyed through outside persuasion, but is based on the information gathered naturally through vision.[39] Merleau-Ponty describes the *voyant-visible* as one "immersed in the visible by his body, itself visible ... ,"[40] who, he says, "opens himself to the world."[41]

For Merleau-Ponty, the *voyant-visible* gathers information through vision while engaging his surroundings in such a way as to be fully visible himself. His perceptibility defines the *voyant-visible* as an actor who is identified as such.

I will employ Merleau-Ponty's *voyant-visible* in two ways. First, I will conceptualize, as an operating principle, the poet as a kind of *voyant-visible*, an artist not wholly removed from the work he creates yet necessarily distinct from his characters in terms of the action of the narrative. Heinze, Otis, and Anderson first showed how Virgil's ability to sympathize with his characters evidences the depth of the poet's subjective style. Heinze suggested that the foundation of Virgil's epic is "the warmth of his sympathy with the emotions of his characters, and . . . the strength of his moral and religious sentiments and of his national feelings. . . ."[42] Heinze refers to this quality elsewhere as Virgil's *Stimmung*, that is, his ability to create a sympathetic tone in which the reader can encounter Virgil's characters.[43] Otis expounded on Heinze's observations in relation to the Nisus and Euryalus episode, concluding that Virgil "is doubly subjective—first in the *empathy* . . . second, in his own *personal reaction* to their emotions."[44] In another classic treatment of the poem, W. S. Anderson notes Virgil's empathy and observes that the narrator's subjective comments reinforce the self-denying behavior of the characters and heighten the reader's sympathetic response.[45]

More important to this discussion, however, is the second way that I employ Merleau-Ponty's concept of the *voyant-visible:* I will emphasize that Virgil creates characters whose vision motivates an active response to their surroundings. These characters do not observe from a removed or secure vantage point but are in the midst of the narrative's action.[46] Thus, from his first appearance, Aeneas emerges as a "see-er" acutely *in touch with the reality of the moment* and *motivated to action by his vision.* The *voyant-visible* is the character—in the *Aeneid*, principally but not exclusively Aeneas—who embraces the challenging situations in which Virgil places him both visually (i.e., using vision as a primary means of discerning the proper course of action) and visibly (i.e., being a part of the action as a principal figure; this is unlike Paris of *Iliad* 3, who is physically removed from his situation [3.380–383]). This activity and engagement based on vision are what Merleau-Ponty refers to as "a living relationship and tension among individuals."[47] The *voyant-visible* interacts with the world thus:

> This subject is no longer alone, is no longer consciousness in general or pure being for itself. He is in the midst of other consciousnesses which likewise have a situation; he *is* for others. . . .[48]

Merleau-Ponty's *voyant-visible* is connected to other living beings, forming a mutual relationship in which each person becomes fully understood only in relation to others.[49] Proper vision, which defines that relationship, motivates the *voyant-visible* to act appropriately in his environment. This proper action is borne out of decision-making based on what is seen and therefore what is real to the viewer, not a "God's-eye view" but a human view on the human plane.

I do not mean that Aeneas' vision is entirely physical or that he is incapable of the kind of internal vision that looks toward the future in a metaphorical sense. Rather that, too, is an aspect of his role as *voyant-visible*. With regard to physical sight, however, Aeneas, as the *voyant-visible*, interacts compassionately with some of those he sees, such as the survivors of the shipwreck in *Aeneid* 1; to others he responds harshly, such as those he encounters on the battlefield in *Aeneid* 10–12. When Aeneas kills, he gives no heed to rhetorical persuasion but relies on visual stimuli. Aeneas' gaze can enable him to show compassion, but the actions motivated by his gaze can also strengthen his resolve, intensify his sense of duty, and, some would argue, cause him to indulge his human fallibility. The *voyant-visible* is capable of deep feeling, whether compassion or anger, based on what he sees.[50]

THEORIA[51]

Although movement beyond focalization to phenomenology represents a widening of the scope of vision within Virgilian narrative, it also imposes certain constraints. This study will not simply treat language related to eyes or vision in Virgil or exclusively examine situations rife with visual imagery. This book will not treat portents, predictions, or apparitions that do not directly relate to the way in which a character gathers information. Nor will it treat the fertile topic of ecphrasis in detail, although it has been considered thoroughly by a number of scholars such as Fowler,[52] Putnam,[53] and others.[54] Furthermore, this study will not consider Virgil's quasi-rococo descriptions such as that of Fama (Book 4), Charon (Book 6), or Allecto (i.e., qua visual creature, Book 7). Though such passages may be visually striking (e.g., the stunning transformation of the ships into nymphs in Book 9), they do not fall within the scope of this analysis. Rather, I will consider in phenomenological terms a number of different episodes in the *Aeneid* that reflect Virgil's shift from rhetoric to vision as the paramount form of communication in the narrative. In addition to gathering information through vision, Virgil's characters communicate through visual signals. Such visual communication was a crucial aspect of Augustan society.

In that society, a number of cultural icons were being established by which Romans could glean information about the new imperial order, various current events, and even the significance of international developments. A Roman of the middle Augustan period, for example, could walk from the Forum Romanum, an area symbolized by the old rostrum, to the curia, where many a debate had raged, to the nearby comitium, where pivotal votes of the Republic had been cast, to Julius Caesar's relatively new forum, the centerpiece of which was a temple dedicated to Venus Genetrix. In this, the first of the imperial fora, public and private were merged, for the structure celebrated Caesar both as public official and as the heir of the Julian *gens* descended from Venus.

Caesar's successor, Octavian, was equally adept at promoting himself within the context of the iconography of late Republican Rome.[55] In the 20s, Augustus was developing and building his own forum to connect his Julian heritage with Aeneas and also to bind the regal and Republican history to Romulus, whose statue was located in the center of the southern exedra of the forum, directly opposite the statue of Aeneas in the northern exedra. These could be seen on either side of the pronaos of the temple of Mars Ultor, the centerpiece of the new forum. Messages were disseminated iconographically to the viewing public in the new Forum Augustum even as the orators of the old Forum Romanum had once poured forth orations from the old rostrum.[56]

In the *Aeneid*, vision transmits messages in a manner similar to the methods by which information was conveyed in Augustan society. Just as Aeneas gathers information by viewing the objects described by Virgil in various ecphrases (e.g., in Books 1, 6, 8), the Roman population under Augustus is likely to have beheld their mythical and historical past in Augustus' forum and, to take another example, on the Ara Pacis. While the beholder probably would not have grasped all the monument's information, the icon's content would have resonated generally with the experience and thoughts of most Roman viewers. The cultural and historical approaches of Zanker and Galinsky thus provide this study with an important point of departure.

Beyond departure, however, lies a journey into the text of the *Aeneid* wherever vision plays a role in Virgil's characterization and his construction of narrative. In that narrative, Virgil's use of vision often points toward the poem's telos. Virgil manipulates sight vis-à-vis his characters to reveal a character's disposition or temperament. For example, a character's confidence in the gods is often strengthened through visual confrontation with a god. Gods can also use vision deceptively to advance their own agendas. In addition, vision can be a means of coordinating the power of past events with the promise of the future. Further, bonds of love in the *Aeneid* are both strengthened and ruptured through vision. Analysis of Dido's and Aeneas' vision aids in analyzing their relationship; both the way they perceive each other and the way they perceive their destinies ultimately cause the break between the two lovers, overriding any last-minute verbal appeals. Vision's outstripping of oratory is also closely associated with the poem's telos, which, as noted above,[57] I regard as the re-foundation of Troy in Rome, paraphrased simply by the well-known phrase from the poem's opening, *dum conderet urbem* (1.5). For this study, then, I proffer the word *telos* as a term to which I will return frequently in my discussion of the importance of visual communication in the *Aeneid*.[58]

Consideration of Virgilian characterization and narrative necessarily involves establishing further terminology, beginning with the English word *vision*, which itself contains several nuances of meaning. It can suggest the physical aspect of sight, a future aspiration or goal, or even a mental capacity. For example, one speaks of foresight, hindsight, insight, and eyesight, all of which can be embraced by the single word vision.[59] The Latin terminology encompasses a similar range of meaning: *uidere* is, of course, the primary Latin word for the act of seeing and chiefly refers to the physical act of sight.[60] Other Latin verbs are also considered in this treatment, including *tueri, aspicere,* and other cognates of *aspicere,* as well as nouns related to both the **spic-*and **uid-*word roots.[61]

Another term important to this study is *imago,* which occurs only once in the *Eclogues* and once in the *Georgics;* it occurs thirty times in the *Aeneid.* Netta Berlin considers this word in the context of *Aeneid* 12.560, where its meaning ranges from the mental picture of an imminent attack (*pugnae . . . maioris imago*) to the faculty of memory itself.[62] Such an interpretation squares nicely with *imago* as an apparition from the past.[63] Elizabeth Block explains *imago* as denoting "those visions that come unbidden into men's minds" or the gods' disguised visitation of men.[64] Other times it can mean a manifestation of a character such as Creusa, whose *imago* appears before Aeneas.[65] Obviously, the term *imago* had many other associations.[66] One important connection to the past is the notion of the *imagines* of a Roman house or funeral procession. When Aeneas sees the *imago* of his father or of Creusa, therefore, there is a poignancy to the word that transcends any English translation.[67]

Finally, one last note on terminology. Words for vision in Latin and in English have a wide range of meaning. Vision can suggest in English a hope for the future as well as the act of sight. We find this dual meaning also in the *Aeneid*. For example, when Aeneas asks Dido, *si te Karthaginis arces / Phoenissam Libycaeque aspectus detinet urbis, / quae tandem Ausonia Teucros considere terra / inuidia est?* (*Aen.* 4.347–350),[68] he associates physical sight with vision, in the broader sense, of his future land. Accordingly, I will seek to analyze both aspects of vision in this study and, in Chapter 4, will enlarge on the passage cited here.

In this study, however, I will not merely analyze Virgil's vision-related language; rather, I will seek to show how Virgil's use of vision reflects the ways in which changes in communication had influenced art and literature. As Merleau-Ponty noted, "The perceived world is the always presupposed foundation of all rationality, all value and all existence."[69] Such a formulation might well be applied to Augustan Rome. The establishment of that city is the telos of Virgil's poem, in which vision's emergence as the dominant form of perception affirms, or at least reflects, the visual supremacy of Augustan society. In general terms, therefore, vision in the *Aeneid* extends beyond mere physical sight to characterize the most profound themes of the narrative.

As Virgil's primary protagonist, Aeneas embodies the attributes of Merleau-Ponty's *voyant-visible:* he is in the world as see-er and as one held up as an icon in the midst of those with whom he interacts. He is a participant in and an engager of his surroundings, not existential or removed from them. Such an "earthy" understanding of the human experience is comparable to the atomism of Lucretius and Philodemus; Virgil was poetically indebted to Lucretius and was among Philodemus' personal friends.[70] The effects of atomic theory on Virgil's poetry have long been recognized by Heinze and others as an aspect of his poetic style.[71]

Lucretian visual theory probably informed the manner in which Virgil conceived of vision. Lucretius' conceptual framework was obviously heavily steeped in the ideas of Epicurus, whose notions were ultimately derived in many ways from pre-Socratic thought. For example, the Epicurean concept of sight was indebted to the Empedoclean idea of effluences (ἀπορροίαι). Empedocles had earlier suggested that effluences enter the eye and that elements in the eye then distinguish light from dark to form the visual image.[72] The atomists Leucippus and Democritus used this theory to suggest that vision is caused by "images" that strike the eye:

εἴδωλα γάρ τινα ὁμοιόμορφα ἀπὸ τῶν ὁρωμένων συνεχῶς ἀπορρέοντα καὶ ἐμπίπτοντα τῇ ὄψει τοῦ ὁρᾶν ᾐτιῶντο. τοιοῦτοι δὲ ἦσαν οἱ περὶ Λεύκιππον καὶ Δημόκριτον.   ALEXANDER, *De sensu* 56.12[73]

[They attributed sight to certain images, of the same shape as the object, which were continually streaming off from the objects of sight and impinging on the eye. This was the view of the school of Leucippus and Democritus.][74]

As it had been for Alcmaeon and some other pre-Socratics,[75] to the atomistic philosopher, vision ultimately concerns touch, as the εἴδωλα would physically contact the eye.[76] Virgil possibly understood vision to be such a tactile process. Yet it is also possible that Virgil considered metaphysical approaches to vision, such as those descended from Platonic philosophy.

In the *Republic*'s myth of the cave, Plato posited a link between philosophy and vision, for awareness of the cave's darkness comes through vision, the greatest gift that human beings receive from the gods (*Timaeus* 47a-b). The *Republic*'s cave (Book 7) provides, in many ways, the primary metaphor of Greek philosophy's quest for truth. Vision brings enlightenment and understanding critical for the greatest good: knowledge itself.[77]

Aristotle considered the notion of εἴδωλα to be improbable, yet his own ideas concerning visual theory are somewhat limited. While he believed that the way the physical act of vision functions is essentially passive (αἱ δὲ ὄψεις παθητικαί, *Problems* 959a24), Aristotle clearly placed vision above all other sensations. This can be seen at the opening of the *Metaphysics*, where Aristotle states that "of all sensations those received by means of the eyes are liked most. For, not only for the sake of doing something else but even if we are not going to do anything else, we prefer, as one might say, seeing to the other sensations."[78] Aristotle's more extensive discussions of vision also connect sight to emotion, an association already present in Greek Orphic thought.[79] While accepting the connection of vision and the emotions, Virgil accepts Aristotle's declaration of vision's primacy among the senses, apparently ignoring the passive way that Aristotle conceives of vision with regard to information gathering. In the *Aeneid*, as in the opening of the *Metaphysics*, vision is conjoined with action.

The Roman Epicureans of the first-century BC did not entirely abandon the Aristotelian association of eyes with emotions. Lucretius' treatment of vision, which occupies much of the early and middle portions of the fourth book of the *DRN*, explains how emotional energy is taken in with the stream of *simulacra* (the Latin translation of εἴδωλα) that strike a person's eye.[80] Philodemus, whose circle of colleagues and friends included Virgil, instead of focusing on how vision can provoke anger, turns the equation around when he describes the anger that a madman's eyes can convey.[81]

Beyond these philosophical circles, the importance of sight as a means of information gathering and of iconography for the conveyance of information was also recognized. Thus, the psychological effect of visual stimulation is also important, for one finds an increased use of vision in communication and entertainment, particularly during the middle to late Republican period. As Rome waxed powerful in the late second and early first century BC, visual arts such as theater flourished in the *urbs*.[82] Statues, often imported from Greece,[83] increasingly adorned the city. Near the beginning of the first century, Roman wall painting had begun to change from the First "incrustation" style to the visually richer Second style that was characterized by various portraits of receded walls, landscapes, and mythological scenes.[84] Art collections became widespread as well. By the early 40s BC, Caesar had begun to gather numerous works of art in the pronaos of the temple of Venus Genetrix within his recently constituted forum,[85] located, symbolically, "in the heart of the city."[86] With increased wealth and political influence came a heightened awareness of the visual arts, and Rome became a primary importer of such arts.

These were some of the ideas about vision that Virgil must have considered as he wrote the *Aeneid*. While I am primarily concerned with the philosophical aspects of vision as applied to the *Aeneid*, the psychological expression of vision in the cultural context of Augustan Rome will also be an aspect of consideration in this discussion, for Virgil's concept of sight was indebted to the intellectual and cultural heritage surrounding him. Now let us turn to Virgil's text to see how he employs vision in the *Aeneid*. We shall consider Virgil's text in phenomenological terms, both ancient and modern.

ANTE ORA PATRUM

Aeneas first speaks amidst a disastrous situation in the darkness of a raging storm that hampers his crew's ability to see. Even without a clear view of their situation, the crew discerns that death is imminent. Their unfortunate situation causes Aeneas to shudder; he cries out in apparent desperation:[87]

> 'o terque quaterque beati,
> quis ante ora patrum Troiae sub moenibus altis
> contigit oppetere! o Danaum fortissime gentis
> Tydide! mene Iliacis occumbere campis
> non potuisse tuaque animam hanc effundere dextra,
> saeuus ubi Aeacidae telo iacet Hector, ubi ingens
> Sarpedon, ubi tot Simois correpta sub undis
> scuta uirum galeasque et fortia corpora uoluit!'   *Aen.* 1.94–101

["O, three and four times blessed
were those who died before their fathers' eyes
beneath the walls of Troy. Strongest of all
the Danaans, o Diomedes, why
did your right hand not spill my lifeblood, why
did I not fall upon the Ilian fields,
there where ferocious Hector lies, pierced by
Achilles' javelin, where the enormous
Sarpedon now is still, and Simois
has seized and sweeps beneath its waves so many
helmets and shields and bodies of the brave!" (M. 1.133–144)]

This first speech that Aeneas makes in the poem calls attention to the relationship of memory and visual image, for the hero evokes an image that harks back to the memory of a previous situation when he proclaims that those who died at Troy "before their fathers' eyes" (95), as Mandelbaum renders the phrase, are truly blessed. This statement helps the reader to discern immediately Aeneas' perception of the situation that encompasses him. He views the storm through the lens of past disasters, specifically those of *Iliad* 12.22–23,[88] knowing that Troy once witnessed many bodies and weapons rolling in the Simois. Aeneas proclaims that he would rather have been seen among mangled corpses at Troy than be the perceiver of the current disaster. Although he escaped death at Troy, he must now witness the plight of his comrades-in-arms in a new disaster on the sea.

Though Aeneas is sailing to a new land, he is here and elsewhere occupied with the past.[89] Odysseus' words provide a model for those of Aeneas:

"νῦν μοι σῶς αἰπὺς ὄλεθρος.
τρισμάκαρες Δαναοὶ καὶ τετράκις οἳ τότ' ὄλοντο
Τροίῃ ἐν εὐρείῃ, χάριν Ἀτρείδῃσι φέροντες.
ὡς δὴ ἐγώ γ' ὄφελον θανέειν καὶ πότμον ἐπισπεῖν
ἤματι τῷ ὅτε μοι πλεῖστοι χαλκήρεα δοῦρα
Τρῶες ἐπέρριψαν περὶ Πηλείωνι θανόντι.
τῷ κ' ἔλαχον κτερέων, καί μευ κλέος ἦγον Ἀχαιοί·
νῦν δέ με λευγαλέῳ θανάτῳ εἵμαρτο ἁλῶναι."[90]   Od. 5.305–312

["My sheer destruction is certain.
Three times and four times happy those Danaans were who died then
in wide Troy land, bringing favor to the sons of Atreus,
as I wish I too had died at that time and met my destiny

13

on the day when the greatest number of Trojans threw their
    bronze-headed
weapons upon me, over the body of perished Achilleus,
and I would have had my rites and the Achaians given me glory."][91]

Like Aeneas, Odysseus speaks in the midst of a storm. But while some of
Odysseus' words compare to those of Aeneas, particularly Virgil's allusion
to the Homeric formula "thrice and four times blessed," Odysseus reaches
a conclusion different from that of Aeneas.[92] Odysseus' concern is for himself[93] and for his own funeral in particular (line 313). With proper burial,
Odysseus says he could have enjoyed in the burial ceremony the *kleos* (glory,
312) that crowns a hero's life. Aeneas has a less self-glorifying perspective
than does Odysseus. Aeneas will be concerned not only with his own sur-
vival and that of his men but that of Troy, as well. His future, like his past,
is to be a national venture.

    This recontextualization of Homeric material both identifies Aeneas as
a hero in the tradition of Odysseus and contrasts him with that same hero.
The allusion goes beyond *Odyssey* 5. Aeneas' invocation of those who died
at Troy before the faces of their fathers (95) suggests a visual image similar to
Odysseus' reaction to the sacking of Troy in the song of Demodocus in *Odyssey* 8. There Demodocus describes a woman who has witnessed her husband's mortal wound (8.526). As she attempts to cling to his body, she is taken
away from one who had fallen "before people and city" (πρόσθεν πόλιος
λαῶν τε, 8.524). This description and Odysseus' tearful response to Demodocus' song are characterized at all points by pathos engendered by the visions
of suffering that the song embodies.[94] Odysseus' grief, like the woman's in
the simile, is engendered by what he sees. Virgil's text, the phrase *ante ora
patrum*, presents an instance of pathos comparable to Homer's visual portrait of violence, loss, and grief in *Odyssey* 8.524.[95] Aeneas views his current situation of possible death in a storm to be less honorable than the
noble but pathetic death of soldiers in battle, with their fathers beholding
the event.

    The vision of past events to which Aeneas refers here parallels his vision
of the disaster of which he is a part. It is significant that Aeneas does not
speak as an observer or as one somehow removed from the plight of his men
in the storm; with his pathetic utterance, he reveals that he willingly involves himself in the struggle.[96] In this situation, Aeneas is a *voyant-visible*
even if, paradoxically, his disturbed *terque quaterque* address comes when
vision has been obscured:

insequitur clamorque uirum stridorque rudentum;
eripiunt subito nubes caelumque diemque
Teucrorum *ex oculis;* ponto nox incubat atra;
intonuere poli et crebris micat ignibus aether
praesentemque uiris intentant omnia mortem.   *Aen.* 1.87–91

　　　　　　　　　[. . . cries
of men, the creaking of the cables rise.
Then, suddenly, the cloud banks snatch away
the sky and daylight from the Trojans' eyes,
black night hangs on the waters, heavens thunder,
and frequent lightning glitters in the air;
everything intends quick death to men. (M. 1.124–130)]

Aeneas makes his opening proclamation, then, precisely when the Trojans have lost their vision of the situation because the storm obscures the very light of day. This not only heightens the sense of obscurity of their seemingly imminent deaths but also adds to the panic of the moment: the cables creak (87), the men cannot see the full force of the winds, the clouds and heaven disappear as night "glooms over"[97] a sea (89) rendered visible only by lightning (*micat ignibus aether*, 90). These are the visions that cause Aeneas to proclaim that those who died before their fathers' eyes were many times blessed. He and his men would have been better off dying visibly *ante ora patrum* (95) than in the figurative and literal obscurity of this dark storm (88–89).

After Aeneas' opening words, Virgil continues to heighten the intensity of the moment in visual terms:

tris Notus abreptas in saxa latentia torquet
(saxa uocant Itali mediis quae in fluctibus Aras,
dorsum immane mari summo), tris Eurus ab alto
in breuia et Syrtis urget, *miserabile uisu*,
inliditque uadis atque aggere cingit harenae.   *Aen.* 1.108–112

[And then the south wind snatches up three ships
and spins their keels against the hidden rocks—
those rocks that, rising in midsea, are called
by the Italians "Altars"—like a monstrous
spine stretched along the surface of the sea.

Meanwhile the east wind wheels another three
off from the deep and, terrible to see,
against the shoals and shifting silt, against
the shallows, girding them with mounds of sand. (M. 1.153–161)]

Some of these vivid images are captured in a well-known depiction of the storm from the fifth-century Codex Vergilius Romanus (Figure 1.1).[98] The manuscript's illustration offers an imaginative interpretation of this passage and features an oversized Aeneas with hands upraised, presumably offering his "terque quaterque" declaration. Virgil's concise expression, *miserabile uisu* (111), however, suggests a visual image more intense than the artist can express. Aeneas' view of the wretchedness of the men in the storm presents a psychological condition that the fifth-century artist does not capture.[99] Virgil delineates Aeneas' appraisal of the situation while also suggesting how the hero is beheld by others. The poet's careful manipulation of and empathy with Aeneas' perspective establishes the hero as *voyant-visible* in this opening scene. As such, Aeneas both sees and is involved with his men, visible even in the dark and gloomy situation in which the Trojans are first seen. Aeneas emerges at the poem's beginning from darkness and disorder.

The storm concludes when Neptune becomes aware of the disturbance:

> Interea magno misceri murmure pontum
> emissamque hiemem sensit Neptunus et imis
> stagna refusa uadis, grauiter commotus, et alto
> *prospiciens* summa placidum caput extulit unda.
> disiectam Aeneae toto *uidet* aequore classem,
> fluctibus oppressos Troas. . . .   *Aen.* 1.124–129

[But Neptune felt the fracas and frenzy;
and shaken by the unleashed winds, the wrenching
of the still currents from the deep seabed,
he raised his tranquil head above the surface.
And he can see the galleys of Aeneas
scattered across the waters, with the Trojans
dismembered by the waves. . . . (M. 1.177–183)]

Neptune's perception of the storm (127) closely follows that of Aeneas; raising his "tranquil head" above the surface of the raging waters, Neptune looks forth upon—one might note well the participle's prefix, which em-

Figure 1.1. *Aeneas amidst the Storm.* From the fifth-century Codex Vergilianus Romanus. Vatican Museum.

phasizes the extension of Neptune's gaze—the storm from a vantage point different from that of Aeneas. Whereas Aeneas sees the chaos and yet can do nothing, Neptune's vision is pacifying. His divine power enables him to take action and bring about a resolution, much like a good speaker who, Virgil goes on to explain, is able to assuage troubled hearts:

> ac ueluti magno in populo cum saepe coorta est
> seditio saeuitque animis ignobile uulgus
> iamque faces et saxa uolant, furor arma ministrat;
> tum, pietate grauem ac meritis si forte uirum quem
> *conspexere,* silent arrectisque auribus astant;
> ille regit dictis animos et pectora mulcet. . . .   *Aen.* 1.148–153

> [And just as often, when a crowd of people
> is rocked by a rebellion, and the rabble
> rage in their minds, and firebrands and stones
> fly fast—for fury finds its weapons—if,
> by chance, they see a man remarkable
> for righteousness and service, they are silent
> and stand attentively; and he controls
> their passion by his words and cools their spirits. . . . (M. 1.209–216)]

Here the perception emphasized is not that of the *pietate grauem . . . uirum* (151) but rather of those who watch and listen to him. The crowd first beholds this man and, only after seeing him, awaits eagerly the words that will calm their hearts. Neptune, then, while being the primary object of this simile, is not quite the only one for whom the comparison is apt, for Aeneas behaves similarly.

The description of the "man remarkable for righteousness and service" anticipates the deportment of Aeneas a few lines later (197–209), when he will rally his men on the Carthaginian shore, telling them that perhaps they will eventually recall their suffering with some pleasure[100] (*forsan et haec olim meminisse iuuabit,* 203).[101] Aeneas comforts his men (*pectora mulcet,* 197) in a manner similar to the speaker of the simile (cf. 153) before putting on a good show of bravery for his men to see (*spem uultu simulat,* 209).[102] Insofar as Aeneas' speech to his men (198–207) represents a tangible example of the speaker of the simile (148–153), oratory and vision join forces in this passage.[103] This alliance of speech and sight, however, begins to fray by the end of the sixth book.

As we move from Neptune's intervention to the narrative of Aeneas and his men, Virgil uses the same visual words (*prospicere*) to describe Neptune surveying the now quiet seas:[104]

> . . . sic cunctus pelagi cecidit fragor, aequora postquam
> *prospiciens* genitor caeloque inuectus aperto
> flectit equos curruque uolans dat lora secundo.　　　*Aen.* 1.154–156

> [. . . so all the clamor of the sea subsided
> after the father, gazing on the waters
> and riding under the cloudless skies, had guided
> his horses, let his willing chariot run. (M. 1.217–220)]

Once Neptune has gathered information through his perspective of the disaster on the sea, he brings necessary calm to the waters. His gaze, twice mentioned (*prospiciens,* 127, 155), compels him to take action in restoring order to the sea. Just as the god's first vision of the winds corresponds to Aeneas' vision of the storm, Neptune's final look at the calm seas compares with Aeneas' inspection of the situation when Virgil, a few lines later, twice presents Aeneas' view of his new surroundings:

> Aeneas scopulum interea conscendit, et omnem
> *prospectum* late pelago petit, Anthea si quem

iactatum uento uideat Phrygiasque biremis
aut Capyn aut celsis in puppibus arma Caici.
nauem in conspectu nullam, tris litore ceruos
prospicit errantis; hos tota armenta sequuntur
a tergo et longum per uallis pascitur agmen.   *Aen.* 1.180–186

[Meanwhile Aeneas climbs a crag to seek
a prospect far and wide across the deep,
if he can only make out anything
of Antheus and his Phrygian galleys, or
of Capys, or the armor of Caicus
on his high stern. There is no ship in sight;
all he can see are three stags wandering
along the shore, with whole herds following
behind, a long line grazing through the valley. (M. 1.251–259)]

Aeneas has emerged from the storm's obscuring of vision, coming to a place
where he can see clearly. Like Neptune, who had come up from the depths
to appraise the situation of the storm, Aeneas has a clear view of his surroundings (*prospectum*, 181). The calm of this scene contrasts with the turmoil of the storm, and Aeneas will now be able to provide for his men, for he
can see a food source (*prospicit*, 185) that will physically and psychologically
strengthen the Trojans.[105] Aeneas' vision is markedly similar to that of the
god, and his perspective, characterized by the same verb (*prospicere*) as Neptune's, leads to action.[106] Aeneas sees his duty and takes action; the action
that vision engenders demonstrates his *pietas*.[107]

The perspective that Aeneas adopts does not celebrate the space between
viewed and viewer or suggest that meaning should be understood in terms
of such space.[108] Instead, a Merleau-Pontian reading of Virgil espouses the
shrinking of that space through vision. The true *voyant-visible* should not
take a detached view of others' situations, such as that seen in the opening of
Lucretius' second book.[109] There, Lucretius explains the importance of being
without care by using the figure of a true Epicurean who watches the plight
of others from a distance:

suaue, mari magno turbantibus aequora uentis,
e terra magnum alterius spectare laborem;
non quia uexari quemquamst iucunda uoluptas,
sed quibus ipse malis careas quia *cernere suaue est.*
suaue etiam belli certamina magna *tueri*

per campos instructa tua sine parte pericli.
sed nil dulcius est, bene quam munita tenere
edita doctrina sapientum templa serena,
despicere unde queas alios passimque *uidere*
errare atque uiam palantis quaerere uitae. . . .   *DRN* 2.1–10[110]

[Sweet it is, when on the great sea the winds are buffeting the waters,
to gaze from the land on another's great struggles; not because it is a
pleasure or joy that anyone should be distressed, but because it is sweet
to perceive from what misfortunes you yourself are free. Sweet is it too,
to behold great contests of war in full array over the plains, when you
have no part in the danger. But nothing is more gladdening than to
dwell in the calm regions, firmly embattled on the heights by the
teaching of the wise, whence you can look down on others, and see
them wandering hither and thither, going astray as they seek the way
of life. . . .]

The storm within Lucretius' passage (*turbantibus aequora uentis*, 2.1) compares to the situation of Aeneas and his men (*uenti . . . / . . . turbine perflant. /
incubuere mari*, 1.82–84).[111] When Virgil has Aeneas recall those who died
at Troy (94–101), he alludes to the second image of Lucretius, the vision of
armies embattled on the plains (*suaue etiam belli certamina magna tueri*,
5). Ironically, Aeneas would picture himself with his men in dangers quite
similar to those of *DRN* 2's prologue.

What Virgilian critics have characterized as the poet's subjective style—
his ability to sympathize with his characters—manifests itself in the gaze
of his characters. Unlike Lucretius, who advocates a distant and secure perspective, Virgil closes the gap between one character and another, the gap
between the character and his or her surroundings. This increased proximity
can encourage a profound range of emotions, from expressions of sympathy and affection to those of concern and anger. Perhaps most significantly,
vision can provoke action; for Aeneas, this action can range from fighting on
the battlefield to rallying men after a disaster.

When Aeneas rallies his men after the storm of Book 1, like the noble
statesman of the simile, he merely makes the best of a terrible situation:

'per uarios casus, per tot discrimina rerum
tendimus in Latium, sedes ubi fata quietas
ostendunt; illic fas regna resurgere Troiae.
durate, et uosmet rebus seruate secundis.'

Talia uoce refert curisque ingentibus aeger
spem uultu simulat, premit altum corde dolorem.   *Aen.* 1.204–209

["Through so many crises and calamities
we make for Latium, where fates have promised
a peaceful settlement. It is decreed
that there the realm of Troy will rise again.
Hold out, and save yourselves for kinder days."
These are his words: though sick with heavy care,
he counterfeits hope in his face; his pain
is held within, hidden. (M. 1.284–292)]

Aeneas projects an image that commands attention and respect. He proves to be neither the glory-seeking Odysseus nor a person shaped by a concern for the *securitas* of recent Roman didactic epic. Informed by, yet separated from, these two intertexts, Aeneas emerges as a palpable, suffering hero with the capacity to mask his own doubt and fear for the good of his people (209). He causes them to perceive him in a way that benefits and sustains them. Beyond mere words of encouragement, Aeneas thus uses his physical appearance to give them a sense of security.

In the midst of a bleak and stormy present and within the context of the tragic past evoked by *terque quaterque beati,* Aeneas finds a way to engender hope in those who look to him for leadership. His unique blend of sympathy and courage is a kind of participatory subjectivity, a concept related to the poet's own sympathetic style. Such psychological proximity to the world in which he lives will characterize Aeneas throughout the poem. The vision of his surrounding circumstances here produces in him a humane and sympathetic response. On other occasions—particularly in the poem's second half—it overrides what he hears, causing him to take severely decisive action.

THE SCOPE OF THE ARGUMENT

Thomas Rakoczy[112] and Raymond Prier[113] have considered vision in Greek poetry, with special attention paid to Homer. While Rakoczy's work centers on the negative aspects of gaze and divine spite, Prier, whose criticism is indebted methodologically to the phenomenologist Edmund Husserl,[114] considers a more varied use of terms for sight, such as Homer's verbs, παπταίνειν and δέρκεσθαι. Prier suggests that these and other terms reveal the nature of comprehension based on visual perception: Homer's reliance on vision aids the construction of meaning in the Homeric poems and influences the nature of perception in the wake of the Homeric epics.

Recent work on aspects of vision as a mode of perception and communication in the *Aeneid* has generated many insightful observations. Licinia Ricottilli has explored how one character's gesture functions vis-à-vis language to convey information to another character. She details the many passages in which words and gestures function in tandem to produce dramatic, even theatrical effects. This combination of speech and gesture evokes response from characters, and Virgil's representation of any given gesture assists and can outstrip the importance of direct discourse.[115]

Other studies, such as that of William Hunt, have noted how visual images seem to become increasingly "more concrete" as the poem progresses.[116] Hunt correctly demonstrates the way that pictures come into sharp focus in the poem. Although Hunt points in the right direction, he uses the terms "picture" and "image" in such a general way[117] that his study does not advance the topic of Virgilian vision very far.[118] The current study posits a tension between rhetoric and vision that develops throughout the *Aeneid*. As I have noted previously, I follow closely the reasoning and evidence of Zanker and Galinsky and seek to apply what Zanker has called "visual language" to Virgil's text, a theory relevant to Roman society during its transition from Republic to Empire.[119] Rome's first emperor used images to convey meaning and to create a kind of political and artistic renaissance in Augustan society, a specific historical moment in which great works of literature and art could occur through the *auctoritas* of that same emperor.[120]

The *Aeneid* reflects this major trend toward visual communication in Augustan society. At the opening of the *Aeneid*, vision complements and fulfills the words of the speaker, as consideration of the simile of the speaker in *Aeneid* 1 makes evident. By the poem's midpoint, vision has moved to a position distinctly opposed to oratory; during the poem's final scene, vision chiefly motivates the action of Aeneas within the narrative in such a way as to suggest that rhetoric has lost much of its effect. I will use several examples from the *Aeneid* to support this thesis. In Chapter 2, I consider a number of instances in which the gods become visible and interact with human beings. Denis Feeney's many lucid observations provide a starting point for my evaluation both of the manner in which gods appear to mortals and of the effects of their appearances.[121]

In the third chapter, I consider how the act of sight functions with regard to temporality, specifically examining how vision seems to broker among past, present, and future in the poem. Vision transcends temporal boundaries to point toward a justification of Rome's existence and the actions that an-

ticipate or help to preserve that existence.[122] Vision offers a means for bringing the future and past together within the cyclical nature of Roman time:
in encountering his past and looking back in that sense, Aeneas can see the
future more clearly.

Chapter 4 argues for an implied contrast between the vision of Dido and
Aeneas as lovers and the vision that Aeneas has of his beloved country.
Interpreting Dido and Aeneas as *voyants-visibles*, I argue that vision fuels
important phases in the lovers' relationship, from their meeting, to their
separation, to the rendezvous in the *campi lugentes*. As they begin to cease
viewing each other sympathetically, however, their relationship begins to
deteriorate, and the hero's vision of his future city replaces his view of her as
the object of his love. Vision in the Dido and Aeneas tale therefore accom-
plishes its ends, first by cooperating with rhetoric and then by responding to
and ultimately supplanting rhetoric.

In the final chapter, I assert that oratory becomes increasingly suspect
and devalued as the poem proceeds. Appeals offered by embassies become
less successful.[123] Pleas for mercy fall on deaf ears. In the final scene of the
Aeneid, vision effects in Aeneas a strong response. Virgil's use of vision is
ultimately causative, prompting action, for the power of images replaces
rhetoric as the motivation for action.

But let us begin with the gods, as does Virgil's poem, for visual perception of the gods causes mortals to reconsider decisions and redirect their own
courses of action.

CHAPTER 2

Ruse and Revelation

VISIONS OF THE DIVINE AND THE TELOS OF NARRATIVE

❧

And did those feet in ancient time
Walk upon England's mountains green?
And was the holy Lamb of God
On England's pleasant pastures seen?

And did the countenance Divine
Shine forth upon our clouded hills?
And was Jerusalem builded here
Among these dark Satanic Mills?

Bring me my Bow of burning gold!
Bring me my Arrows of desire!
Bring me my Spear! O Clouds, unfold!
Bring me my Chariot of fire!

I will not cease from Mental Fight,
Nor shall my Sword sleep in my hand,
Till we have built Jerusalem
In England's green and pleasant land.[1]

WILLIAM BLAKE, "Jerusalem,"
from *Milton*

In the preface to his *Milton*, William Blake offers a lyric precursor to his longer edition of *Jerusalem*.[2] Blake brings the fantastic visions seen in the Old and New Testament books of prophecy down to earth, specifically to England. By intentionally intertwining British topographical features with Biblical references, he transforms the world of prophecy into a clear and present reality for his British reader.[3]

Blake couches his poetic program in the form of a question. He asks whether the divine presence could have appeared in England and then proposes a related agenda for action: the prophet will struggle to transform England into Jerusalem, the land that the Lamb once physically occupied. These rhetorical questions obliquely establish the Lamb of God as a *voyant-visible*, depicted in a country that, though initially dark and foreboding, is to be positively refashioned as Jerusalem in the midst of England. Blake's decision to work toward this goal of transforming England into a new holy land, shown by the repeated imperatives of the third stanza, is effected through the very thought of such a vision of the Lamb.

Like Blake's Lamb of God whose "countenance divine" inspires, Virgil's gods sometimes participate in the narrative of the *Aeneid* and motivate Virgil's characters. In this chapter, I shall discuss the manner in which the gods are seen by and see human beings. Divine intervention demands and provokes swift human response, and the sight of a god moves the poem toward its telos.[4] I will consider how a character's sight of the gods—particularly Aeneas' vision of Mercury—affects his actions. In Aeneas' encounters with the divine, visual aspects of the narrative tend to outweigh words, particularly as the epic progresses. A god's presence provokes response more than do a god's verbal instructions. Visual deception, in such cases, is justified insofar as it points to the poem's telos.

I have divided the presentation of this topic into three sections. The first encompasses passages in which the gods are involved with some form of visual deception; for example, the gods' appearances may be altered. In the second section of the chapter, I shall consider visual encounters with the supernatural that are not deceptive. In such cases, the gods are correctly perceived as divine beings by their human contacts, and vision of the divinity validates divine communication. The expected result is immediate human compliance, not merely religious awe.[5] For Aeneas and Turnus, the degree to which each responds to the vision of a god tells us something about each character's reliance upon and compliance with visual stimuli.

Finally, I shall use the third section of this chapter to examine how Octavian/Augustus appears as an example of a semidivine character and offers a living example of the ideal *voyant-visible*. The structural position of visions of and allusions to Augustus in the *Aeneid* does not so much inspire Aeneas to fulfill his destiny in refounding Troy as it foreshadows the refounding of Rome by Augustus. Aeneas is not cognizant of the importance of the figure of the emperor whom he beholds, but his vision of him nevertheless justifies ex post facto the poem's telos. Let us begin, however, with a discussion of another encounter in which Aeneas is not fully aware of whom he beholds, namely, his own mother, in Book 1.

SEEN/UNSEEN
Virgin Mother

After Aeneas has regrouped his people on the Libyan shores, he and Achates explore the nearby area. In doing so, Aeneas encounters his mother,[6] who is disguised as a virgin huntress, much like Athena's appearance to Odysseus in the *Odyssey*.[7] When they meet, Venus speaks to Aeneas:

cui mater media sese tulit obuia silua
uirginis os habitumque gerens et uirginis arma
Spartanae, uel qualis equos Threissa fatigat
Harpalyce uolucremque fuga praeuertitur Hebrum.

. . .

ac prior 'heus,' inquit, 'iuuenes, monstrate, mearum
uidistis si quam hic errantem forte sororum
succinctam pharetra et maculosae tegmine lyncis,
aut spumantis apri cursum clamore prementem.'

Aen. 1.314–317, 321–324

[But in the middle of the wood, along
the way, his mother showed herself to him.
The face and dress she wore were like a maiden's,
her weapons like a girl's from Sparta or
those carried by Harpalyce of Thrace
when she tires out her horses, speeding faster
even than rapid Hebrus as she races.

. . .

And she speaks first:
"Young men there! Can you tell me if by chance
you have seen one of my sisters pass—she wore
a quiver and a spotted lynx's hide—
while she was wandering here or, with her shouts,
chasing a foaming boar along its course?" (M. 1.443–450, 455–460)]

Virgil's presentation of Venus' appearance, even down to the details of her ethnicity and her dress, suggests how she will be beheld by Aeneas. Her maidenly external appearance reverses Dido's psychological state: Venus appears externally as a "virgin" but is internally the goddess of love, while Dido is externally a woman but internally compels herself to remain faithful to Sychaeus, and in that sense is a "virgin."[8] Venus' appearance as a Thracian or Spartan girl (316) seems somewhat out of place in Africa, something that Aeneas would presumably notice, and her non-Libyan status is not well explained by commentators. R. D. Williams' suggestion that Spartan girls have a certain "physical toughness"[9] is apt enough but does not account for the geographical displacement.[10]

Aeneas states that he has not seen the sisters, and he does not offer to look for them. Rather, his attention is focused on the way the huntress with whom he now is conversing sounds and appears:[11]

'nulla tuarum audita mihi neque uisa sororum,
o quam te memorem, uirgo? namque haud tibi uultus
mortalis, nec uox hominem sonat; o, dea certe
(an Phoebi soror? an Nympharum sanguinis una?),
sis felix nostrumque leues, quaecumque, laborem. . . .'   *Aen.* 1.326–330

["I have not seen or heard your sister, maiden—
or by what name am I to call you, for
your voice is not like any human voice.
O goddess, you must be Apollo's sister
or else are to be numbered with the nymphs!
Whoever you may be, do help us, ease
our trials. . . ." (M. 1.462–468)]

So striking are her facial features that the very detail that Virgil had pointedly mentioned, namely, the appearance of Venus' face (315), is precisely the object upon which Aeneas fixes his vision (327). Aeneas remarks that her features do not seem to be mortal, and, though he does not recognize her as his mother, he is able to infer her divine status.

At the conclusion of Venus' speech, Aeneas identifies himself, ironically explaining that he has progressed on his journey because of his goddess-mother's help (381–382).[12] The encounter between Aeneas and Venus concludes with Venus' revelation of her true identity as she turns away:

Dixit et auertens rosea ceruice refulsit,
ambrosiaeque comae diuinum uertice odorem
spirauere; pedes uestis defluxit ad imos,

et uera incessu patuit dea. ille ubi matrem
agnouit tali fugientem est uoce secutus:
'quid natum totiens, crudelis tu quoque, falsis
ludis imaginibus?'   *Aen.* 1.402–408

[These were the words of Venus. When she turned,
her neck was glittering with a rose brightness;
her hair anointed with ambrosia,
her head gave all a fragrance of the gods;
her gown was long and to the ground; even
her walk was sign enough she was a goddess.
And when Aeneas recognized his mother,
he followed her with these words as she fled:
"Why do you mock your son—so often and
so cruelly—with these lying apparitions?" (M. 1.573–582)]

This is an ironic, almost comical anagnorisis. Only at the close of the encounter does Aeneas fully recognize his mother.[13] The verb *agnouit* (406)
shows that Aeneas has taken note of the way she walks (*uera incessu patuit dea*, 405) and of her huntress' garb as it is transformed into the *palla* of
a divinity.[14] As in the beginning of their interchange, Virgil emphasizes the
way the two appear to each other when he makes Aeneas call attention to
their mutual gaze, charging his mother with using false visions of herself to
mock him (407–408).

Virgil causes Aeneas to pose the narratologically provocative question
as to why he is in fact deceived by "lying apparitions." The answer would
seem to be that deception is necessary for Venus to convey information
about Dido to Aeneas without the distraction that the epiphany of a goddess would have engendered. Recognition of Venus might have prompted
Aeneas to seek the direct help and guidance that she chooses to provide less
directly, for Venus understands that, to achieve his destiny, Aeneas must first
undergo trials. He must meet Dido in the precise circumstances that Venus
has arranged; these circumstances depend on deception, even if that means
a mother must deceive her son.[15]

As *voyant-visible*, Aeneas does not always need to understand fully what
he sees; even limitations imposed on his vision support the narrative's telos.
Vision and cognizance do not always occur concurrently, yet vision can anticipate and create a context for proper understanding when the appropriate
moment presents itself.

Deception to Disclosure: A Hero's Welcome ex nube

As Aeneas enters Carthage, he has been conveniently concealed in a cloud that allows him to see others but protects him from being seen, a situation analogous to that of Venus earlier in this same book. Dido and her attendants see Aeneas, as he emerges from this cloud, with the same clarity with which he had been observing the Carthaginian court, a coincidence that confirms his status as *voyant-visible*. The protective cloud's creator is Venus, who, as the Homeric Aphrodite, once concealed Paris in just such a manner (*Il.* 3.373–383). As Aeneas views the city, he first regards his surroundings from within the cloud:

> at Venus obscuro gradientis aëre saepsit,
> et multo nebulae circum dea fudit amictu,
> cernere ne quis eos neu quis contingere posset
> moliriue moram aut ueniendi poscere causas.   *Aen.* 1.411–414

> [But as goddess, Venus cloaks
> Aeneas and Achates in dark mist;
> she wraps them in a cape of cloud so thick
> that none can see or touch them or delay
> their way or ask why they had come. (M. 1.586–590)]

The first of the negative final clauses, *cernere ne quis eos . . . posset* (413) reveals a manipulation of vision: Venus wants Aeneas to be able to enter the city unseen and to observe it without the interference of strangers. Unlike the rescue of Paris in *Iliad* 3, where Aphrodite specifically hid Paris for his protection, Venus conceals Aeneas so that he can gather information.

As Aeneas and Achates enter the city, they behold Dido speaking with Ilioneus and the other Trojans. Achates reminds Aeneas that Venus' words have now been visually corroborated (583–585). Having seen the confirmation of Venus' words, Aeneas is now ready to confront Dido. Venus herself withdraws the cloud and exposes Aeneas to Dido's astonished gaze:

> uix ea fatus erat cum circumfusa repente
> scindit se nubes et in aethera purgat apertum.
> restitit Aeneas claraque in luce refulsit
> os umerosque deo similis; namque ipsa decoram
> caesariem nato genetrix lumenque iuuentae
> purpureum et laetos oculis adflarat honores.   *Aen.* 1.586–591

[Yet he was hardly done when suddenly
the cloud that circled them is torn; it clears
away to open air. And there Aeneas
stood, glittering in that bright light, his face
and shoulders like a god's. Indeed, his mother
had breathed upon her son becoming hair,
the glow of a young man, and in his eyes,
glad handsomeness. (M. 1.825–832)]

Surrounded by light (*claraque in luce*, 588), Aeneas' statuelike pose (*restitit*, 588)[16] and radiant appearance easily catch Dido's eye. In the following two lines (590–591), Virgil describes Venus' role in creating this first impression. Not only has the goddess initially concealed her son from Dido, but she has also influenced the way that Aeneas first is made visible to the queen, causing him to appear *deo similis* (589).[17]

Venus' actions are comparable to those of Athena when she causes Odysseus to appear to Nausicaa in *Odyssey* 6:

τὸν μὲν Ἀθηναίη θῆκεν, Διὸς ἐκγεγαυῖα,
μείζονά τ' εἰσιδέειν καὶ πάσσονα, κὰδ δὲ κάρητος
οὔλας ἧκε κόμας, ὑακινθίνῳ ἄνθει ὁμοίας.
ὡς δ' ὅτε τις χρυσὸν περιχεύεται ἀργύρῳ ἀνὴρ
ἴδρις, ὃν Ἥφαιστος δέδαεν καὶ Παλλὰς Ἀθήνη
τέχνην παντοίην, χαρίεντα δὲ ἔργα τελείει,
ὣς ἄρα τῷ κατέχευε χάριν κεφαλῇ τε καὶ ὤμοις.   Od. 6.229–235

[Then Athene, daughter of Zeus, made him seem taller
for the eye to behold, and thicker, and on his head she arranged
the curling locks that hung down like hyacinthine petals.
And as when a master craftsman overlays gold on silver,
and he is one who was taught by Hephaistos and Pallas Athene
in art complete, and grace is on every work he finishes,
so Athene gilded with grace his head and his shoulders.]

The principal similarity of the two passages concerns the way each hero is perceived, though, as Austin notes, this is no mere translation, mediated, as it is, through an intervening allusion to Apollonius (*Arg.* 4.1309–1349).[18] Yet the principal intertext here is the Homeric passage, from which Virgil draws some of the details of hero meeting heroine.[19] Athena increases Odysseus' attractiveness so that Nausicaa will give him assistance,[20] whereas, in Virgil, Venus makes Aeneas appear especially handsome to thwart Juno's plans.

In the *Aeneid*, Venus is as artistic as she is cunning, careful to emphasize Aeneas' comeliness:

quale manus addunt ebori decus, aut ubi flauo
argentum Pariusue lapis circumdatur auro.   *Aen.* 1.592–593

[such grace as art can add
to ivory, or such as Parian marble
or silver shows when set in yellow gold. (M. 1.832–834)]

Here Virgil resumes further details from the Homeric model cited above (*Od.* 6.232–234). Though the description of Aeneas' enhanced stature (1.588–591) is clearly attributable to Venus, the goddess is not specifically compared to an artisan as Athena is in the *Odyssey*. This omission, along with the impersonal "hands" (*manus*, 592) and Virgil's use of the passive voice (*circumdatur*, 593), may indicate that he wishes to emphasize Aeneas' natural comeliness rather than merely Venus' ability to enhance.

Aeneas' dramatic emergence from the cloud engenders in Dido a sense of amazement (*obstipuit primo aspectu*, 613[21]). Aeneas' miraculous physical materialization causes in Dido not merely a humane response; it also leads her to fall in love with him, fulfilling Venus' desire to impede Juno's plans. The power of vision and visual deception seen here will characterize and qualify the relationship of these lovers, just as deception and vision are aspects of Aeneas' relationship with Venus. Aeneas' sudden appearance transforms him from invisible voyeur to *voyant-visible*, and his attractiveness evokes a compassionate gaze that will lead to an emotional connection with Dido (*magnoque animum labefactus amore*, 4.395). This bond begins with Dido's vision of Aeneas.

Unseen Love

Venus is well aware of the emotional bond that she has begun to forge between Dido and Aeneas, and her words anticipate that union in Book 1 when she details her plan for Dido (*magno Aeneae mecum teneatur amore*, 1.675).[22] Venus explains to Amor that she intends to substitute him for Ascanius. This proposal creates a contrast between visibility and concealment, for the exchange of the two boys effects an ironic perceptual tension whereby Love is simultaneously both hidden and seen. Venus' use of visual stimuli in the account contrasts with Juno's pronouncement of the affair to be a marriage (126) and with Dido's further articulation of the same (*coniugium uocat,* 4.172).[23] Juno's pronouncement and Dido's interpretation are not so effective as Venus' use of visual deception and the vision of Mercury, the latter of which ultimately redirects Aeneas' course.

Venus decides to influence Dido's affections in order to forestall further acts by Juno.[24] Venus' intention is to deceive (*capere ante dolis,* 673), and she employs language that reflects the siege of a city (*cingere flamma,* 673) to explain her strategy. While Venus uses the visual ruse of disguise to achieve her goal, Juno will attempt to bring about a marriage through her words: *conubio iungam stabili propriamque dicabo. / hic hymenaeus erit* (4.126–127).[25] The tricks of Juno are not so carefully cloaked and deceptive as those of Venus, and Venus is thus able to perceive clearly Juno's plans.[26] Insofar as Juno's devices fulfill Venus' strategy, Venus willingly assents to Juno's request (127–128).

Venus soon proposes to Amor the course of action that she has in mind: she will hide Ascanius away in sleep (680), while Amor will adopt Ascanius' appearance, specifically, his facial features (684). In the lines that follow, Dido's vision is emphasized, for she and her company marvel at the gifts and at Iulus; the queen, unable to find satisfaction by looking, continues to stare:

> mirantur dona Aeneae, mirantur Iulum,
> flagrantisque dei uultus simulataque uerba,
> pallamque et pictum croceo uelamen acantho.
> praecipue infelix, pesti deuota futurae,
> *expleri mentem nequit ardescitque tuendo*
> Phoenissa, et pariter puero donisque mouetur.   *Aen.* 1.709–714

> [They marvel at Aeneas' gifts, at Iülus
> the god's bright face and his fictitious words—
> and at the cloak, the veil adorned with saffron
> acanthus borders. And above all, luckless
> Dido—doomed to face catastrophe—
> can't sate her soul, inflamed by what she sees;
> the boy, the gifts excite her equally. (M. 1.990–996)]

Though both gifts and giver are regarded as astounding (709), Virgil chiefly emphasizes the deception of the "burning" god at the banquet (710). With a pathetic comment about her destiny (712), Virgil notes that Dido, too, burns (713–714). The deceptive vision of Amor in this passage produces Venus' desired results.

The childlike god then completes his task by moving from visual to sensory contact with the banqueters, especially the queen:[27]

> . . . reginam petit. haec oculis, haec pectore toto
> haeret et interdum gremio fouet inscia Dido
> insidat quantus miserae deus.   *Aen.* 1.717–719

> [Then he seeks out the queen.
> Her eyes cling fast to him, and all her heart;
> at times she fondles him upon her lap—
> for Dido does not know how great a god
> is taking hold of her poor self. (M. 1.999–1003)]

Virgil draws out the movement, beginning with the queen's eyes (717) and moving down to her breast and lap (718).[28] Dido's handling of Amor here obviously has erotic overtones.[29] Love works his way into Dido to achieve the bond between her and Aeneas that, we recall, is intended to prevent Aeneas from harm (671–672); this very relationship, if distracting for a time, will ultimately remind Aeneas of his mission.

In the gods' hands, deceptive vision causes even the strongest characters to be distracted, or, in the case of Dido, tragically deceived. For Aeneas, however, there are further visions that will cause him to focus afresh on the true vision of his own and his people's destiny.[30] When vision, deceptive or otherwise, moves the narrative toward the poem's telos, the gods, it would seem, are at liberty to employ visual ruses to deceive even the epic's most noble characters.

Somnus and Palinurus

En route to that telos, there are many disturbing moments when Aeneas or his men lose focus and suffer harm. Sometimes loss of focus occurs when vision succumbs to rhetorical persuasion. One such example is found in *Aeneid* 5, when the words of Somnus, who is disguised as Phorbas, attempt to overcome the vision of Palinurus.

The tale begins as this god disguises himself as Phorbas and appears to Palinurus, the helmsman to whom Aeneas has entrusted head position in the fleet (5.835–842). The sleepiness (*placida . . . quiete*, 836) that introduces the episode is the perfect setting for *leuis* Somnus to come gliding down from the stars (837). Night brings the darkness that precludes vision,[31] and, as he arrives, Somnus ironically acts as a ray of light, displacing the darkness (*aëra dimouit tenebrosum et dispulit umbras*, 839).

Before falling asleep, Palinurus encounters the false Phorbas, who reminds Palinurus of his familial origin through the patronymic:

'Iaside Palinure, ferunt ipsa aequora classem,
aequatae spirant aurae, datur hora quieti.
pone caput fessosque oculos furare labori.
ipse ego paulisper pro te tua munera inibo.' *Aen.* 5.843–846

["Palinurus, son of Iasus,
the seas themselves bear on the fleet; the breezes
blow steadily; this is a time for rest.
Lay down your head and steal your tired eyes
from trials; and for a brief while I myself
will take your place, your duties." (M. 5.1113–1118)]

By addressing Palinurus as Iasides, Somnus evokes a connection with Troy, for Iasius was one of Troy's legendary founders and the grandfather of Laomedon,[32] whose duping of Neptune and Apollo led to a human sacrifice.[33] This family connection is important because it suggests a history of deception that precedes this incident. Furthermore, this deception leads in both instances to human sacrifice. Somnus' address of Palinurus conjures up a lineage that had encompassed a significant affront to Neptune,[34] who, a few lines earlier, had stated that there would be a sacrifice (*'unus erit tantum amissum quem gurgite quaeres; / unum pro multis dabitur caput,'* 5.814–815).[35] Neptune seems to allude to the old curse of the human sacrifice that he and Apollo once required of the Trojans, as do Somnus' opening words.

Palinurus' death is described as a struggle to stay awake and thus specifically to maintain the vision that he needs to guide the ships:

cui uix attollens Palinurus lumina fatur:
'mene salis placidi uultum fluctusque quietos
ignorare iubes? mene huic confidere monstro?
Aenean credam (quid enim?) fallacibus auris
et caeli totiens deceptus fraude sereni?' *Aen.* 5.847–851

[Palinurus,
who scarcely lifts his eyes, makes this reply:
"And are you asking me to act as if
I did not know the face of this calm sea
and its still waves? Do you ask me to trust
this monster? Why should I confide Aeneas
to the deceiving winds—I who have been
cheated so often by the treachery
of tranquil skies?" (M. 5.1118–1126)]

Palinurus' effort to keep his eyes open is emphasized by the adverb/participle combination of *uix attolens* (847). Further, adjectives such as *placidi* and *quietos* (848) heighten the sense of sleepiness that Somnus brings and recall Virgil's description of the somnolent setting of this event (*placida . . . quieta*, 836). Palinurus' rejection of Phorbas' suggestion and his resolve to fix his eyes on his task roughly parallel the dogged determination of Odysseus' aural resistance to the Sirens' song. Interestingly, Palinurus is steering the ship precisely toward the Sirens' abode at the time of his encounter with Somnus (*iamque adeo scopulos Sirenum aduecta subibat*, 864 ["Now, swept along, it neared / the Sirens' reefs" (M. 5.1142–1143)]).

Palinurus' physical effort and words concertedly resist the *loquelae* (842) of Phorbas. Here Palinurus' resolve to maintain his visual clarity would have prevailed over Phorbas' words, had not the god resorted to further measures:

talia dicta dabat, clauumque adfixus et haerens
nusquam amittebat oculosque sub astra tenebat.
ecce deus ramum Lethaeo rore madentem
uique soporatum Stygia super utraque quassat
tempora, cunctantique natantia lumina soluit.   *Aen.* 5.852–856

[He held the tiller fast;
not once did he let loose his grasp; his eyes
were fixed upon the stars. But—look—the god
now shakes a bough that drips with Lethe's dew,
drenched with the stupefying power of Styx,
on Palinurus' temples; as he struggles,
his swimming eyes relax. (M. 5.1126–1132)]

Because the god's words are not sufficient to overcome Palinurus' resolve, Somnus must resort to a different method (854–856). Vision (*oculos . . . tene-*

bat, 853) fails Palinurus only under the influence of the Stygian power (*uique ... Stygia,* 855). Here, at the book's end, in an event associated with sacrifice (Neptune's *unum pro multis,* 815), Palinurus hesitates when struggling to keep his focus. The conjunction of the notions of sacrifice and focus parallels, in many ways, the presentation of Dido in Book 4 as the "sacrifice" that allows Aeneas to focus on the true land of his calling.[36] Thus, Dido's and Palinurus' "sacrifices" are necessary to point toward the goal of the poem and spur Aeneas to fulfill his destiny.

GODS REVEALED
Turnus and Allecto

Now I would like to turn the argument away from the vision of gods that is deceptive but fixed upon the telos of the narrative to the argument that deception leads to direct and fully disclosed visions of the divine. These, too, point toward the poem's outcome, albeit obviously. Let us begin with Turnus' encounter with the Fury Allecto who, though she first deceives him, shortly and ironically reveals her true identity. Virgil uses this revelation to introduce Turnus and begin a characterization that will culminate in the poem's final scene: Turnus understands, too late, what he has done, and his last-minute appeal does not suffice.

Having resolved to turn to chthonic forces to achieve her goals (*flectere si nequeo superos, Acheronta mouebo,* 7.312 ["if I / cannot bend High Ones, then I shall move hell" (M. 7.412–413)]), Juno seeks out Allecto. Juno issues her orders (*dissice compositam pacem, sere crimina belli,* 339 ["break this settled peace; / sow war and crime" (M. 7.448–449)]), and Allecto proceeds to Amata's threshold, infusing the queen with hate and rage in a dramatic fashion. Though Allecto is never actually beheld by Amata, she is most certainly beheld by her next victim, Turnus. Allecto appears to Turnus as Calybe, the priestess of Juno:

> tectis hic Turnus in altis
> iam mediam nigra carpebat nocte quietem.
> Allecto toruam faciem et furialia membra
> exuit, in uultus sese transformat anilis
> et frontem obscenam rugis arat, induit albos
> cum uitta crinis, tum ramum innectit oliuae;
> fit Calybe Iunonis anus templique sacerdos,
> et iuueni ante oculos his se cum uocibus offert. . . . *Aen.* 7.413–420

[There Turnus lay
asleep, beneath his high roof, in black night.
Allecto sets aside her savage features
and Fury's body; she transforms herself,
becoming an old woman, furrowing
her filthy brow with wrinkles, putting on
white hair and headband, then an olive bough;
she now is Calybe, the aged priestess
of Juno and her temple. And she shows
herself before the young man with these words. . . . (M. 7.550–559)]

Turnus is first described in the *Aeneid* as a warrior with his eyes closed in sleep (415). His lack of vision, upon his introduction, contrasts with Aeneas' ability to see (cf. 1.111) the struggle of his men even though he is caught with them in the sea storm (*Aen.* 1.94–123). Although commentators do not always acknowledge its significance,[37] Calybe is a fitting name for Allecto to hide behind, as it emphasizes the visual deception; in Greek, Calybe can mean "covering" and is related, of course, to a word implying obstruction of sight, καλύπτειν.[38] This "covered over" Allecto appears as an old woman with white hair (417) that contrasts sharply with the dark night (414) from which she emerges.

Calybe touches on some tender subjects. She begins by raising the question as to whether Turnus' military labors have been wasted.[39] Allecto asks specifically whether Turnus will submit to having his rule transferred to the Greeks (*Dardaniis transcribi*, 422).[40] Her questions, followed by stinging imperatives (*i . . . offer te . . . periclis / . . . i, sterne acies . . .* , 425–426), suggest that Turnus has lost focus of his duty. Allecto emphasizes Turnus' failure to act with accusing remarks that recall those of Dido to Aeneas (4.381–382).[41]

Calybe enjoins Turnus to prepare an army, to burn the Trojan ships (429–431), and to educate Latinus about the proper choice of son-in-law (433–434). Turnus' response, characterized by the participial phrase *uatem inridens*, is, at best, smug. Stating that the news has not escaped his ears, Turnus refutes Calybe's allegation about his fear, exhorting her to attend to her own duty, religion (*cura tibi diuum effigies et templa tueri; / bella uiri pacemque gerent quis bella gerenda*[42]). Turnus' statement identifies him with Hector as the warrior who will counter Aeneas' Achilles, for Turnus cites Hector's statement that war will be a care for men (πόλεμος δ' ἄνδρεσσι μελήσει, *Il.* 6.492).[43]

Allecto drops her disguise as Calybe, revealing the full fury of her power:

> Talibus Allecto dictis exarsit in iras.
> at iuueni *oranti* subitus tremor occupat artus,
> deriguere oculi: tot Erinys sibilat hydris
> tantaque se facies aperit; tum flammea torquens
> lumina cunctantem et quaerentem dicere plura
> reppulit. . . . Aen. 7.445–450

[Allecto blazed in anger at his words.
But even as he spoke, a sudden trembling
clutched at the limbs of Turnus, his eyes stared:
the Fury hisses with so many serpents,
so monstrous is the face she shows. She turned
her flaming eyes and thrust him, faltering, back,
as he tried to say more. (M. 7.589–595)]

Once he recognizes her as a goddess, Turnus entreats Allecto. Servius (ad loc.) connects the participle (*oranti*, 446) with *orator*, and Horsfall notes that in Virgil's day it would have been an archaism to use *orare* to mean "speak."[44] While Turnus' words incite Allecto, the interaction between Allecto and Turnus is portrayed mainly in visual terms. Turnus' eyes grow fixed (447), and a sudden trembling enters his body as he entreats her (446). Her fiery eyes give him pause, and his attempt to speak is futile (449). One might compare this description of Turnus to Aeneas, whose gaze induces Dido to flee in Book 4:

> . . . aegra fugit seque ex *oculis* auertit et aufert,
> linquens multa metu *cunctantem et multa parantem*
> *dicere.* Aen. 4.389–391

[. . . heartsick, she shuns
the light of day, deserts his eyes; she turns
away, leaves him in fear and hesitation,
Aeneas longing still to say so much. (M. 4.533–535)]

Aeneas responds to Dido, who seeks refuge from his gaze, in the same way that Turnus responds to Allecto: he hesitates, wishing to say more (448–449). Such a description also anticipates the depiction of Aeneas at the poem's close; on that occasion, Aeneas turns to a hesitating and beseeching Turnus, who begs Aeneas to spare him out of regard for Daunus his father (12.932–933). In the last description, as in the first (7.446), the verb *orare* appears.

Virgil uses this verb to frame his description of Turnus, showing his tendency to resort to hesitation and entreaty in critical situations. In the poem's final scene, Aeneas also hesitates but overcomes his hesitation by action.

These internal allusions inform Turnus' character and also suggest, particularly after Book 7, that vision is able to evoke a formidable response. Allecto's words have another effect as she admonishes Turnus to have regard for her identity:

'en ego uicta situ, quam ueri effeta senectus
arma inter regum falsa formidine ludit.
respice ad haec: adsum dirarum ab sede sororum,
bella manu letumque gero.'
sic effata facem iuueni coniecit et atro
lumine fumantis fixit sub pectore taedas.   *Aen.* 7.452–457

       ["Then look
at me—undone by rust, fruitless of truth,
whom old age plays upon with cheating terrors
among the quarrels of kings! Just look at me!
I come here from the home of the dread Sisters,
And in my hand I carry death and wars."
And saying this, she cast a torch at Turnus,
Fixing the firebrand within his breast,
And there it smoked with murky light. (M. 7.597–605)]

Allecto instructs Turnus to consider her origin and, to emphasize her point, begins to reveal her thoughts with visual imperatives (*en,* 452, *respice,* 454). She also mimics his quips about her age and her ignorance of warfare. Employing a stark oxymoron well suited to Hades' torches,[45] Virgil adds that Allecto hurls a firebrand with a "dark light" (546–547) at Turnus' chest. Such burning darkness ultimately envelops Turnus' reasoning.

Allecto's display of her true identity to Turnus offers an important clue for consideration of his character. His reaction is characterized by entreaty, an attempt to talk his way out of trouble. From his first introduction to his final appearance, Turnus is a person who often resorts to entreaty when threatened. Let us now consider how Aeneas reacts when he encounters a god revealed.

Mercury

Perhaps the most important encounter with a god in the *Aeneid* is that of Aeneas' vision of Mercury, which occurs in the fourth book. This episode points clearly toward the poem's telos, for this vision of the god refocuses Aeneas upon his mission. The epiphany of Mercury informs Aeneas' sense of both duty and destiny.

The episode begins when Jupiter, inspired by Iarbas' request to take note of the situation in Carthage,[46] turns his eyes toward Carthage and the lovers who have forgotten their reputation.[47] Jupiter pointedly tells Mercury that Aeneas comes up short because he is failing to keep his destiny in proper perspective:

> 'uade age, nate, uoca Zephyros et labere pennis
> Dardaniumque ducem, Tyria Karthagine qui nunc
> exspectat fatisque datas non *respicit* urbes,
> adloquere et celeris defer mea dicta per auras.' *Aen.* 4.223–226

> ["Be on your way, my son, call up the Zephyrs,
> glide on your wings, speak to the Dardan chieftain
> who lingers now at Tyrian Carthage, paying
> not one jot of attention to the cities
> the Fates have given him. Mercury, carry
> across the speeding winds the words I urge." (M. 4.298–303)]

The verbs *expecto* and *respicio* share a common visual root that intimates that Aeneas has lost sight of his goal. The latter verb will occur again eleven lines later in Jupiter's discourse, framing his instructions to Mercury:

> 'quid struit? aut qua spe inimica in gente moratur
> nec prolem Ausoniam et Lauinia *respicit* arua?
> nauiget! haec summa est, hic nostri nuntius esto.' *Aen.* 4.235–237

> ["What is he pondering, what hope
> can hold him here among his enemies,
> not caring for his own Ausonian sons
> or for Lavinian fields. He must set sail.
> And this is all; my message lies in this." (M. 4.314–318)]

Just as Aeneas is to have regard for the city promised by Hector (*moenia quaere / magna . . .* , 2.294–295), he must also have regard for (or look back upon) a vision that itself looks forward. The verb *respicio* is important here.[48] At the beginning of Book 5, Aeneas and his men will look back upon burning Carthage (5.3) as well as, later, on the cloud of smoke generated by the Trojan women's attempt to burn the ships (5.666). Here in Book 4, when Mercury brings him Jupiter's command to have regard for his destiny, Aeneas must confirm the future by looking back to the past. In the terminology of Merleau-Ponty, Aeneas has temporarily lost status as a *voyant-visible*, for he has lapsed in his role as the one who sees.

As Mercury now descends over Atlas, he brings with him his psychopompos' wand that can deprive mortals of vision by sleep or death (*lumina morte resignat*, 244). Mercury will instead restore Aeneas' vision, but only after the god himself has observed Aeneas building walls and citadels:

> ut primum alatis tetigit magalia plantis,
> Aenean fundantem arces ac tecta nouantem
> conspicit. atque illi stellatus iaspide fulua
> ensis erat Tyrioque ardebat murice laena
> demissa ex umeris, diues quae munera Dido
> fecerat, et tenui telas discreuerat auro.   *Aen.* 4.259–264

> [As soon as his winged feet have touched the outskirts,
> he sees Aeneas founding fortresses
> and fashioning new houses. And his sword
> was starred with tawny jasper, and the cloak
> that draped his shoulders blazed with Tyrian purple—
> a gift that wealthy Dido wove for him;
> she had run golden thread along the web. (M. 4.346–352)]

Aeneas has become noticeable in the wrong way. While his appearance is not nearly so effeminate as Iarbas had described him to Jupiter,[49] nevertheless, Aeneas does not yet seem Roman.[50] Instead, Aeneas has focused too much on his own appearance (262–263) rather than on keeping his vision trained on the proper future city.

Following Jupiter's instructions, Mercury remonstrates with Aeneas in the same visual language that Jupiter had used, encouraging Aeneas to have regard for Ascanius' future:

> '. . . Ascanium surgentem et spes heredis Iuli
> *respice*, cui regnum Italiae Romanaque tellus
> debetur.' tali Cyllenius ore locutus

mortalis uisus medio sermone reliquit
et procul in tenuem *ex oculis euanuit* auram.
 At uero Aeneas *aspectu obmutuit* amens,
arrectaeque horrore comae et uox faucibus haesit. *Aen.* 4.274–280

           ["... remember
Ascanius growing up, the hopes you hold
for Iulus, your own heir, to whom are owed
the realm of Italy and land of Rome."
So did Cyllene's god speak out. He left
the sight of mortals even as he spoke
and vanished into the transparent air.
This vision stunned Aeneas, struck him dumb;
his terror held his hair erect; his voice
held fast within his jaws. (M. 4.366–375)]

The expression *aspectu obmutuit*, as Sara Mack once noted, implies "sharp reaction" to the appearance of the god.[51] Earlier, Iarbas had asked Jupiter to behold (208) the affair of Dido and Aeneas, and Jupiter had then informed Mercury that Aeneas has lost perspective (225, 236). Mercury, having himself beheld Aeneas' situation (261), soon appears to Aeneas to admonish him to look to his duty (275). Having thus instructed Aeneas, Mercury disappears from view (277–278), leaving Aeneas awestruck by his appearance (279).

Although he says nothing at the appearance of the god, Aeneas clearly desires to leave Carthage (*ardet abire fuga*, 281). In spite of his intention, Aeneas does not take action immediately. Rather, uncertain and hesitant, he debates about the proper course of action (*heu quid agat?*, 283). The primary reason for this is that the intoxication of his affair with Dido is so strong that a single visit from the god is not sufficient to overcome it. The power of vision has not yet reached fruition in the epic. Though the combination of Mercury's rhetoric and Aeneas' vision of the god has had some effect, Aeneas is still hesitant and ambivalent (283–284).[52]

Mercury again appears to Aeneas, who has delayed his departure despite having completed all necessary preparations. In this second encounter, Virgil emphasizes Mercury's appearance, a description delayed from their first meeting:

huic se forma dei uultu redeuntis eodem
obtulit in somnis rursusque ita uisa monere est,
omnia Mercurio similis, uocemque coloremque
et crinis flauos et membra decora iuuenta. . . . *Aen.* 4.556–559

[And in his sleep a vision of the god
returned to him with that same countenance—
resembling Mercury in everything:
his voice and coloring and yellow hair
and all his handsome body, a young man's—
and seemed to bring a warning once again. (M. 4.770–775)]

Although Aeneas explains to Dido why he must leave, Mercury must appear to him again in a dream to hasten his departure. This extended description lends a greater visual presence to a god who can so easily melt into the breeze. Mercury asks Aeneas whether he sees the dangers that beset him. He resumes this visual thread with a warning of what will come with the dawn if Aeneas does not depart immediately. Mercury also laces his speech with far more visual imagery than his previous admonition contained:

'nate dea, potes hoc sub casu ducere somnos,
nec quae te circum stent deinde pericula *cernis,*
demens, nec Zephyros audis spirare secundos?
illa dolos dirumque nefas in pectore uersat
certa mori, uariosque irarum concitat aestus.
non fugis hinc praeceps, dum praecipitare potestas?
iam mare turbari trabibus saeuasque uidebis
conlucere faces, iam feruere litora flammis,
si te his attigerit terris Aurora morantem.'   *Aen.* 4.560–568

["You, goddess-born, how can you lie asleep
at such a crisis? Madman, can't you see
the threats around you, can't you hear the breath
of kind west winds? She conjures injuries
and awful crimes, she means to die, she stirs
the shifting surge of restless anger. Why
not flee headlong, while there is time?
You soon will see the waters churned by wreckage,
ferocious torches blaze, and beaches flame,
if morning finds you lingering on this coast." (M. 4.776–785)]

Mercury poses a rhetorical question to Aeneas in visual terms, for the perils that beset the hero are plain to see. Furthermore, Mercury's visibility gives his character credibility. By the time Mercury reappears, now in a dream, Aeneas seems to have learned that an apparition of a god is not to be taken lightly. He submits to the god, induced to do so by the power of the vision (*subitis exterritus umbris,* 571) and by the warnings of impending danger. Aeneas' view of Mercury and the god's portrayal of the future stir Aeneas to quit Libya and to seek his fated land.

While the first appearance of the god caused Aeneas to be quiet and confused, Mercury's second epiphany produces obedience and action. Mercury appears not only because Jupiter has sent him and commanded him to do so but also because Aeneas must learn something that Turnus, as we shall see later, never learns. Aeneas has discovered that one should act in response to the power of the visual message; by contrast, Turnus fails to realize that action is better than supplication. The proper response to the vision of a god is immediate action.

Contrasting Visions: Tiber and Aeneas, Iris and Turnus

In the poem's second half, Venus, Tiber, and Iris all make candid appearances to either Aeneas or Turnus;[53] Venus and Iris both appear to the heroes during the daytime, while Tiber approaches Aeneas as he sleeps at night. The openness of each encounter is affirming: the viewing hero is to note not merely the message that the divinity bears but the effect of the divinity's appearance. More importantly, as we saw in the case of Mercury's revelation, the viewer is to act in a timely manner upon the admonition that the divinity brings.

These general observations with respect to the passages in question find support in the text beginning with the encounter of Turnus and Iris. After appearing as Beröe to the Trojan women in Sicily, Iris' next true epiphany occurs in Book 9,[54] when she is sent by Juno to speak with Turnus. When Iris arrives, she finds Turnus sitting in a sacred grove:

> Atque ea diuersa penitus dum parte geruntur,
> Irim de caelo misit Saturnia Iuno
> audacem ad Turnum. luco tum forte parentis
> Pilumni Turnus sacrata ualle sedebat.
> ad quem sic roseo Thaumantias ore locuta est:
> 'Turne, quod optanti diuum promittere nemo
> auderet, uoluenda dies en attulit ultro.'   *Aen.* 9.1–7

> [And while far off these things were happening,
> Saturnian Juno down from heaven sent
> Iris to daring Turnus. As it chanced,

he then was resting in a sacred glen,
the forest of his ancestor, Pilumnus.
The rose-lipped daughter of Thaumas spoke to him:
"Turnus, that which no god had dared to promise
in answer to your prayers, circling time
has brought unasked." (M. 9.1–9)]

On this occasion, there is no baroque description of Iris' descent, such as that of Book 5.[55] In Book 9, Iris simply appears to Turnus, just as Venus did to Aeneas in Book 8:

> At Venus aetherios inter dea candida nimbos
> dona ferens aderat; natumque in ualle reducta
> ut procul egelido secretum flumine uidit,
> talibus adfata est dictis seque obtulit ultro. . . .　　　*Aen.* 8.608–611

[But Venus, the bright goddess, bearing gifts,
drew near in airy clouds; and when far off
she saw her son in a secluded valley,
withdrawn beside a cooling stream, then she
showed herself freely to him, saying this. . . . (M. 8.788–792)]

These two episodes share common features. Both Aeneas and Turnus are secluded, and, while neither prays for an epiphany per se, each is in a place appropriate for such an encounter.[56] Both are situated in sacred groves beside a stream, although Turnus' proximity to a stream is not apparent until after Iris has ascended.[57] In the description of Turnus and Iris, the phrase *en attulit ultro* (9.7) evokes the description of Venus' open revelation of herself to Aeneas in the previous book (*seque obtulit ultro*, 8.611). Virgil contrasts the manner in which, in each scene, a human being's view of a goddess bolsters the hero's spirit.

Once Turnus has received her, Iris explains precisely why she has come. She tells Turnus that Aeneas has left for the Palatine (9.8) and explicitly urges him to act:

> 'quid dubitas? nunc tempus equos, nunc poscere currus.
> rumpe moras omnis et turbata arripe castra.'　　　*Aen.* 9.12–13

["Then why hesitate?
Enough delays! Now is the time to call

for horse and chariot! Now lay hands upon
the panicked Trojan camp." (M. 9.14–17)]

Iris forthrightly declares her mission: inasmuch as Aeneas is away, she has
come to call Turnus to swift action. Philip Hardie rightly associates *tem-
pus* (12) with the Greek notion of καιρός, an association that heightens the
urgency of the action requested.[58] While in the twelfth book we find Turnus
opportunistically taking initiative (12.96), he takes no immediate action on
this occasion.

This lack of swift response is notable, not because Turnus is lazy—indeed he normally is eager to seize opportunity[59]—but because he is temporarily unresponsive, even though he has encountered a divinity. Nor is he
ignorant of the fact that he has been speaking with a goddess, even if his address of her as *decus caeli* may suggest that he is not entirely sure that she
is Iris:[60]

'Iri, decus caeli, quis te mihi nubibus actam
detulit in terras? unde haec tam clara repente
tempestas? medium *uideo* discedere caelum
palantisque polo stellas. sequor omina tanta,
quisquis in arma uocas.'   *Aen.* 9.18–22

["O Iris, heavens' glory, who has sent you
down from the clouds to me on earth? From where
this storm of sudden brightness in the air?
I see the heavens' center opening
and stars that wander all about the pole.
I follow such an omen and whoever
it is who now has called me to take arms." (M. 9.22–28)]

Turnus explicitly states that he sees heaven rending itself, whence came
Iris' glory. Turnus' vision of the goddess echoes both Achilles' address to Iris
in the *Iliad* (18.182) and Aeneas' response to Mercury, considered above.[61]
Though Turnus says that he follows *tanta omina* (21), his stated compliance
is not immediate:

et sic effatus ad undam
processit summoque hausit de gurgite lymphas
multa deos orans, onerauitque aethera uotis.   *Aen.* 9.22–24

[And as he spoke, he reached the riverbank,
scooped water from the swirling stream, and praying
long to the gods, loaded the air with vows. (M. 9.29–31)]

In response to the *tempestas* (20) of Iris' epiphany, which R. D. Williams has noted is not unlike the subsequent description of the revelation of the Great Mother (9.110),[62] Turnus decides to continue to pray (*multa deos orans*, 24). Yet is this the best course of action for a hero? When Aeneas encounters his mother in Book 8, he scrutinizes the contents of the weapons he receives (*atque oculos per singula uoluit,* / *miratur,*[63] 8.618–619) and then girds himself for martial conflict, donning the symbols of his future (731). Turnus' course of action, however, is delayed by much prayer;[64] as Hardie has noted,[65] the phrase *onerauit . . . uotis* (24) has a ponderous feel to it.[66]

In a manner similar to other visions such as those of Hector (Book 2), the Penates (Book 3), Mercury's second appearance (Book 4), and Anchises (Book 5),[67] the vision of Tiber comes when Aeneas is sleeping:

. . . Aeneas, tristi turbatus pectora bello,
procubuit seramque dedit per membra quietem.
huic deus ipse loci fluuio Tiberinus amoeno
populeas inter senior se attollere frondes
uisus (eum tenuis glauco uelabat amictu
carbasus, et crinis umbrosa tegebat harundo),
tum sic adfari. . . .   *Aen.* 8.29–35

[. . . Aeneas, restless over bitter war,
stretched out along the riverbank beneath
the cold, let late-come rest seep through his limbs.
The river god himself, old Tiberinus
lord of that place and gentle stream, rising
from poplar leaves, then stood before Aeneas;
thin linen covered him with sea-green dress,
and shady reeds were covering for his head.
He spoke. . . . (M. 8.35–43)]

Though Mandelbaum's translation does not adequately render the visual force of *uisus* (33), Aeneas sees clearly in his dream. Virgil offers almost rococo details of the god's grey-green garb and crown of reeds. Once Father Tiber has begun to speak, he gives many reassurances of Aeneas' destiny, supported by visual confirmations:

'hic tibi certa domus, certi (ne absiste) penates.
neu belli terrere minis; tumor omnis et irae
concessere deum.
iamque tibi, ne uana putes haec fingere somnum,
litoreis ingens inuenta sub ilicibus sus
triginta capitum fetus enixa iacebit,
alba solo recubans, albi circum ubera nati.'   *Aen.* 8.39–45

["... for here your home and household gods are sure.
Do not draw back or panic at war's threats;
the rage and anger of the gods are done.
And now, lest you should think these are but empty
fictions sleep has feigned, you shall discover
a huge white sow stretched out upon the ground
along the banks beneath the breaching ilex,
together with a new-delivered litter
of thirty suckling white pigs at her teats." (M. 8.48–56)]

There has been a good deal of debate as to the validity of Tiber's formulation (40–41) that the anger of the gods has subsided. At best, this is a wishful statement;[68] at worst, a lie.[69] The latter suggestion seems more plausible because here, as in other instances, a god's visible, undisguised appearance (such as Mercury in Book 4, Venus in Book 8, or Iris in Book 9) indicates the deity's wish to speak openly and honestly: it is not the deceptive vision of Venus in Book 1, Cupid in Book 4, or Iris in Book 5. Here in Book 8, Tiber gives Aeneas a specific sign—the sow (43), the fruition of Helenus' prophecy of Book 3 from which lines 43–45 are repeated verbatim—to prove his credibility. As the fulfillment of both Tiber's and Helenus' words, the sow provides visual confirmation and validation of Aeneas' mission and is characterized as amazing to see (*oculis mirabile monstrum*, 81).

Moreover, Tiber calls attention to his own aspect to confirm his words by the vision that Aeneas now beholds:

'surge age, nate dea, primisque cadentibus astris
Iunoni fer rite preces, iramque minasque
supplicibus supera uotis. mihi uictor honorem
persolues. ego sum pleno *quem* flumine *cernis*
stringentem ripas et pinguia culta secantem,
caeruleus Thybris, caelo gratissimus amnis.'   *Aen.* 8.59–64

["Come now, goddess-born,
arise and, as the stars first set, be sure
to offer fitting prayers to Juno; let
your humble gifts defeat her threats and anger.
And when you are a victor, honor me.
I am *the one you see* touching the banks
with floods dividing fat and well-tilled fields.
I am the blue-green Tiber, river most
beloved of the heavens." (M. 8.75–83)]

Having advised Aeneas to offer sacrifices to Juno, Tiber now calls on Aeneas to behold his peculiarly fluvial aspect and attributes. His further instructions intimate that his words (40–41) have been an optimistic interpretation of divine *tumor et irae* and that Juno preserves at least some anger (hence the injunction to overcome the wrath that remains, 60–61). Tiber then explicitly identifies himself through his physical appearance (*strigentem . . . secantem*) and his visual qualities (*caeruleus*),[70] calling attention to the fact that Aeneas does see him (62).[71] Virgil's *figura etymologica*, involving the shared etymology of *caeruleus* and *caelo*, emphasizes this god's visibility.[72]

Questions as to the optimism or pessimism of Tiber's words now become less important than the validation that his physical appearance and the discovery of the sow provide. The epic has moved away from deceptive visions of a false Troy at Buthrotum, where Aeneas received the prediction of the sow, to true vision of the true Latium, which Tiber and the sow represent.[73] In the earlier prophecy concerning the sow (3.394), Helenus had told Aeneas that the Trojans would eat their tables, a sign that was visually confirmed after they arrived in the promised land (7.116). Verbal prophecy, there, too, is fulfilled by visual signals.

Aeneas responds to the vision of the god and of the sow with action. At the conclusion of the episode, Aeneas will load Tiber with gifts (76) and not with the requests that Turnus gives to the heavens (9.24). Aeneas has learned much since his encounter with Mercury, when the god interrogated him about his inactivity (*Aen.* 4.283–284).[74] Subsequent to that encounter, we saw earlier, Aeneas showed that he understands that action is the most appropriate response to a god's epiphany. After Mercury's second appearance (4.554–570), Aeneas responds by drawing his sword and cutting the ships' cables (*uaginaque eripit ensem*, 4.579), an act comparable to the martial action in which he will engage after receiving weapons from Venus at the conclusion of Book 8.

When Turnus finally does comply with the god's commands, he is described as a river:

> ... medio dux agmine Turnus:
> ceu septem surgens sedatis amnibus altus
> per tacitum Ganges aut pingui flumine Nilus
> cum refluit campis et iam se condidit alueo.   *Aen.* 9.28, 30–32

> [... and at the center of the line is Turnus,
> their captain—even as the silent Ganges
> that rises high with seven tranquil streams,
> or Nile when his rich flood ebbs from the fields
> and he at last sinks back into his channel. (M. 9.36–40)]

In fact, he is described as one of two rivers, either a flooding Ganges or a receding Nile. This back and forth, flowing motion suggests Turnus' indecisiveness, and the fact that these are not local deities suggests his "otherness." This ambivalence of Turnus must be contrasted to Aeneas, who complies with Father Tiber's commands and thus effects a close relationship with an indigenous river. Appearance, too, is important in this passage: Aeneas is not present in Latium but nevertheless appears to be the stalwart defender of a city (9.43–49),[75] while Turnus, though Italian by birth, appears as a foreign, specifically eastern, presence. As such, he comes across the plain in a visible display:

> hic subitam *nigro* glomerari puluere nubem
> prospiciunt Teucri ac *tenebras* insurgere campis.
> primus ab aduersa conclamat mole *Caicus:*
> 'quis globus, o ciues, caligine uoluitur *atra?*'   *Aen.* 9.33–36

> [And here the Teucrians can see a sudden
> cloudbank that gathers with black dust and darkness
> that rises from the plains. And from a rampart
> Caicus is the first to cry aloud:
> "My countrymen, what rolling mass is this
> of gloom and darkness?" (M. 9.41–46)]

As they approach, Turnus' troops appear dark to the Trojans. The Trojan who recognizes them, Caicus, has a name that suggests darkness,[76] and he is the appropriate watchman for a number of reasons. Caicus' name is identical to the name of a specifically eastern river from Mysia that was certainly known to Virgil, for Virgil includes it in his catalogue in *Georgics* 4.[77] As Turnus has previously been compared to an eastern river, it is fitting that one with such a name identifies Turnus' advance. Moreover, his very name, though tri-syllabic, is nonetheless evocative of *caecus* ("blind"). This similarity resonates with the tenebrous description of the Italian troops (*nigro . . . puluere*, 33; *tenebras*, 34; *caligine . . . atra*, 36).

Though Turnus was meticulous to acknowledge Iris (18) and to pray (24),[78] he did not respond with appropriate action. Iris' epiphany reveals not the bold Turnus suggested at the passage's opening (*audacem*, 9.3)[79] but the imprecating[80] Turnus that the reader will persistently encounter by the epic's conclusion. Aeneas, by contrast, responds to encountering his mother by donning weapons that symbolize the future that he now carries on his shoulders, as he will shortly return to battle to take action required to make that future a reality.

Gods who act as *voyants-visibles* accomplish their agendas, and the sight of a god is less a call to marvel than it is to respond. Divine visions justify previous omens, offer guidance, and confirm faith. The one who sees must act and not equivocate.

A GOD IN THE MIDST

Rome's first emperor also appears in the *Aeneid* as a type of divinity, and his numinous status obtains throughout Virgil's poetic career. When Augustus appears directly or by allusion in Virgilian narrative, he is situated *in mediis rebus*, whether in the approximate center of a vignette or of the entire poem. Center position is apparently significant, suggesting Augustus' centrality to the new epoch in which Virgil wrote his poem.

Despite such centrality, visions of Augustus do not propel Aeneas toward the narrative's telos in the same way that a vision of a god does; rather, visions of and allusions to Augustus propel the reader toward acceptance of the meaning of the *Aeneid*'s telos in the context of Augustan culture. I do not mean to suggest that Virgil unequivocally admires Augustus or that the *Aeneid* should be viewed as a poem that merely advances the nascent empire's political manifesto. Rather, I would suggest that Virgil's use of vision connected with Augustus, whether in descriptions of the emperor within the *Aeneid* or merely through allusion to him, reminds the reader that the fulfillment of *dum conderet urbem* has been realized in Augustan culture.

Simply put, had the *Aeneid* been a work of mere panegyric, it would likely have begun with an address to the emperor or, at the very least, would have included a description of him as *castus et sanctus et diis simillimus* (Pliny, *Panegyricus*, 17). Rather, Augustus is first introduced in the *Aeneid* in the catalogue of future Romans near the end of Book 6, the approximate middle of the poem. In that passage, Aeneas, from his vantage point in the present, views Augustus and many other personages important to Rome's future history:

'huc *geminas* nunc *flecte acies*, hanc *aspice* gentem
Romanosque tuos. hic Caesar et omnis Iuli
progenies magnum caeli uentura sub axem.
hic uir, hic est, tibi quem promitti saepius *audis*,
Augustus Caesar, diui genus, aurea condet
saecula qui rursus Latio regnata per arua
Saturno quondam, super et Garamantas et Indos
proferet imperium. . . .'   *Aen.* 6.788–795

["Now turn your two eyes here, to look upon
your Romans, your own people. Here is Caesar
and all the line of Iulus that will come
beneath the mighty curve of heaven. This,
this is the man you heard so often promised—
Augustus Caesar, son of a god, who will
renew a golden age in Latium,
in fields where Saturn once was king, and stretch
his rule beyond the Garamantes and
the Indians. . . ." (M. 6.1044–1053)]

Though Anchises first enjoins Aeneas to see the founders of Rome (788),[81] the focus soon shifts to Augustus (792). In a passage that clearly suggests Augustus' connection with divinity (792), Anchises admonishes Aeneas to behold Augustus: he is introduced as the *diui genus* who will refashion the Golden Age[82] and foster a rebirth of Saturnian happiness (793–794). The sight of Augustus provides tangible evidence of what was hitherto only rumored (791).

Anchises' interpretation of this vision of Augustus is also significant. Augustus is explicitly compared to two figures, Hercules and Bacchus:

nec uero *Alcides* tantum telluris obiuit,
fixerit aeripedem ceruam licet, aut Erymanthi
pacarit nemora et Lernam tremefecerit arcu;
nec qui pampineis uictor iuga flectit habenis

Liber, agens celso Nysae de uertice tigris.
et dubitamus adhuc uirtutem extendere factis,
aut metus Ausonia prohibet consistere terra? *Aen.* 6.801–807

[For even Hercules himself had never
crossed so much of the earth, not even when
he shot the brazen-footed stag and brought
peace to the groves of Erymanthus and
made Lerna's monster quake before his arrows;
nor he who guides his chariot with reins
of vine leaves, victor Bacchus, as he drives
his tigers down from Nysa's steepest summits.
And do we, then, still hesitate to extend
our force in acts of courage? Can it be
that fear forbids our settling in Ausonia? (M. 6.1061–1071)]

Why these two figures? Let us begin with Bacchus. Virgil does not describe Bacchus strictly in terms of his intoxicating qualities or even in terms of the pervasiveness of viticulture;[83] rather, he portrays the train of Dionysus as symbolic of his power over the natural world.[84]

This passage is not the first in which the astute reader of Virgil has seen Bacchus associated with Caesar. Sixteen lines before the close of *Georgics 2*, Virgil describes a "happy farmer," weary from the day and, in the company of his friends, crowning a wine bowl and pouring a libation to Bacchus:

ipse dies agitat festos fususque per herbam,
ignis ubi *in medio* et socii cratera coronant,
te libans, Lenaee. . . . *G.* 2.527–529

[The master himself
Keeps holiday, and sprawling on the grass,
With friends around the fire to wreathe the bowl,
Invokes you, Lord of the Winepress, offering
Libation. . . .][85]

These lines are the reader's final glimpse of the god to whom Virgil dedicates the second book. Some sixteen lines into the next book, we see a different god, Caesar, "in the middle," where he has a temple (*in medio mihi Caesar erit templumque tenebit*, *G.* 3.16).[86] The transition from the world of *Georgics* 1 and 2 to that of *Georgics* 3 and 4 heralds and in some ways thematically anticipates the transition between the two halves of the *Aeneid*.[87] The god Bacchus, celebrated with simple pleasures and rural, homespun games, closes *Georgics* 2, whereas Octavian, along with Rome (*pulcherrima Roma*, 2.534) and Pales (*magna Pales*, 3.1), opens *Georgics* 3. There Octavian is celebrated with Pindaric/Olympic fashion and a hundred chariots. While Bacchus is venerated with fire in the middle and with the crowning of a bowl of "Bacchus," Virgil celebrates the beauty of an idyllic shrine and the power of a public celebration in the Pindaric fashion. Virgil's position as heir of the Greek poetic tradition[88] gives significance to the event.

Moreover, the hero first mentioned at the opening of *Georgics* 3 is Hercules:

> . . . quis aut Eurysthea durum
> aut inlaudati nescit Busiridis aras?   *G.* 3.4–5

[Who has not heard about the grim Eurystheus
Or those notorious altars of Busiris?]

Bacchus and Hercules are frequently associated in the Augustan period.[89] Like Bacchus, Hercules is part of a crescendo leading to the portrait of Octavian in *Georgics* 3. Bacchus had ended Book 2 "in the middle," while Hercules begins Book 3 as an example of material too hackneyed to treat. Virgil quickly moves on to the theme of a living god in his temple, honored in the Pindaric style. For different reasons, both Hercules and Bacchus are fitting parallels with Octavian. Both are men who become gods, both perform heroic exploits, and both have vast and powerful sway.[90]

In *Aeneid* 6, the comparison of Augustus to Bacchus is also couched in terms of the description of his train: Bacchus drives his lion-drawn car with vine-shoot reins. Virgil describes not the liquid Bacchus but the visual one as *uictor* here (804). Other elements astutely posited by scholars such as Eduard Norden,[91] followed by commentators such as Austin and Williams, are true as well: in terms of viticulture, at least, Bacchus shares an important characteristic with Hercules and Augustus: all three are *filii divi*. There are yet other good reasons that Augustus can be appropriately associated with Bacchus. Suetonius records a legend about Augustus' birth, of which Virgil may well have known:

> Quo natus est die, cum de Catilinae coniuratione ageretur in curia et
> Octauius ob uxoris puerperium serius affuisset, nota ac uulgata res est
> P. Nigidium comperta morae causa, ut horam quoque partus acceperit,
> affirmasse dominum terrarum orbi natum. Octauio postea, cum

per secreta Thraciae exercitum duceret, in Liberi patris luco barbara
caerimonia de filio consulenti, idem affirmatum est a sacerdotibus,
quod infuso super altaria mero tantum *flammae emicuisset,* ut
supergressa fastigium templi ad caelum usque ferretur, unique omnino
Magno Alexandro apud easdem aras sacrificanti simile prouenisset
ostentum   *Aug.* 94.5.1–12

["The day he was born the conspiracy of Catiline was before the House,
and Octavius came late because of his wife's confinement; then Publius
Nigidius, as everyone knows, learning the reason for his tardiness and
being informed also of the hour of the birth, declared that the ruler of
the world had been born. Later, when Octavius was leading an army
through remoter parts of Thrace, and in the grove of Father Liber
consulted the priests about his son with barbarian rites, they made the
same prediction; since such a pillar of flame sprang forth from the wine
that was poured over the altar, that it rose above the temple roof and
mounted to the very sky, and such an omen had befallen no one save
Alexander the Great, when he offered sacrifice at the same altar."][92]

The first part of this story, at least, is presented by Suetonius as if it were
common knowledge (*nota ac uulgata*). We cannot know with certainty, of
course, whether Virgil knew this tale or the second part about the shrine
of Liber. The association with Bacchus at *Aeneid* 6 may, at any rate, suggest
that Virgil did. The omen about Augustus' birth, as described in Suetonius,
connects that event with a story associated with Alexander the Great, who
was, of course, also associated specifically with Hercules and Dionysus.[93]

Accordingly, even though the analogy is not precise between the unborn
Octavian and the oracle-receiving Alexander, a connection between them is
clear enough.[94] A similar, if more allusive transition between halves of the
poem occurs in the *Aeneid.* Having compared Augustus to both Hercules
and Bacchus at the close of *Aeneid* 6, Virgil alludes to the emperor in the
opening scenes of *Aeneid* 7:

tum satus Anchisa delectos ordine ab omni
centum oratores *augusta* ad moenia regis
ire iubet, ramis uelatos Palladis omnis,
donaque ferre uiro pacemque exposcere Teucris.

. . .

iamque iter emensi turris ac tecta Latinorum
ardua cernebant iuuenes muroque subibant.   *Aen.* 7.152–155, 160–161

[Then Anchises' son
gives orders that a hundred emissaries,
men chosen from each rank, be sent—to go
before the king's majestic walls; all should
be shaded by Minerva's boughs and bring
gifts to the king and ask peace for the Trojans.

. . .

By now the Trojan band had found its way;
they saw the Latin towers and high roofs,
they neared the walls. (M. 7.196–201, 208–210)]

Aeneas sends an embassy of one hundred *oratores*, used here in the Ennian sense of "spokesman."[95] While Fordyce dismisses the number of one hundred as "heroic color,"[96] and Horsfall regards it as a "conventional large number,"[97] the high number suggests at the very least that Aeneas executes diplomacy in dramatic fashion. The number befits the city's *augusta moenia* and its steep roofs and towers that the Trojans behold (160–161). King Latinus appears to them seated on his throne:

> ille intra tecta uocari
> imperat et solio medius consedit auito.
> *tectum augustum*, ingens, centum sublime columnis
> urbe fuit summa, Laurentis regia Pici,
> horrendum siluis et religione parentum.   *Aen.* 7.168–172

[Latinus orders that the strangers be
invited to the palace. At its center
he sat on his ancestral chair of state.
It was a stately dwelling, wide and high
and hundred-columned, towering above
the city; once the palace of Laurentian
Picus, an awesome place both for its forests
and for the sanctity of ancient worship. (M. 7.220–227)]

This palace would befit an emperor such as Augustus,[98] and a number of commentators have called attention to repeated use of the adjective *augustus*. This adjective occurs only in this passage in the *Aeneid* and only once, possibly,[99] in his other poetry.[100] Virgil is careful to give highly visual details of the palace: it is atop the city in a wooded area regarded with awe by past generations. Such sights hold the attention of the embassy that has come at Aeneas' request "to bring gifts . . . and ask for peace" (155; M. 7.200–201).

The way that the Trojans comply with Aeneas is one final hint that the vision they see here, in the middle of the poem, is that of the emperor's house. At first blush, the embassy's compliance is natural enough, for they are on a uniquely important mission. But that we should see Augustus' home lurking behind this portrait of Latinus' palace is perhaps further suggested by a turn of phrase used by Virgil to describe the compliance of Aeneas' hundred ambassadors: *haud mora, festinant iussi rapidisque feruntur / passibus* (156–157 ["There is no lingering: they hurry off, / all carried by their rapid steps" (M. 7.202–203)]). With the juxtaposition of *mora* and *festinant*, we may see a reflection of a well-known expression of Augustus, σπεῦδε βραδέως ["Make haste slowly"] (Suet. *Aug.* 25.4). In the midst of a description of the "august house," this juxtaposition may be more than merely coincidental[101] and would offer a clever paronomasia on Augustus' familiar expression. Accordingly, although Augustus is not present in the narrative per se, the august house and Virgil's possible allusion to one of Augustus' household expressions here in the midst of the *Aeneid* combine to evoke the emperor's *genius* in a way unmatched by even direct reference.

Our last vision of Augustus in the *Aeneid* occurs precisely in the middle of the description of the shield in the eighth book:[102]

> haec inter tumidi late maris ibat imago
> aurea, sed fluctu spumabant caerula cano,
> et circum argento clari delphines in orbem
> aequora uerrebant caudis aestumque secabant.
> *in medio* classis aeratas, Actia bella,
> cernere erat, totumque instructo Marte uideres
> feruere Leucaten auroque effulgere fluctus.
> hinc Augustus agens Italos in proelia Caesar
> cum patribus populoque, penatibus et magnis dis,
> stans celsa in puppi, geminas cui tempora flammas
> laeta uomunt patriumque aperitur uertice sidus.   *Aen.* 8.671–681

> [Bordering these scenes,
> he carved a golden image of the sea,
> yet there were blue-gray waters and white foam
> where dolphins bright with silver cut across
> the tide and swept the waves with circling tails.

Across the center of the shield were shown
the ships of brass, the strife of Actium:
you might have seen all of Leucata's bay
teeming with war's array, waves glittering
with gold. On his high stern Augustus Caesar
is leading the Italians to battle,
together with the senate and the people,
the household gods and Great Gods; his bright brows
pour out a twin flame, and upon his head
his father's Julian star is glittering. (M. 8.869–883)]

Virgil calls attention to the visual quality of the narrative with words and expressions such as *imago* (671), *cernere erat* (676), and *uideres* (676).[103] Augustus' temples pour forth twin flames, confirming his divinity through allusion to the Julian star, a comet that was taken to betoken Julius Caesar's divine status. This comet's flight occurred when Augustus was holding funeral games in honor of Caesar.[104] This vision of Augustus establishes his godhead yet again, and it is no surprise that his highly visible victory occurs "in the middle" of the shield's images (675).[105]

Aeneas sees Augustus on the shield, but we know from the two-line tag that abruptly closes Book 8 that he does not understand what he sees (730–731). The reader, however, does. That reader understands the identification of Augustus with Dionysus and Hercules, recognizes Latinus' palace as a precursor of Augustus' future home, and perhaps even catches the clever paronomasia on Augustus' frequent admonition to make haste slowly. Now the reader sees Augustus both as a victor and as one who preserves his people, the heir of Aeneas. For Augustus, the victory occurs at the battle of Actium, as depicted on the shield that Aeneas will bear during his final duel with Turnus. If Aeneas sees, at the poem's climax, the story of the Daenaids on Pallas' buckler, Turnus sees Augustus at the center of the shield carried by the one who looms over him. Augustus, portrayed in the Underworld in *Aeneid 6*, alluded to in palatial architecture (*Aen.* 7), and embossed on a shield (*Aen.* 8), is visible and present in the *Aeneid* and is a symbol of victory in the poem's final scene.

Whatever Virgil's personal politics might have been, Augustus is seen not as a god from Olympus but as the heir of Aeneas. With a visibility that engenders the reverence suggested by his august name, he is, as the leader of his society, the character central to the poem's acknowledgment of the Augustan experience and central to the reader's acceptance of the poem's telos that establishes the city reestablished by Rome's first emperor and second founder, Caesar Augustus. In the person of Augustus, therefore, Virgil constitutes a physical flesh-and-blood *voyant-visible* who will follow in the way that Aeneas had begun, walking amidst the city he has resurrected, like the Christ of Blake's "Jerusalem," in a "green and pleasant land."

CHAPTER 3

Vision Past and Future

❧

Sic pater Anchises, atque haec mirantibus addit:
'aspice . . .'   VIRGIL, *Aen.* 6.854–855

Methought I saw my late epousèd saint,
Brought to me like Alcestis from the grave,

Whom Jove's Great Son to her sad husband gave,
Rescued from death by force, though pale and faint,

Mine as whom washed from spot of child-bed taint,
Purification in the Old Law did save,

And such, as yet once more I trust to have
Full sight of her in heaven, without restraint,
Come vested all in white, pure as her mind:

Her face was veiled, yet to my fancied sight,
Love, sweetness, goodness, in her person shined
So clear, as in no face with more delight.

But O as to embrace me she inclined
I waked, she fled, and day brought back my night.
                    JOHN MILTON, "Sonnet XXIII"

In the twenty-third sonnet of John Milton, past, present, and future are
brought into a harmonic balance through Milton's vision of his late wife.

The poet constructs the narrative around her apparition as she comes to him "like Alcestis from the grave." Vision brokers between temporal modes: in the present, Milton's persona sees his past wife in anticipation of a complete and future vision of her (7–8). To use terminology by now familiar,[1] he plays the role of a *voyant-visible* who transcends time. As the poem ends, the persona of the husband, the heir of Virgil's Orpheus or Aeneas, wakes to darkness in a powerful closing brushstroke emphasizing the harsh reality of Milton's blind existence outside the world of poetry.

In the *Aeneid*, the sequence of events that make up time is at the service of, or at least moderated by, vision. As in Milton's sonnet, vision can be a liaison between temporal modes. Visions from the past deepen a character's understanding of the present and can even anticipate that character's vision of the future.

Visions of the past tend to point toward the future just as future-oriented vision is often an aspect of a view from the past. Such visions, whether future in past or past in future, consistently provide a rationale for Rome's existence and for the actions that anticipate or preserve that existence. Accordingly, future vision is sometimes aetiological, other times cosmological, and is often ultimately associated with Rome's foundation.

Several examples to be considered in this chapter reveal these aspects of future and past vision: Aeneas' view of Hector in Book 2 and of the Penates in Book 3, Andromache's vision of a bygone Troy (also in Book 3), Aeneas' viewing of the Underworld's denizens in Book 6, and his beholding of the future site of Rome in Book 8. Each of these anticipates Rome's destiny, providing a justification for its foundation and existence. Hector's apparition in *Aeneid* 2, contrasting with the injunction that the Penates later issue to Aeneas, offers a point of departure.

HECTOR AND THE PENATES

Complex temporal sequencing closes the second book and opens the third. Aeneas is in the midst of explaining, before Dido and her court, his eyewitness account of the Trojan past, an account laced with visions pertaining to his calling or Rome's future destiny. Accordingly, while the visions that Aeneas presents form part of his own city's past, the details of Trojan history anticipate and expound a future vision of Rome. Two complementary examples from Aeneas' account, namely, those of Hector and the Penates, offer Aeneas an explanation of his mission. In each case, vision surpasses words, pointing toward the hero's destiny and the telos of Rome's foundation.

In Delos, Aeneas and his men consult the oracle for instructions about their future. As they approach the oracle, they feel the earth shake and hear the voice of the god:

> summissi petimus terram et uox fertur ad auris:
> 'Dardanidae duri, quae uos a stirpe parentum
> prima tulit tellus, eadem uos ubere laeto
> accipiet reduces. antiquam exquirite matrem.
> hic domus Aeneae cunctis dominabitur oris
> et nati natorum et qui nascentur ab illis.' *Aen.* 3.94–98

> [We bow low
> upon the ground. A voice is carried to us:
> "O iron sons of Dardanus, the land
> that gave you birth, the land of your ancestors,
> will welcome you again, returned to her
> generous breast. Seek out your ancient mother.
> For there Aeneas' house will rule all coasts,
> as will his sons' sons and those born of them." (M. 3.123–130)]

One notices immediately in these words a pendulum-like sway between the past origins of the Trojan race (94–95) and the glorious future domain of the *domus Aeneae*. These components allude to the *auctoritas* and *imperium* of Aeneas' heirs such as Caesar and Augustus, who are the sons of the sons referred to in line 98. When the injunction to seek out the ancient mother (*antiquam exquirite matrem*, 96) is reasonably but incorrectly interpreted by Anchises as referring to Crete (3.102–117), the Trojans there commence the foundation of a city, replete with many of the marks of a civilized society. Only after the Trojans have suffered a plague do the Penates appear to Aeneas to clarify the oracle of Delian Apollo.

The Penates come to Aeneas at night, an appropriate time for visions of this type:[2]

> Nox erat et terris animalia somnus habebat:
> effigies sacrae diuum Phrygiique penates,
> quos mecum a Troia mediisque ex ignibus urbis
> extuleram, uisi ante oculos astare iacentis
> in somnis multo manifesti lumine, qua se
> plena per insertas fundebat luna fenestras. . . . *Aen.* 3.147–152

> ["Night. Sleep held every living thing on earth.
> The sacred statues of the deities,

the Phrygian household gods whom I had carried
from Troy out of the fires of the city,
as I lay sleeping seemed to stand before me.
And they were plain to see in the broad light
where full moon flowed through windows in the walls." (M. 3.197–203)]

Here the Penates, "plain to see in the broad light" (151), interrupt Aeneas as
he sleeps. Aeneas builds up to this vision by explaining how he had rescued
and carried the Penates from burning Troy. Before recounting the words of
the Penates, Aeneas carefully affirms for his audience that he, in fact, has
seen the Penates standing before his eyes (150), a detail that, after he has related the gods' instructions, he again asserts:

talibus attonitus uisis et uoce deorum
(nec sopor illud erat, sed coram agnoscere uultus
uelatasque comas praesentiaque ora uidebar . . .)   *Aen.* 3.172–174

["These visions and the voice of gods were too
astonishing: I did not dream, I knew
their faces and the fillets in their hair,
those trusted images that stood before me." (M. 3.228–331)]

Aeneas' words are emphatic: most certainly he has personally seen this vision, which then redirected the Trojans' course, for he emphasizes that he
even seemed to recognize the facial features and the hair of the Penates.[3] The
emphasis on Aeneas' vision, which frames the Penates' speech, reassures
Aeneas' hearers that the words he recollects are true.

The Penates begin to address Aeneas by asserting that they have not come
by their own authority:

'quod tibi delato Ortygiam dicturus Apollo est,
hic canit et tua nos en ultro ad limina mittit.
nos te Dardania incensa tuaque arma secuti,
nos tumidum sub te permensi classibus aequor,
idem uenturos tollemus in astra nepotes
imperiumque urbi dabimus. tu moenia magnis
magna para longumque fugae ne linque laborem.'   *Aen.* 3.154–160

['Unasked, Apollo sends us to your threshold;
for here he prophesies just as he would

had you again traced back the seas to Delos.
We followed you, your men, from burning Troy
and crossed the swollen waters in your care
together with your ships; and we shall raise
your children to the stars and build an empire
out of their city. For the great make ready
great walls, do not desert the tedious
trials of your journeying.' (M. 3.205–214)]

The Penates desire this epiphany to connect past and future: they have been
with Aeneas through the destruction of Troy (156) and have traversed the sea
with him; with an immediate transition to the future tense, they say that
they will extol Aeneas' descendants (158) while giving the future city *imperium* (159). The Penates, known in Rome also as the *di magni*, fittingly ask
Aeneas to prepare "great" walls for the "great ones."[4] In that future city, the
Penates will have a temple on the Velia, among those restored by Augustus
(*aedem deum Penatium in Velia . . . feci*, RG 19), who by this act connected
himself with the city's origins.[5]

The second part of the Penates' injunction is also linked to Aeneas' own,
immediate future. The *longum . . . laborem* (160) to which they refer suggests
that Aeneas' journey will encompass a great amount of time and distance.
They declare that Apollo does not want the present circumstances to obtain (*non haec tibi litora suasit / Delius . . . Apollo*, 161–162). Aeneas and the
Trojans are thus to face the future, even though the future actually looks to
the past:

> est locus, Hesperiam Grai cognomine dicunt,
> terra antiqua, potens armis atque ubere glaebae;
> Oenotri coluere uiri; nunc fama minores
> Italiam dixisse ducis de nomine gentem.
> hae nobis propriae sedes, hinc Dardanus ortus
> Iasiusque pater, genus a quo principe nostrum.   *Aen.* 3.163–168

[There is a place the Greeks have named Hesperia—
an ancient land with strong arms and fat soil.
The men who lived there were Oenotrians;
but now it is said that their descendants call
the country "Italy" after their leader.
That is the home for us. Iasius—

our father, founder of the Trojan race—
and Dardanus were both born there. (M. 3.217–224)]

From their opening line, the Penates show their awareness of the epic past, as the allusion to Ennius' *est locus Hesperiam quam mortales perhibebant* shows.[6] As Troy's "cupboard deities," they represent the oldest aspect of that city.[7] Having shared in the journey with Aeneas toward the preordained land, the Penates are especially suited to bring past and future together. Servius records that the Penates were believed to have originated in either Troy or Samothrace.[8] The reference to both Dardanus and Iasius would seem to allow either of these possibilities,[9] alluding to the Penates' connection with the remote history of Troy while simultaneously looking to the future, as the contrast between the phrases *non haec . . . litora* (161) and *hae nobis propriae sedes* (167) implies. Ironically, the vision that Aeneas has of the Penates, one so powerful that he twice emphasizes that he saw them firsthand, itself contains a vision of the past, *terra antiqua* (164).

The Penates' address also contains a well-known internal allusion. The words of the Penates at 163–166 are repeated verbatim from Ilioneus' speech presented to Dido in the first book (1.530–533). When the Penates speak to Aeneas, Ilioneus' speech has not yet "happened" chronologically, although it has, of course, occurred sequentially in the poem. The Penates' apparition provides a connection between past and future, for they repeat words from an event yet to take place. Specifically, they refer to an ancient land that, paradoxically, is yet to come: this country is the land of the Trojans' ultimate origins.

The reference to Ennius' *est locus Hesperiam* that introduces this four-line sequence puts the allusion in the proper context: just as Ennius' material, part of the "epic past," is reused in Virgil's poem, so the Penates, as elements of the Trojan past, will be preserved and adapted for the Roman future. Further, the deliberate repetition of the words of Ilioneus—whose distinctly Trojan name is here worth mentioning[10]—must be considered in this light. Aeneas' description of the cupboard deities therefore encompasses a description of the future that Dido has heard once already. Accordingly, Aeneas' exposition to the queen and her court of his vision of the Penates in Crete should have clarified, for them and for himself, his own destiny and obligation to his future land.

Another echo in the Penates' address is a line from the vision of Hector in Book 2. This internal allusion reveals Aeneas' destiny as preserver of the Trojan race and culture. In echoing Hector's line, the Penates show that they are a part of that destiny, for Hector had first instructed Aeneas to take the household gods from Troy to the promised land:

> 'sacra suosque tibi commendat Troia penatis;
> hos cape fatorum comites, his *moenia* quaere
> *magna* pererrato statues quae denique ponto.'   *Aen.* 2.293–295

> ['But Troy entrusts
> her holy things and household gods to you;
> take them away as comrades of your fortunes,
> seek out for them the great walls that at last,
> once you have crossed the sea, you will establish.' (M. 2.400–404)]

As the city's spokesman, Hector makes it clear that Troy, personified as a goddess, entrusts these household gods to Aeneas. Hector commands Aeneas to take the Penates as comrades and to seek "great walls" for them, even as the Penates themselves command in Book 3. The Penates resume this notion of founding great walls by alluding to Hector's lines, which themselves contain elements of the poem's prologue.[11] In so doing, they point toward the poem's telos.

Aeneas' encounter with Hector bears other resemblances to that of the Penates. First, it begins with a setting similar to that of the Penates' appearance, with careful attention to the circumstances and the time of the revelation:[12]

> *Tempus erat* quo prima quies mortalibus aegris
> incipit et dono diuum gratissima serpit.
> *in somnis*, ecce, *ante oculos* maestissimus Hector
> *uisus* adesse mihi largosque effundere fletus,
> raptatus bigis ut quondam, aterque cruento
> puluere perque pedes traiectus lora tumentis.   *Aen.* 2.268–273

> ["It was the hour when for troubled mortals
> rest—sweetest gift of gods that glides to men—
> has just begun. Within my sleep, before
> my eyes there seemed to stand, in tears and sorrow,
> Hector as once he was, dismembered by
> the dragging chariot, black and bloodied dust;
> his swollen feet were pierced by thongs." (M. 2.371–377)]

Brooks Otis notes that it is not the power of Hector's words here that have the most effect, but rather the power of the vision of him: "Once [Aeneas] sees, his reaction is instinctive and immediate."[13] Aeneas carefully explains that Hector appeared "before his eyes," as did the Penates (3.150). Further, both Hector and the Penates appear to Aeneas "in dreams" (22.270; cf. 3.151), and both offer a charge of destiny to Aeneas. As Philip Hardie notes, this vision provides an important transition in "epic succession," for a hero of the older epic transfers the gods to the new poem's hero.[14] Although Hector is a ghost from the epic past, the vision of him informs Aeneas' present and future.

Emphasizing his role as the beholder of the vision, Aeneas pauses to recall the details of Hector's appearance and thus reveals his feelings at the sight of the apparition:

ei mihi, qualis erat, quantum mutatus ab illo
Hectore qui redit exuuias indutus Achilli
uel Danaum Phrygios iaculatus puppibus ignis!
squalentem barbam et concretos sanguine crinis
uulneraque illa gerens, quae circum plurima muros
accepit patrios.   *Aen.* 2.274–279

[Oh this
was Hector, and how different he was
from Hector back from battle, putting on
Achilles' spoils, or Hector when he flung
his Phrygian firebrands at Dardan prows!
His beard unkempt, his hair was thick with blood,
he bore the many wounds he had received
around his homeland's walls. (M. 2.377–384)]

Aeneas is the compatriot to whom the future will be entrusted. He begins with the compassionate exclamation *ei mihi* (274) and then reveals his grief at Hector's changed appearance. But the vision is more than merely an affirmation of Aeneas' sympathy; it is also the vehicle for transition of leadership between Hector, the past protector of the city, and Aeneas, the future leader of the Trojan race.

Though he did not first address the Penates, Aeneas here seems to speak first. After an "Ennian" introduction (*uidebar / compellare uirum et maestas expromere uoces*, 279–280),[15] Aeneas addresses the hero:

'o lux Dardaniae, spes o fidissima Teucrum,
quae tantae tenuere morae? quibus Hector ab oris
exspectate uenis? ut te post multa tuorum
funera, post uarios hominumque urbisque labores
defessi *aspicimus!* quae causa indigna serenos
foedauit uultus? aut cur haec uulnera *cerno?*'   *Aen.* 2.281–286

['O light of Troy, o Trojans' trusted hope!
What long delay has held you back? From what
seashores, awaited Hector, have you come?
For, weary with the many deaths of friends,
the sorrows of your men, your city, how
our eyes hold fast to you! What shameful cause
defaced your tranquil image? Why [do I see] these wounds?'
    (M. 2.386–392)[16]]

That the vision of Hector disorients Aeneas can be seen in his troubled address of that hero. Having inquired of Hector whence he has come, Aeneas states that he sees him only after many funerals (283–284). Aeneas then pointedly mentions the strikingly visual quality of Hector's wounds (*cerno*, 286) but, in his stupor, is unable to recall the death of Troy's greatest warrior (285).[17]

The Ennian introduction of Aeneas' speech represents part of a wider allusive program involving passages from the *Annales* and other apposite texts of that poet that also emphasize some visual qualities in the encounter. For example, Aeneas' address to Hector encompasses an allusion to Ennius' tragedy *Alexander*, in which play Paris had addressed Hector as Troy's "light":[18]

O lux Troiae, germane Hector,
quid ita cum tuo lacerato corpore
miser es aut qui te sic *respectantibus*
tractavere nobis?   *Alexander* 76–79[19]

[O my own brother, Hector, you light of Troy, how is it you are thus made pitiful with your torn body? And who are they who have thus dragged you before our very eyes?]

Virgil's allusion to Ennius connects Aeneas' past with the Homeric past both by learned reference and by his positive description of Hector in Ennian terms as the "light of Troy."[20] Through this allusion, Virgil emphasizes the closeness of the relationship between Aeneas and Hector, suggestively construing Aeneas in a quasi-fraternal relationship with Hector. Furthermore, as does Aeneas in Book 2, the Paris of Ennius' text emphasizes the visual aspect of the encounter (*respectantibus . . . nobis*, 78–79). Aeneas regards Hector with the empathetic gaze of a brother and successor. Aeneas' questions about Hector's wounds, strengthened by the intertextual resonance with Ennius, call attention to the physical act of sight; Aeneas' view of Hector, if surprisingly uninformed, is nonetheless characterized by pathos and care for his friend.

As Aeneas continues in his description of the encounter, he receives from Hector the injunction to flee, together with a charge for the future:

> ille nihil, nec me quaerentem uana moratur,
> sed grauiter gemitus imo de pectore ducens,
> 'heu fuge, nate dea, teque his' ait 'eripe flammis.
> hostis habet muros; ruit alto a culmine Troia.
> sat patriae Priamoque datum: si Pergama dextra
> defendi possent, etiam hac defensa fuissent.'   *Aen.* 2.287–292

> ["He wastes no words, no time on useless questions—
> but drawing heavy sighs from deep within,
> 'Ah, goddess-born, take flight,' he cries, 'and snatch
> yourself out of these flames. The enemy
> has gained the walls; Troy falls from her high peak.
> Our home, our Priam—these have had their due:
> could Pergamus be saved by any prowess,
> then my hand would have served.'" (M. 2.393–400)]

Austin points out that Hector does not answer Aeneas' sleep-induced, and therefore somewhat inappropriate, questions. Instead, with a passionate groan (*imo de pectore*, 288), he explains to Aeneas what is really happening. Hector moves from present commands (289), to a statement of the present reality (290), to what might have happened (291–292) and, finally, in the lines quoted above, to the instructions about the future. Aeneas should take the Penates and build great walls after crossing the sea (293–295).

Having given this charge, Hector presents Aeneas with the household gods and more:

> sic ait et manibus uittas Vestamque potentem
> aeternumque adytis effert penetralibus ignem.

. . .

excutior somno et summi fastigia tecti
ascensu supero atque *arrectis auribus asto.* . . .

Aen. 2.296–297, 302–303

[So Hector speaks; then from the inner altars
he carries out the garlands and great Vesta
and, in his hands, the fire that never dies.

. . .

I start from sleep and climb the sloping roof
above the house. I stand, alerted. . . . (M. 2.405–407, 412–413)]

The gifts suggest the unique power of the vision; the passing on of the garlands and Vesta's flame is symbolic of the transition between the memory
of past reality and the hope of future possibilities. It is not surprising that
Aeneas listens to Hector *arrectis auribus* (303), far too succinctly translated
by Mandelbaum as "alerted." One will not fail to recall that this phrase harks
back to the manner in which the crowd, in the simile of Book 1, had similarly listened to the voice of the statesman (1.152). Hector's appearance, along
with that of the Penates, is inspiring, just as is that of the great statesman of
the first book (*si . . . quem / conspexere, silent,* 151–152).

To sum up: in Aeneas' encounters with Hector and with the Penates,
vision complements and indeed surpasses the effect of words alone: each
confirms and establishes what has been said. By contrast, Anchises, as a
mere hearer of words and not as one who sees a vision, has been confused
about the oracular pronouncement (3.103–117). Though all the Trojans hear
the words of the oracle, Aeneas alone sees the vision of the Penates that clari-
fies, inspires, and provides a connection between past and future. The situation with Hector is similar to that of the Penates. In learning from Hector's
vision, Aeneas will also bear the tangible symbols of past and future. Precisely because Aeneas has seen both of these visions, he can lead correctly.

The passages quoted above offer several clues about how Virgil uses vision
to construct his future-oriented grand narrative. As the epic unfolds, further
visual examples appear, connecting past with future and ultimately pointing
toward the poem's telos. One of the more remarkable examples of how vision
connects past and future occurs when Aeneas describes for Dido's court his
encounter with Andromache.

HINDSIGHT TO FORESIGHT: ANDROMACHE AND AENEAS

As Aeneas continues the account of his travels, he includes a tale in which vision betokens sadness as well as hope. In this passage, Andromache's false vision of the present is produced by her view of the past. Aeneas' visit to Buthrotum allows him to reaffirm his vision of the future by witnessing first-hand how destructive self-deception can be. Aeneas emerges as a *voyant-visible*, beheld as a symbol of Troy's future while able to see the future more clearly than Andromache, whose false vision of Troy in Buthrotum inappro-priately relies on past images.

Describing his arrival in Buthrotum, Aeneas explains how he met Andro-mache while she was making offerings at the cenotaph of Hector:

> progredior portu classis et litora linquens,
> sollemnis cum forte dapes et tristia dona
> ante urbem in luco falsi Simoentis ad undam
> libabat cineri Andromache manisque uocabat
> Hectoreum ad tumulum, uiridi quem caespite inanem
> et geminas, causam lacrimis, sacrauerat aras.   *Aen.* 3.300–305

> [Just then—when I had left the harbor and
> my boat, drawn up along the beaches—there,
> within a grove that stood before the city,
> alongside waves that mimed the Simois
> Andromache was offering to the ashes
> a solemn banquet and sad gifts, imploring
> the Shade of Hector's empty tomb that she
> had raised out of green turf with double altars
> and consecrated as a cause for tears. (M. 3.389–397)]

Aeneas draws attention to the vision of the false Simois that he had seen just before entering Buthrotum. Andromache was calling out to an unseen world at Hector's tomb, an empty structure representing her past (304).[21] Aeneas' language reinforces the pathos of this experience as he describes the sacrifice on the twin altars as cause for tears.

Aeneas' entrance into this world was, he explains, a kind of intrusion that Andromache could not fully fathom, even though she could see him plainly:

> ut me *conspexit* uenientem et Troia circum
> arma amens *uidit*, magnis exterrita monstris

deriguit *uisu in medio*, calor ossa reliquit,
labitur, et longo uix tandem tempore fatur. . . .   *Aen.* 3.306–309

[And when, distracted, she caught sight of me
and saw our Trojan armor all around her,
in terror of these mighty omens, she
grew stiff [in the midst of the sight];[22] heat left her bones; she fell,
      fainting.
But after long delay, at last she asks. . . . (M. 3.398–402)]

When she perceives Aeneas' approach, Andromache grows terrified, and she
soon becomes emotional (*impleuit clamore locum*, 313–314). Overwhelmed,
her body temperature decreases. She is "freezing" in the midst of beholding Aeneas (308), whereupon she immediately swoons (309), the very thing
Homer's Andromache did in the *Iliad* when beholding Hector's lifeless body:

αὐτὰρ ἐπεὶ πύργον τε καὶ ἀνδρῶν ἷξεν ὅμιλον,
ἔστη παπτήνασ' ἐπὶ τείχεϊ, τὸν δὲ νόησεν
ἑλκόμενον πρόσθεν πόλιος· ταχέες δέ μιν ἵπποι
ἕλκον ἀκηδέστως κοίλας ἐπὶ νῆας Ἀχαιῶν.
τὴν δὲ κατ' ὀφθαλμῶν ἐρεβεννὴ νὺξ ἐκάλυψεν,
ἤριπε δ' ἐξοπίσω, ἀπὸ δὲ ψυχὴν ἐκάπυσσε.
τῆλε δ' ἀπὸ κρατὸς βάλε δέσματα σιγαλόεντα, . . .   *Il.* 22.462–468[23]

[But when she came to the bastion and where the men were gathered
she stopped, staring, on the wall; and she saw him
being dragged in front of the city, and the running horses
dragged him at random toward the hollow ships of the Achaians.
The darkness of night misted over the eyes of Andromache.
She fell backward, and gasped the life breath from her, and far off
Threw from her head the shining gear that ordered her headdress. . . .][24]

Andromache's vision had taken her, on that occasion, near the brink of death
(467) as she viewed with her own eyes her beloved Hector on the Trojan
plain. In the *Aeneid*, Andromache "steps readily into that domain of death,"[25]
for she is entirely prepared to believe that Aeneas has come from that realm.
Virgil's Andromache seems to commence where Homer's heroine had ended:
both her despondency and her hope are based on what she sees.

Because Aeneas' appearance has so startled her, Andromache questions
the veracity of what she sees:

'uerane te facies, uerus mihi nuntius adfers,
nate dea? uiuisne? aut, si lux alma recessit,
Hector ubi est?' dixit, lacrimasque effudit et omnem
impleuit clamore locum. uix pauca furenti
subicio et raris turbatus uocibus hisco:
'uiuo equidem uitamque extrema per omnia duco. . . .'   *Aen.* 3.310–315

[Are you, born of a goddess, a true body,
a real messenger who visits me?
Are you alive? Or if the gracious light
of life has left you, where is Hector?' So
she spoke. Her tears were many and her cries
filled all the grove. She is so frenzied, I—
disquieted—must stammer scattered words:
'Indeed I live and drag my life through all
extremities. . . .' (M. 3.403–411)]

Her vision of Aeneas seems to come from this past, and thus Andromache
wonders if he can be "true." The vision that Andromache has of Aeneas is
of a living person, as Virgil's use of the word *uiuo* (315) explains. This attitude contrasts sharply with Andromache's devotion to the dead (*manisque
uocabat / Hectoreum ad tumulum*, 3.303–304).[26] David Quint has shown that
Virgil reverses Homer's description of Odysseus' journey to the shades; instead of a katabasis, Aeneas discovers Andromache, who mistakenly views
him as a shade.[27]

Andromache's primary concern is, fittingly, not for Aeneas but for Hector (312), whom she presumes Aeneas recently to have seen. She ponders
whether Aeneas could be a vivid ghost in her otherwise vague fantasy world.
Aeneas understands her bewilderment and, between her emotional out-
bursts, addresses her misunderstanding, reassuring her that she beholds a
true person living in the present:

'. . . ne dubita, nam *uera uides*.
heu! quis te casus deiectam coniuge tanto
excipit, aut quae digna satis fortuna reuisit,
Hectoris Andromache? Pyrrhin conubia seruas?'
deiecit uultum et demissa uoce locuta est. . . .   *Aen.* 3.316–320

['. . . do not doubt—I am real.
But you, what fate has overtaken you,

divided from so great a husband, or
what kindly fortune comes again to Hector's
Andromache? Are you still wed to Pyrrhus?'
Her eyes downcast, she spoke with murmured words . . .

    (M. 3.411–416)]

In contrast to Aeneas' statement about himself, Aeneas (as will later, Andromache herself [488]) defines her in terms of her Trojan past and through her relationship with Hector.[28] Ironically, Aeneas' statement that Andromache sees "true things" (320) is at once accurate and erroneous. On the one hand, inasmuch as her world is a construct of false visions of Troy, Andromache's vision is, generally, anything but true; on the other hand, when she sees Aeneas she sees a "true thing," for the living Aeneas is real, a true and tangible *voyant-visible*. Virgil characterizes Andromache's response to Aeneas in terms of how she directs her gaze (*deiecit uultum*, 320). Servius understands her response in terms of her shame at being admonished for her status as concubine (*decenter, quia de concubitu admonita est*).[29] The casting down of one's eyes upon meeting an individual may reflect social custom[30] or possibly might suggest a touch of sadness that goes beyond mere personal embarrassment. When introduced in Book 1, Dido, too, had cast down her gaze as she addressed Aeneas' men: *tum breuiter Dido uultum dimissa profatur* (1.561).[31]

Aeneas seems neither to grasp fully the pathos of her downward gaze (320) nor to hear in her words sentiments similar to those that, in Book 1, he had himself advanced in his *terque quarterque* address (1.94–101). Nevertheless, when Aeneas departs, he uses words similar to Andromache's own, thereby seemingly acknowledging that he understands, to some degree, her peculiar devotion to the past:

. . . 'uiuite felices, quibus est fortuna peracta
iam sua: nos alia ex aliis in fata uocamur.
uobis parta quies: nullum maris aequor arandum,
arua neque Ausoniae semper cedentia retro
quaerenda.'   *Aen.* 3.493–497

['Your fate is here, then live it happily.
But we are called from one fate to another.
For you can rest: no need to plow the seas
Or seek the fleeing fields of Italy. . . .' (M. 3.643–646)]

On one level, Aeneas' words take up Andromache's, for he now resumes the pathetic recollection of Polyxena that Andromache had mentioned earlier (*o felix una ante alias Primeia uirgo* . . . , 321), reversing it so as to enjoin Andromache and all those in this ghost town to "live happily" (493).[32] Consciously or unconsciously, he inverts Andromache's own pathetic speech. But Aeneas' farewell speech also epitomizes and reflects the many contrasts—or doubles, as Bettini has called them—of this episode.[33] First, Aeneas seems to suggest that an almost Epicurean security has been established for these colonists of new Troy. This happiness (*uiuite felices* [493] . . . *uobis parta quies* [495]) contrasts sharply with the care that Aeneas' offspring will have (*maneat nostros ea cura nepotes*, 505). His descendants' charge will be to make another Troy, one that does not merely seek to recapture the shadowy past but instead provides the true foundation of a Roman future that, if not yet fully formed, is nevertheless as true as Andromache's vision of Aeneas had been.

Further, the passage contrasts the ever-receding fields of Ausonia that need not be sought by the Buthrotans (*neque Ausoniae semper cedentia retro / quaerenda*, 496–497) with the Hesperian land that Aeneas will link to theirs:

> 'effigiem Xanthi Troiamque *uidetis*
> quam uestrae fecere manus, melioribus, opto,
> auspiciis, et quae fuerit minus obuia Grais.
> si quando Thybrim uicinaque Thybridis arua
> intraro gentique meae data moenia *cernam*,
> cognatas urbes olim populosque propinquos,
> Epiro Hesperiam (quibus idem Dardanus auctor
> atque idem casus), unam faciemus utramque
> Troiam animis: maneat nostros ea cura nepotes.'   *Aen.* 3.497–505

> ['Here *you can see* the image of new Xanthus
> and of the Troy your hands had built beneath
> more kindly auspices, I hope—a city
> less open to the Greeks than was old Troy.
> If ever I shall enter on the Tiber
> And on the lands that lie along the Tiber
> *And see* the ramparts given to my race,
> Then we, in time to come, shall build one Troy
> In spirit from our sister cities in

Epirus and Hesperia and from
Our kindred peoples—those who share one founder
In Dardanus and share one destiny.
May this become the care of all our sons.' (M. 3.647–659)]

Aeneas' vision looks to the future. The Buthrotans see their river and city in the present (*uidetis*, 497). Aeneas, by contrast, will have to wait to see his river and city (*Thybrim uicinaque Thybridis arua*, 500; *cernam*, 501).[34] A single Troy encompassing the past (as symbolized by Buthrotum) and the future (as symbolized by Rome) will ultimately unite these two visions (504–505).

Andromache nostalgically sees the faces and images of her past. Even the *parua Troia*—so like the real thing that Aeneas openly acknowledges the similarity—is simply an image to be seen, a visual double of the destroyed city. Andromache's farewell speech to Aeneas that precedes the lines just considered elucidates the way she beholds past and future:

'accipe et haec, manuum tibi quae monimenta mearum
sint, puer, et longum Andromachae testentur amorem,
coniugis Hectoreae. cape dona extrema tuorum,
o mihi sola mei super Astyanactis imago.
sic oculos, sic ille manus, sic ora ferebat;
et nunc aequali tecum pubesceret aeuo.'   *Aen.* 3.486–491

['Receive these, too, my boy: memorials
of my own handiwork; and let them serve
as witness to Andromache's long love
as wife of Hector. Take with you these last
gifts of your people—you, the only image
that still is left of my Astyanax:
so did he bear his eyes, his hands, his face;
so would he now be entering his youth,
were he alive, his years the same as yours.' (M. 3.633–641)]

Derived from the root for memory,[35] *monimenta* (486) is a loaded term,[36] as even Andromache's gift is a visual reminder of a lost past. Her vision fixes now on Ascanius. He does not appear to her to be the *imago* of the future hope of Rome but of someone from her past, her own dead son, Astyanax (489). She began the episode by mistakenly viewing Aeneas as a shade and speaking with a sad, downcast gaze, and she fittingly concludes the episode by beholding the future's future (Ascanius), again confusing that vision with the lost future of the past (Astyanax).[37]

The confused gazing of this heroine gives Aeneas fresh urgency for his own mission. Andromache's vision of the past is as keen as that of Aeneas' vision of the future, and, while his grasp on the past will loosen as he fulfills his destiny, hers will abide: she cannot live *felix*, Aeneas' injunction to do so notwithstanding. Andromache's introspective, downward glance suggests grief and perhaps even shame caused by her fixation upon the past, a fixation that prevents her vision from fully understanding the present or looking forward to the future. This encounter is, in the final analysis, at least as much concerned with the future-oriented vision of Aeneas as it is concerned with the past vision of Andromache, to whom he strangely appears as a living *voyant-visible* in an otherwise symbolically dead world.

IMAGO CREUSAE

Aeneas' description of his final encounter with his wife Creusa differs starkly from the encounter with Andromache. Andromache assumes Aeneas to be an unreal vision from her past. While the vision of Creusa that Aeneas sees evokes the past, it also points toward his own future, a future closely linked to that of the city he will found. The vision of Creusa thus consoles and encourages Aeneas, but her role has changed from wife and lover to counselor from his past, not unlike Anticlea, who, as a vision in the *Odyssey*, similarly counseled and consoled Odysseus.[38]

As the narrator, Aeneas will tell this story and every tale in the second and third books from his own particular point of view, as Friedrich Klingner once noted somewhat emphatically.[39] Thus Aeneas explains, from his own vantage point, how, once he realized that Creusa was missing, he filled the byways with shouts as he looked for her in the gloom:

> ausus quin etiam uoces iactare per umbram
> impleui clamore uias, maestusque Creusam
> nequiquam ingeminans iterumque iterumque uocaui.
> quaerenti et tectis urbis sine fine ruenti
> infelix simulacrum atque ipsius umbra Creusae
> uisa mihi ante oculos et nota maior imago.
> obstipui, steteruntque comae et uox faucibus haesit.   *Aen.* 2.768–774

["And more, I even dared to cast my cries
across the shadows; in my sorrow, I—

again, again, in vain—called for Creüsa;
my shouting filled the streets. But as I rushed
and raged among the houses endlessly,
before my eyes there stood the effigy
and grieving shade of my Creüsa, image
far larger than the real. I was dismayed;
my hair stood stiff, my voice held fast within
my jaws." (M. 2.1036–1045)]

Aeneas' calling out is to no avail, suggesting *prima facie* the inefficacy of speech versus vision. Aeneas specifies that Creusa appeared before his eyes and notes that the power of her vision caused his voice to catch in his throat (774). Beyond mere point of view, Virgil carefully emphasizes a contrast between Aeneas' ineffectual calling and the power of the appearance of Creusa's *imago* before his eyes (773). In contrast to his prior shouting (768–770), Aeneas is so struck by this vision that he is unable to reply to the image of his wife. He gives much attention to describing precisely how she appeared to him, an image literally larger than life (773).

Creusa, a vision of Aeneas' immediate past, now charges Aeneas with instructions about his future in Latium[40] (*illic res laetae regnumque et regia coniunx / parta tibi . . .* , 783–784 [There, days of gladness lie in wait for you: / a kingdom and a royal bride (M. 1056–1057)]).[41] Creusa quickly turns to some specific details of that future, namely, the general *res laetae* and his *regia coniunx* (783). The mention of his future wife has a certain poignancy in this context, coming so soon after Creusa's address of Aeneas as *dulcis coniunx* (777). The participle *parta* (784), too, has drawn the attention of commentators. Conington notes that " 'partus' is peculiarly used of things that are virtually, though not actually realized."[42]

This vision of Creusa, like Mercury's second appearance to Aeneas, points toward his future. But this *imago* is, like Aeneas' encounter with Hector's shade, a window to his past. As *voyant-visible*, Aeneas encounters in Creusa a person from his past of whom he had literally lost sight; he failed to look for her as he escaped from Troy.[43] Now, however, she, too, emerges as *voyant-visible*, in her "beatified" state surpassing even Aeneas as one who sees and is seen, for her clairvoyance allows her to see the future in a way that Aeneas cannot.[44] Creusa charges Aeneas to seek a future family, and she offers a promise of better days to come. While looking upon Creusa's *imago*, which represents his Trojan past, Aeneas now hears about his Roman future (*regnum*, 783). Creusa directs Aeneas not to escape disaster but to pursue his own and the poem's telos, which is the foundation of a new Troy.

As Creusa continues, we learn that her own destiny is not to be that of so many Trojan women condemned to serve in the Greek world as spoils of war:

'*non ego* Myrmidonum sedes Dolopumue superbas
aspiciam aut Grais seruitum matribus ibo,
Dardanis et diuae Veneris nurus;
sed me magna deum genetrix his detinet oris.
iamque uale et nati serua communis amorem.'   *Aen.* 2.785–789

['I am not
to see the haughty homes of Myrmidons
or of Dolopians, or be a slave
to Grecian matrons—I, a Dardan woman
and wife of Venus' son. It is the gods'
great Mother who keeps me upon these shores.
And now farewell, and love the son we share.' (M. 2.1058–1064)]

Creusa now refers to her own future vision, stating explicitly that she will not look upon (*aspiciam*, 786) the enemy's haughty abodes. This important detail reveals Creusa's dignity; it evokes the sad fate of many a captive woman while at the same time it contrasts such a fate with Creusa's religious destiny in the service of the Great Mother. Creusa's image will fade away as Aeneas' epic past gives way to his epic future. Her final words explicitly instruct Aeneas to maintain the love of their son (*nati serva communis amorem*, 789), whose future represents a link to their past union.

Aeneas reacts to this vision of Creusa by thrice attempting to embrace her:

'ter conatus ibi collo dare bracchia circum;
ter frustra comprensa manus effugit imago,
par leuibus uentis uolucrique simillima somno.'   *Aen.* 2.792–794

["Three times
I tried to throw my arms around her neck;
three times the Shade I grasped in vain escaped
my hands—like fleet winds, most like a winged dream."
(M. 2.1067–1070)]

After her explanation of her situation and instructions about Aeneas' future, Creusa recedes into thin air before his eyes (790–791) like a gentle wind or a dream. This description and Aeneas' attempt to embrace her three times evoke other famous Virgilian departure scenes, especially that of Orpheus and Eurydice (*G.* 4.485-489) and that of Aeneas and Anchises (*Aen.* 6.700-702). In each of these episodes, vision serves as the liaison between past and future. For Orpheus, a backward glance leads to his wife's second death, whereas, in the *Aeneid*, it is precisely the opposite: Aeneas' failure to look back upon Creusa when leaving the city results in his losing her.[45] Aeneas cannot embrace Anchises in Book 6 because he cannot cling to the past. In Book 2, Aeneas has already begun to lose his Trojan past when he encounters Creusa's *imago*.

Such scenes, of course, do not belong uniquely to Virgil. The oldest model for our passage is certainly *Iliad* 23, where Achilles attempts to embrace Patroclus' ghost (ὠρέξατο χερσὶ φέλησιν, / οὐδ'ἔλαβε· ψυχὴ δὲ κατὰ χθονὸς ἠΰτε καπνὸς ᾤχετο τετριγυῖα, 99-101).[46] Anticlea provides perhaps an even more telling model in *Odyssey* 11:

Ὣς ἔφατ', αὐτὰρ ἐγώ γ' ἔθελον φρεσὶ μερμηρίξας
μητρὸς ἐμῆς ψυχὴν ἑλέειν κατατεθνηυίης.
τρὶς μὲν ἐφορμήθην, ἑλέειν τέ με θυμὸς ἀνώγει,
τρὶς δέ μοι ἐκ χειρῶν σκιῇ εἴκελον ἢ καὶ ὀνείρῳ
ἔπτατ'· ἐμοὶ δ' ἄχος ὀξὺ γενέσκετο κηρόθι μᾶλλον,
καί μιν φωνήσας ἔπεα πτερόεντα προσηύδων·   *Odyssey* 11.204-209

['So she spoke, but I, pondering it in my heart, yet wished
to take the soul of my dead mother in my arms. Three times
I started toward her, and my heart was urgent to hold her,
And three times she fluttered out of my hands like a shadow
Or a dream, and the sorrow sharpened at the heart within me
And so I spoke to her and addressed her in winged words. . . .']

Virgil's *ter conatus . . . / ter frustra comprensa . . . imago* (792-793) is clearly indebted to the Homeric anaphora of lines 206-207. The simile that immediately follows in *Aeneid* 2 (*par leuibus uentis uolucrique simillima somno*, 794) imitates the Homeric "like unto a shadow or even a dream" (207). Even Odysseus' reaction of grief (ἐμοὶ δ' ἄχος ὀξύ, 208) is recalled rather precisely by Aeneas' sorrowful state (*lacrimantem et multa volentem / dicere*, 790-791).

The Homeric intertext invites a wider comparison as it concerns how Creusa's *imago* provides a visual link between Aeneas' past and future. The conversation between Odysseus and his mother, Anticlea, which follows immediately upon the lines cited above, gives us insight into the Aeneas-Creusa encounter.[47] Anticlea offers her son her own version of *noli me tangere:*

Ὣς ἐφάμην· ἡ δ' αὐτίκ' ἀμείβετο πότνια μήτηρ·
"ὤ μοι, τέκνον ἐμόν, περὶ πάντων κάμμορε φωτῶν,
οὔ τί σε Περσεφόνεια, Διὸς θυγάτηρ, ἀπαφίσκει,
ἀλλ' αὕτη δίκη ἐστὶ βροτῶν, ὅτε τίς κε θάνῃσιν·
οὐ γὰρ ἔτι σάρκας τε καὶ ὀστέα ἶνες ἔχουσιν,
ἀλλὰ τὰ μέν τε πυρὸς κρατερὸν μένος αἰθομένοιο
δάμνατ', ἐπεί κε πρῶτα λίπῃ λεύκ' ὀστέα θυμός,
ψυχὴ δ' ἠΰτ' ὄνειρος ἀποπταμένη πεπότηται.
ἀλλὰ φόωσδε τάχιστα λιλαίεο· ταῦτα δὲ πάντα
ἴσθ', ἵνα καὶ μετόπισθε τεῇ εἴπῃσθα γυναικί."   Od. 11.215-224

['So I spoke, and my queenly mother answered me quickly:
"Oh my child, ill-fated beyond all other mortals,
this is not Persephone, daughter of Zeus, beguiling you,
but it is only what happens, when they die, to all mortals.
The sinews no longer hold the flesh and the bones together,
and once the spirit has left the white bones, all the rest
of the body is made subject to the fire's strong fury,
but the soul flitters out like a dream and flies away. Therefore
you must strive back toward the light again with all speed; but
      remember
these things for your wife, so you may tell her hereafter." ']

Here is the background for Virgil's description of the vision of Creusa that he encounters at line 794. Odysseus' mother instructs the hero to depart in haste from this encounter and to tell his wife what he has learned (223–224). Anticlea's words resemble the language that Creusa uses to refer to Aeneas' future wife at *Aeneid* 2.783–784.

Creusa has assumed the role of Anticlea and, in that sense, has acquired some maternal characteristics. Aeneas interacts with a vision of one now in the service of the Great Mother. Indeed, Creusa's instructions to Aeneas to preserve the love of their son raises the question of guardianship, an issue perhaps fitting for an attendant of the Great Mother.[48] Aeneas' vision of Creusa therefore indicates a spiritual metamorphosis of her character from devoted wife and lover to advice-giving mother-figure. This vision softens, to some extent, the discomfiture of having to explain that there will be a *regia coniunx* in the new land (783).

In sum, Aeneas views Creusa as Orpheus views Eurydice, as several self-references to the *Georgics* 4 passage suggest.[49] By assuming the advice-giving role of Anticlea, however, Creusa also presents Aeneas with the image of the human mother that he never had.[50] The future vision of *res laetae regnumque* (783) that Creusa unfolds is charged with elements of Aeneas' past identity. Whereas, in *Aeneid* 1, Venus merely tells Aeneas about Dido and her kingdom without giving him a full sense of his mission, the vision of Creusa, who has taken on the role of Anticlea, speaks to Aeneas the details of his future, including his future wife. Thus Creusa's own vision of the future, presented by her who is herself a vision of Aeneas' past, creates, through vision, a temporal *mise en abyme*. In the nexus of this *mise en abyme*, Creusa sends Aeneas on his way with information pertinent to his own and Troy's destiny.

Allusion to Homer in the midst of this visual encounter redefines Aeneas' relationship with Creusa. His vision of her collapses temporal boundaries, for, in beholding his past, Aeneas again learns of his future. And Aeneas' vision of his past does more than merely inform his future: it charges it with a sense of purpose.

VISION AND TEMPORAL MODALITY IN AENEAS' KATABASIS

We have already considered some of the ways in which vision has allowed Aeneas to confront both past and future. Aeneas' katabasis is not merely another in a series of such visions. Rather, when Aeneas descends into the Underworld to confront his past one last time, he reaches a critical turning point in his reception of images. Aeneas' reaction to the Juno temple frieze in Book 1 and his account of his wanderings in Books 2 and 3 demonstrate that, by the time he visits Anchises in Book 6, he has already begun to leave his past behind. When Aeneas engages in a final dialogue with his father in Book 6, the poem begins to shift toward the future, for much of what Aeneas and his father behold is yet to come. Aeneas' dialogue with his past encompasses a series of explicated visions of the future. These future visions consist of persons and events that are consequent to and justify ex post facto the foundation of Rome.

Virgil's description of Aeneas' encounter with his father begins as Anchises teaches with verbal explanations (759), and the account closes as Anchises pointedly directs Aeneas' vision toward the future (788–789). The future will rely on visual images, much as the past (e.g., the temple representations of *Aeneid* 1) relied on visual images. Just as Aeneas took comfort from images of his past, he will not find encouragement and learn lessons about the future through visions. Anchises' words provide a commentary on these visions that makes them intelligible to Aeneas in a way that an ecphrasis of the future, such as the shield of Book 8, cannot.

Several visual tokens connect Book 6 with previous visual vignettes involving past and future and lead to Anchises and Aeneas' confrontation with the future. As Aeneas approaches the river Styx, he observes an image that recalls the *ante ora patrum* pronouncement discussed in the first chapter. Aeneas sees a throng of those who have died and are still awaiting transport to the other side:

> huc omnis turba ad ripas effusa ruebat,
> matres atque uiri defunctaque corpora uita
> magnanimum heroum, pueri innuptaeque puellae,
> impositique rogis iuuenes *ante ora parentum*. . . .   *Aen.* 6.305–308

> [And here a multitude was rushing, swarming
> shoreward, with men and mothers, bodies of
> high-heated heroes stripped of life, and boys
> and unwed girls, and young men set upon
> the pyre of death before their fathers' eyes. . . . (M. 6.402–406)]

In Book 1, Aeneas specifically stated that those who died at Troy were more blessed than those who would perish on the seas (1.94–96). Now, in lines closely imitative of the katabasis of the Orpheus of Virgil's *Georgics*,[51] Aeneas confronts the sad image of parents who behold their children placed on pyres. The Underworld will be an informative place where visions of the past impinge upon Aeneas. There also the image of premature death reminds the hero (and the reader) of the deep sense of loss associated with death. Aeneas' vision never becomes so optimistic as to lose a connection with the past, a state underscored here by the description of parental loss.

As Aeneas proceeds, the Sibyl calls attention to sad images, many from Aeneas' past. She notes that Aeneas sees an unburied throng (*Cocyti stagna alta uides* . . . , 323; *haec* . . . , *quam cernis, inops inhumataque turba est*, 325). These visual references set the tone for Aeneas' discovery of his former helmsman, Palinurus (*cernit ibi maestos* . . . , 333; *maestum cognouit in umbra*, 340). Palinurus explains that he had died violently after seeing the shore of Italy (357), and, by evoking symbols of Aeneas' past and future (*per genitorem oro, per spes surgentis Iuli*, 364), he requests proper burial.[52]

These visual tokens evoke memories of Aeneas' family, preparing him to encounter, in Anchises, the symbol of his past.

Vision provides a medium for Aeneas to engage the past, for Aeneas sees images that evoke memories of events from the first six books. After encountering Dido in the *campi lugentes*, Aeneas enters the "happy places" (6.638–639) where he beholds a number of scenes[53] that are, strictly speaking, outside the purview of his own epic history (656–677). After seeing so many reminders of his travels and other striking portrayals of various aspects of the Underworld, Aeneas at last confronts his own past in the form of his father:

> isque ubi tendentem aduersum per gramina uidit
> Aenean, alacris palmas utrasque tetendit,
> effusaeque genis lacrimae et uox excidit ore:
> 'uenisti tandem, tuaque exspectata parenti
> uicit iter durum pietas? datur ora tueri,
> nate, tua et notas audire et reddere uoces?'   *Aen.* 6.684–689

> [And when he saw Aeneas cross the meadow,
> he stretched out both hands eagerly, the tears
> ran down his cheeks, these words fell from his lips:
> "And have you come at last, and has the pious
> love that your father waited for defeated
> the difficulty of the journey? Son,
> can I look at your face, hear and return
> familiar accents?" (M. 6.905–912)]

Anchises first sees Aeneas and then, with tears welling up, speaks to him, calling attention to the visual and verbal aspects of the encounter (688–689). Sight stirs emotion and then provokes conversation. The sight of Aeneas had long been anticipated by Anchises, as he had often envisioned the reunion with his son:

> 'sic equidem ducebam animo rebarque futurum
> tempora dinumerans, nec me mea cura fefellit.'   *Aen.* 6.690–691

> ["So indeed I thought,
> imagining this time to come, counting
> the moments, and my longing did not cheat me." (M. 6.912–914)]

Anchises explains that he had been marking the time until Aeneas' arrival. His patient anticipation offers an imaginative conflation of present, past, and future, all revolving around Anchises' reflection (*ducebam animo*) and sense of expectation (*rebarque futurum*). Their mutual anticipation finds fulfillment in the vision with which father and son behold each other, as Aeneas explains with the words *tua me, genitor, tua tristis imago, / saepius occurrens haec limina tendere adegit . . .*[54] (6.695–696; cf. also 684–685). Visions have informed both: the father had envisioned the future meeting, while his son Aeneas had seen frequent images of the past in dreams. Now as future (son) and past (father) meet, they bring with them their thoughts. These thoughts (Aeneas' of the past and Anchises' of the future) reverse what each man symbolizes. Soon Anchises will rightly call Aeneas a Roman (851), turning Aeneas' attention toward the future.[55] But before Anchises does so, Aeneas tries to embrace him:

> ter conatus ibi collo dare bracchia circum;
> ter frustra comprensa manus effugit imago,
> par leuibus uentis uolucrique simillima somno.   Aen. 6.700–702

> [Three times
> he tried to throw his arms around Anchises'
> neck; and three times the Shade escaped from that
> vain clasp—like light winds, or most like swift dreams. (M. 6.924–927)]

These lines, which directly echo his attempt to embrace Creusa at 2.793–794, underscore Aeneas' evanescent visions of his past, visions that can only briefly point toward the fulfillment of his destiny.[56] Aeneas' failure to embrace his father's *imago* does not prevent him from continuing to look, as the line that follows shows (*interea uidet Aeneas*, 703).[57] As if a substitute for physical embrace, vision acts as the vehicle by which Aeneas engages Anchises and, therefore, his past, and vision is also the means by which Aeneas anticipates and views his future. Anchises will offer a commentary on these future images as if they were *elogia* comparable to the *imagines maiorum* of a Roman house or affixed to the bases of publicly displayed statues.[58] Paul Zanker has suggested that *Aeneid* 6 should be compared with the statues in the *exedrae* of the Forum Augustum,[59] an idea that squares well both with the images Aeneas sees and with the commentary that his father provides.[60]

To view this panoply of figures and offer his "elogia," Anchises takes Aeneas and the Sibyl to a lookout point:

> Dixerat Anchises natumque unaque Sibyllam
> conuentus trahit in medios turbamque sonantem,
> et tumulum capit unde omnis longo ordine posset
> aduersos legere et uenientum discere uultus.   *Aen.* 6.752–755

> [Anchises ended, drew the Sibyl and
> his son into the crowd, the murmuring throng,
> then gained a vantage from which he could scan
> all of the long array that moved toward them,
> to learn their faces as they came along. . . . (M. 6.994–998)]

R. D. Williams' note aptly glosses *legere* as "scan,"[61] for clearly Virgil intends that Aeneas, as directed by Anchises, witness his future. Such a temporal confluence works well vis-à-vis Virgil's development of the doctrine of metempsychosis. Yet the emphasis rests not so much on the teaching of this doctrine as it rests on Aeneas' perception of his future. This perception is underscored by Aeneas' being taken to an appropriate vantage point. Thence he views these future generations as they come along in a group. Harriet Flower has noted that these figures appear as if the *imagines* in a long funeral procession.[62] Yet these *imagines* are figures from Aeneas' future.

Anchises will add to these visions an explanation:

> 'Nunc age, Dardaniam prolem quae deinde sequatur
> gloria, qui maneant Itala de gente nepotes,
> inlustris animas nostrumque in nomen ituras,
> expediam dictis, et te tua fata docebo.'   *Aen.* 6.756–759

> ["Listen to me: my tongue will now reveal
> the fame that is to come from Dardan sons
> and what Italian children wait for you—
> bright souls that are about to take your name;
> in them I shall unfold your fates." (M. 6.999–1003)]

With the last of these lines, Anchises emphasizes that he will instruct Aeneas about what he sees, for, as Virgil has already emphasized, he is *inscius* (711). Yet it is apparently not important that Aeneas understand fully everything he sees; rather, the overwhelming power of the images before him, with Anchises' slender commentary, should suffice for him to grasp, to some extent, the import of what he sees.

With several visual prompts (*uides*, 760; *aspice*, 771; *uiden*, 779), An-

chises reviews a stream of Romans who approach Aeneas, beginning with
the kings (760–780). Denis Feeney has demonstrated that the stream of noble
Romans in this *Heldenschau* is not entirely unmuddied:[63] sons who fall short
of their fathers' standards are included in the list, as is allusion to Caesar's
and Pompey's civil wars (830–835). Feeney does not conclude, however, that
the remedy for this civil strife is Caesar Augustus, even though the emperor
is explicitly likened to the dominating yet civilizing forces of Hercules and
Bacchus (801–805):[64]

> 'huc geminas nunc flecte acies, hanc aspice gentem
> Romanosque tuos. hic Caesar et omnis Iuli
> progenies magnum caeli uentura sub axem.
> hic uir, hic est, tibi quem promitti saepius audis,
> Augustus Caesar, diui genus, aurea condet
> saecula qui rursus Latio regnata per arua
> Saturno quondam, super et Garamantas et Indos
> proferet imperium. . . .'   *Aen.* 6.788–795

> ["Now turn your two eyes here, to look upon
> your Romans, your own people. Here is Caesar
> and all the line of Iulus that will come
> beneath the mighty curve of heaven. This,
> this is the man you heard so often promised—
> Augustus Caesar, son of a god, who will
> renew a golden age in Latium,
> in fields where Saturn once was king, and stretch
> his rule beyond the Garamantes and
> the Indians—" (M. 6.1044–1053)]

Aeneas should "turn his eyes" in the direction of the family of the Caesars
and behold his Romans (788), yet his focus is soon upon the *diui genus*.
Space (*magnum caeli uentura sub axem*, 790) and time (*saecula*, 793) sur-
round Aeneas' vision of this person, whose introduction is marked by the
staggered repetition of the demonstrative (791). Anchises associates Augustus with the restoration of the Golden Age (*condet* / . . . *rursus*, 792–793) and
the propagation of the empire (794–795). In this vision, Aeneas beholds the
one figure on whom the rebirth of Rome in Virgil's own day depends.[65]

After Aeneas has seen (e.g., *uis uidere*, 817–818; *aspice*, 825) the Tarquins
and the figures from Republican times, including the Decii and, markedly,
in light of the empress' family connections, the Drusi,[66] Anchises closes

his catalogue with "a vivid, animated . . . introduction"[67] of the *gens Fabia* (*quo fessum rapitis, Fabii?*) followed by an allusion to Ennius, thus calling attention to Quintus Fabius Maximus' famous tactics of delay.[68] Anchises then offers some curious words that introduce the best known and most frequently quoted line of advice that he gives Aeneas in the poem:[69]

> 'excudent alii spirantia mollius aera
> (credo equidem), uiuos ducent de marmore uultus,
> orabunt causas melius, caelique meatus
> describent radio et surgentia sidera dicent:
> tu regere imperio populos, Romane, memento
> (hae tibi erunt artes), pacique imponere morem,
> parcere subiectis et debellare superbos.' *Aen.* 6.847–853

> ["For other peoples will, I do not doubt,
> still cast their bronze to breathe with softer features,
> or draw out of the marble living lines,
> plead causes better, trace the ways of heaven
> with wands and tell the rising constellations;
> but yours will be the rulership of nations,
> remember, Roman, these will be your arts:
> to teach the ways of peace to those you conquer,
> to spare defeated peoples, tame the proud." (M. 6.1129–1137)]

After Anchises' description of Greek (*alii*) superiority in the visual arts, he turns specifically to oratory, suggesting that even here the Greeks have outstripped the Romans. "What would Cicero have made of this?" the reader asks.[70] Indeed, not without reason are commentators such as Austin deeply troubled by this line. Williams puts it mildly when he writes, "It seems that Anchises does less than justice in these matters to his own people."[71] While perhaps few will object to most elements in this list, oratory categorically stands out.

Why does Anchises devalue Roman oratory? He does so in part, it would seem, because Anchises wants to subordinate all of these arts to Rome's destiny, as lines 851–853 reveal. While other arts mentioned are concerned merely with living, rule by *imperium* and the setting of "the stamp of civilized usage upon peace" (852)[72] are the "arts" that the Romans must practice.[73] With his famous closing line (853), Anchises states that Aeneas should be merciful to those already subject to him (the force of the perfect participle) but conquer the proud. Anchises relegates oratory to such a diminutive status that it pales in comparison to the more important historical visions that Aeneas beholds.[74]

But this is only part of the contrast. Oratory's insignificance is further underscored by the words that Anchises adds immediately afterwards:

> Sic pater Anchises, atque haec mirantibus addit:
> '*aspice*, ut insignis spoliis Marcellus opimis
> ingreditur uictorque uiros *supereminet* omnis.
> hic rem Romanam magno turbante tumultu
> sistet eques, sternet Poenos Gallumque rebellem,
> tertiaque arma patri suspendet capta Quirino.'   *Aen.* 6.854–859

[So, while Aeneas and the Sibyl marveled,
father Anchises spoke to them, then added:
"And see Marcellus there, as he advances
in glory, with his splendid spoils, a victor
who towers over all! A horseman, he
will set the house of Rome in order when
it is confounded by great mutiny;
he will lay low the Carthaginians
and rebel Gaul; then for a third time father
Quirinus will receive his captured arms." (M. 6.1138–1147)]

The image of Marcellus is pointedly visual, for he is himself a towering victor, and the spoils of his victory are on public display. In reference to Marcellus, Anchises proclaims, "Behold the victor," and he does so with an Ennian tone (855–856).[75] Marcellus' victory over Virdomarus at Clastidium in 222 BC exemplifies the principles outlined by Anchises. Aeneas must remember (851) and see (855). The first of these imperatives carries four infinitives that Anchises offers for stable Roman rule.

The first infinitive phrase, *regere imperio*, summarizes the three that follow. The imperative (*memento*) that introduces the infinitives is important, too, for it shows that ruling must be done by memory: one must have a clear picture of the past in order to regulate the present or future; for example, one might show leniency to the subject, for memory of one's own misfortunes can evoke pity. The correspondence of the last infinitive phrase, *debellare superbos*, anticipates the poem's closing, where Aeneas will do this very thing. It is also located hard by the next imperative of Anchises, *aspice* (855), with which admonition Anchises returns to the *Heldenschau* proper.[76] By so doing, he reveals that it is the sight of the great figures of the "past"

—though for him and Aeneas, of course, this past is the future—whereby one rules and indeed lives well (*pacique imponere morem,* 852). Marcellus, who towers conspicuously over all as once Rome appeared to Tityrus (*Ecl.* 1: *uerum haec tantum alias inter caput extulit urbes / quantum lenta solent inter uiburna cupressi,*[77] 24–25), is the next figure to whom Anchises directs Aeneas' vision. Aeneas continues to behold the future, which under Marcellus' name is tinged with victory (856) as well as with grief (868–886).

To sum up: The great *Heldenschau* and perhaps the depth of wisdom of Anchises' words have caused Aeneas and the Sibyl to marvel. As they do so, Anchises' next words give a further challenge to oratory, which he has relegated merely to arts admired by Hellenophiles. The Romans' ability to rule and their ability to behold for themselves, to see and to learn from seeing rather than from being persuaded, will supplant oratory.

Aeneas' trip to the Underworld is, in one respect, necessarily "visual." The sights of persons and legendary places there spontaneously evoke a graphic description that would characterize any katabasis. When one considers the many references to vision in the episode, however, a pattern emerges. Anchises, who embodies Aeneas' past, repeatedly calls attention to Aeneas' vision of the future. As Anchises teaches and explains, he repeatedly emphasizes the Roman future, with special attention to Aeneas' vision of his descendant Augustus, the *diui genus*, around whom time and space revolve (790–793). Anchises will soon return to the age-old comparison of Greek and Roman, but with an important new twist: oratory, which normally the Romans would have claimed to have perfected, is added to the list of merely decorative arts. Anchises replaces oratory with the charge to rule, based on the recollection of certain precepts. He swiftly adds the need for vision, citing the victor Marcellus as an example (855), upon whose descendant Aeneas will pointedly gaze just five lines later (*ire uidebat / egregium forma iuuenem,* 860–861).

Another episode in Book 8 expands upon this vision; the future is again cast in terms of the past, and Aeneas' gaze provides him a means for gaining an understanding of future events through reflection on the past.

SITE/SIGHT OF ROME

In Book 8, after the chorus of Salii sings of the exploits of Hercules and the priests offer sacrifice, Aeneas and Evander tour the site of future Rome. Evander plays the role of second father and mentor to Aeneas, teaching him as Anchises had in *Aeneid* 6.[78] For Evander and Aeneas, vision serves as a frame for the encounter with the future. Virgil carefully draws attention to Evander's visual assessment of Aeneas when they first meet and to Evander's recollection of how Anchises had appeared when he met Evander in Arcadia many years previously.[79] This encounter is paradoxical not only because Aeneas views the site of monuments not yet monumental but also because he sees these future monuments while learning about their past history from Evander. This passage, then, is the material counterpart to the prosopographical retinue of *Aeneid 6*.

In the center of the episode, Aeneas comes to the Porta Carmentalis (338). Both this gate, with its eponymous deity, and the reference to Janus (357), the god of gates, have symbolic significance.[80] The Porta Carmentalis represents oral communication (*carmen*), while Janus, the double-faced deity, suggests vision both prospective and retrospective. As Anchises had deemphasized oratory in *Aeneid 6* when presenting visions of the Roman future, these portal references and the conversation between Aeneas and Evander direct the hero away from a reliance on the spoken word and toward a confidence in the reality of things seen.

Setting out from the festival, Evander, Aeneas, and Pallas pass the time in friendly conversation:

> . . . et comitem Aenean iuxta natumque tenebat
> ingrediens uarioque uiam sermone leuabat.
> miratur facilisque oculos fert omnia circum
> Aeneas, capiturque locis et singula laetus
> exquiritque auditque uirum monimenta priorum.   *Aen. 8.308–312*

> [. . . he kept Aeneas and his son
> beside him as companions as he walked
> while lightening the way with varied talk.
> Aeneas marvels; eagerly he turns
> his eyes on everything Evander notes:
> he is so captivated by the place
> that, glad, he seeks and, one by one, he learns
> the chronicles that tell of men of old. (M. 8.403–410)]

As they walk and talk, Aeneas carefully surveys the area (310) and inquires about what he sees. Though he unwittingly beholds the future, he asks about the past. Vision provides a connection between the past, about which Aeneas learns, and the future, about which the Roman reader already has knowledge.[81] In this connection the word *monimenta* is important, derived as it is from the Indo-European root **men-*, which suggests the visual retention of the past in one's memory.[82]

Evander enlarges upon the origins of the Latin people, explaining how Saturnus, dispelled from Olympus by Jove, fled with his son and dwelt among this rustic people:

> 'is genus indocile ac dispersum montibus altis
> composuit legesque dedit, Latiumque uocari
> maluit, his quoniam latuisset tutus in oris.
> aurea quae perhibent illo sub rege fuere
> saecula: sic placida populos in pace regebat,
> deterior donec paulatim ac decolor aetas
> et belli rabies et amor successit habendi.'   *Aen.* 8.321–327

>   ["He made a nation
> of those untamed and scattered in high mountains
> and gave them laws. And he chose Latium
> as name, because he had lain safely hidden
> along these coasts. The golden age they tell of
> was in the time of this king, for he ruled
> his tribe in tranquil peace. But by degrees
> an age depraved and duller took its place,
> with war's insanity and love of gain." (M. 8.420–428)]

Here Virgil, through Evander, makes an etymological connection between Latium and *latuisset*, explaining the origin of the place in terms of the god's hidden presence. The region of Latium, therefore, suggests Saturnus' inability to be seen. The degeneration of the people is explained also in visual terms: the Golden Age gives way to a colorless age (*decolor aetas*) characterized by greed and the madness of strife.[83]

Explaining his own exile, however, Evander states that he was led by the warnings of his mother, the nymph Carmentis:

> 'me pulsum patria pelagique extrema sequentem
> Fortuna omnipotens et ineluctabile fatum
> his posuere locis, matrisque egere tremenda
> Carmentis nymphae monita et deus auctor Apollo.'
> Vix ea dicta, dehinc progressus monstrat et aram

et Carmentalem Romani nomine partam
quam memorant, nymphae priscum Carmentis honorem,
uatis fatidicae, cecinit quae prima futuros
Aeneadas magnos et nobile Pallanteum.   *Aen.* 8.333–341

    ["All-able fortune and my fate,
the inescapable, have driven me,
when banished from my country, across far seas
to settle here. The warning of my mother,
the nymph Carmentis, and the urgings of
our patron god, Apollo, spurred us on."
His words were scarcely done when, moving on,
he points out both the altar and the gate
the Romans call Carmental, ancient tribute
in honor of the nymph Carmentis, fate-
foretelling prophetess, the first to sing
the greatness of Aeneas' sons and future
of noble Pallanteum. (M. 8.434–446)]

Carmentis instructed Evander about his destiny and predicted the future Aeneidae. Through the figure of Carmentis, present, past, and future are brought into a single vision, that of the Porta Carmentalis, a monument that Aeneas can clearly behold. This gate commemorates a past event and, at the same time, reminds the viewer of the future that the nymph had predicted.

As he continues his tour, Aeneas sees the copse that affords asylum between the Capitoline and Palatine (342),[84] and the Lupercal (343), with an etymological explanation of how its name is connected with Arcadian Pan.[85] Other sites, too, are mentioned, from the Argiletum (345) to the Tarpeian rock (347) to the Capitoline Hill, where, Evander explains, Arcadian shepherds were thought to have seen Jove (352–353). These topographical details look forward to a day when they will be refounded as landmarks in the context of Augustan Rome. They also look back, however, to the past, and Aeneas views them as tangible reminders of that past. Aeneas then sees the last of the public monuments described by Evander:

'haec duo praeterea disiectis oppida muris,
reliquias ueterumque *uides monimenta* uirorum.
hanc Ianus pater, hanc Saturnus condidit arcem;
Ianiculum huic, illi fuerat Saturnia nomen.'   *Aen.* 8.355–358

["And farther on
you see two towns with ruined walls, the relics
and the memorials of ancient men:
for father Janus built this city, that
was built by Saturn; and the name of one,
Janiculum; Saturnia, the other's." (M. 8.464–469)]

Evander's invocation of Aeneas' vision (*uides*, 356) is similar to Anchises' directive in Book 6 for Aeneas to behold his fellow Romans, specifically the *diui genus* (6.792). Here, Evander's words recall the earlier description of Aeneas' marveling at the monuments of bygone generations (8.310–312); moreover, this second reference to the *monimenta* creates a frame for the tale through the visual connotations that the root of *monimenta* encompasses.[86] Evander's tour also evokes the notion of ancient memory techniques described by Cicero in *De oratore*.[87] Discussing such mneumo-technics, Frances Yates writes, "The word [. . .] hardly conveys what the artificial memory of Cicero may have been like, as it moved among the buildings of ancient Rome, seeing the places, seeing the images stored on the places, with a piercing inner vision which immediately brought to his lips the thoughts and words of his speech."[88] Now, pointedly, at the end of his description of these monuments, Evander calls attention to Aeneas' sight before Saturn's Capitoline citadel and the Hill of Janus, the gate-god.

Janus, the visually bidirectional god of bridges and gates, fittingly culminates an episode with a prominent visual component. Just as Aeneas made his exodus from the Underworld through a gate[89] and into the martial challenges of Books 7–12, so the sight of the specific monuments of Rome's destiny offers Aeneas a transition between past and future. Janus' two faces afford him vision of both what lies behind and what is left to come. Janus' presence at the episode's culmination also explains why, among so many important Roman topographical features, Virgil emphasizes the Janiculum.

Janus' two-way vision recalls the experience that Aeneas has in seeing the monuments of ancient men. These records of an ancient past also lie upon the future site of Rome. Aeneas has thus become a kind of time-defying *voyant-visible*, for he sees future topographical monuments superimposed upon the geography of the past. The two gates—that of Janus, who represents gates and two-way vision, and the Porta Carmentalis—present a contrast. The latter is associated with the nymph who, Evander says, specifically sang of the future (340); the paronomasia between *cecinit* and *carmentalis* is typical of Virgilian *lepos*.[90]

Carmentis' song had been important in setting the stage for the present reality of the Aeneidae's arrival, even as her *monita* (336), like Apollo's, had directed Evander's steps. Yet by the end of the passage, significantly, Janus' *monimenta* (356) have replaced Carmentis' *monita*. For Aeneas, the gate-god that he sees last is especially important, particularly with regard to the narrative's telos, the future city reflected here in the vision of future Rome. Through the reference to Janus, whom Evander puts on a par with Saturnus (357–358) as one of the city's founding deities, the visible city emerges as predicted by Carmentis, expounded upon by Evander, and beheld by Aeneas. Carmentis sings of the future while Janus allows vision of both past and future. Aeneas, himself here visible amidst these monuments, is able, as a *voyant-visible*, to participate in the future by vision. That vision will be brought to fruition in the "future monuments" that he now sees.

CONCLUSION

In the *Aeneid*, vision offers a means for bringing the future and past together. Aeneas' visions of both Hector and the Penates, who are intimately associated with his past, give him a mandate for his future. Creusa has a similar effect, particularly with regard to Aeneas' domestic affairs and the line of succession through him to their common son, Ascanius. Only when Aeneas encounters Andromache is Aeneas' sense of mission temporarily obfuscated, for the visit to Buthrotum is a false vision of the past and, therefore, a diversion from his ultimate journey. Yet, even here, vision of the future eventually prevails as Aeneas promises, based on his own vision of the future (*moenia cernam*, 501), to join Buthrotum to Rome.

When Aeneas descends to the Underworld in Book 6 and encounters his past, he cannot embrace it, but it can instruct him about how to view his future. Anchises explicitly enjoins Aeneas to look closely at scores of future Romans; such visions give Aeneas the sense of purpose that he needs to accomplish his mission. Most importantly, Aeneas is to remember (*memento*, 851), a word that in the context of the review of these *imagines* of the future's past has a poignant tone. "To remember" means to be linked to the past visually[91] and to allow memory to govern one's governing, even as the imperative *memento* governs four dependent infinitives (6.851–853).[92] Evander's explanation of the site and sights of future Rome in Book 8 has a similar effect as Aeneas gazes upon and learns about a past that will inform and shape his own and Rome's future. Evander's story involves two gates associated with aspects of Roman history.

Virgil uses vision to broker time to suggest that one cannot look ahead without looking back. While Glenn Most's arguments for a kind of selective memory have merit,[93] my understanding of Aeneas' visions of his past is different: it seems Aeneas' visions of the past blend that past with the future, transcending temporal confines and informing his ability to make decisions in the present. Aeneas' vision of a future that would have been the past for a contemporary of Virgil is balanced within the text by Aeneas' view of his own past, as exemplified by his encounters with Hector, Creusa, and the Penates. These images of the past inform and give meaning to Aeneas' and Rome's future.

CHAPTER 4

Hic amor

LOVE, VISION, AND DESTINY

❦

> I met a lady in the meads,
> Full beautiful, a fairy's child;
> Her hair was long, her foot was light,
> And her eyes were wild.
> . . .
> I saw pale kings, and princes too,
> Pale warriors, death pale were they all;
> They cried—"La belle dame sans merci
> Hath thee in thrall!"
>
> KEATS, "La Belle Dame sans Merci:
> A Ballad," 13–16, 37–40

In Keats' "La Belle Dame sans Merci," a lonely knight-at-arms encounters a dryadlike girl whose eyes capture his gaze. Although he symbolically endeavors to overcome her waywardness by closing her "wild" eyes with kisses, the knight senses that the relationship cannot endure. In his dreams, the knight can see the "death-pale" succession of lovers from the girl's past. By the end of the poem, the knight has become a *voyant-visible*, able to see another's past and present while anticipating the dangerous future that awaits him should he remain where "the sedge is wither'd from the lake / and no birds sing" (3–4, 47–48).

Virgil uses similar visual imagery in the *Aeneid* to illustrate the creation and destruction of Dido and Aeneas' relationship. Virgil interweaves visual description with amatory allusions, contrasting vision and love of Aeneas' future country with the lovers' glances and the present reality of their love affair. From their initial meeting, the way that Aeneas and Dido look at each other reveals that the development of their relationship will be indebted, in some measure, to the vision each has of the other. Aeneas' focus on Dido temporarily obscures his vision of the land of his calling. Other significant passages in the *Aeneid* also reflect this pattern; near the poem's conclusion, Aeneas' future vision of Rome[1] conflicts with Turnus' vision of Lavinia.[2]

We can begin to examine the connection between Dido and Aeneas by contextualizing their initial meeting. *Prima facie*, Venus arranges the meeting of Dido and Aeneas to secure aid for her son in Carthage. Nevertheless, Dido and Aeneas' relationship extends beyond a mere political alliance because of Venus' desire to thwart Juno's plans to dissuade Aeneas from his mission (671–672). The pair's tender glances clash with the imperial visions of each for their respective countries, and each must eventually choose a primary object of vision. As Aeneas ceases to view his relationship with Dido as his central focus, his vision of Rome is reestablished, for such vision replaces the amatory gaze that had existed between himself and Dido.[3]

Application of Merleau-Ponty's theory of the *voyant-visible* elucidates the importance of vision during each phase of Dido and Aeneas' relationship, from meeting, to separation, to rendezvous in the *campi lugentes*. Virgil juxtaposes vision and verbal communication to illustrate the widening gap between the two, and consideration of Dido and Aeneas' changing views of each other and of the future helps the reader to evaluate the evolution and eventual disintegration of the relationship. Analysis of the first encounter of Dido and Aeneas, with attention to an interesting remark by Servius on the passage, will provide understanding of the importance of vision in their relationship.

ALIUD GENUS OFFICII: VISION AND THE SECOND FAVOR

From the initial meeting of Dido and Aeneas, Virgil effects a synergy of vision and language. Dido's first sight of Aeneas produces in her a response that befits both a noble ruler and a sympathetic human being. Dido's gaze transforms Aeneas from hidden voyeur to *voyant-visible*, to whom Dido reacts with thoughtful speech. By contrast, Aeneas' vision of Dido temporarily obscures the understanding that he has of his own destiny. Although he initially reciprocates Dido's passion and devotion in the context of their relationship, Aeneas eventually looks afresh to his duty and true calling.

In *Aeneid* 1, Dido addresses the Teucrian refugees with words of great encouragement and distinct compassion:

Tum breuiter Dido uultum demissa profatur:
'soluite corde metum, Teucri, secludite curas.
res dura et regni nouitas me talia cogunt
moliri et late finis custode tueri.
quis genus Aeneadum, quis Troiae nesciat urbem,
uirtutesque uirosque aut tanti incendia belli?'   *Aen.* 1.561–566

[Then Dido softly, briefly answers him:
"O Teucrians, enough of fear, cast out
your cares. My kingdom is new; hard circumstances
have forced me to such measures for our safety,
to post guards far and wide along our boundaries.
But who is ignorant of Aeneas' men?
Who has not heard of Troy, its acts and heroes,
the flames of that tremendous war?" (M. 1.791–798)]

In explaining the reason for the border guards, Dido is able to create an empathetic tone, and her gracious words gladden the hearts of her visitors. Her
manner of self-presentation also identifies her as a gentle host; as she addresses the men, Dido directs her eyes downward in the manner of Hyp-
sipyle before Jason in Apollonius' *Argonautica*.[4] Servius auctus comments
on Dido's posture with the words, *dicendo autem 'uultum demissa' aliud
genus officii adiecit*.[5] Dido's body language, the commander suggests, indicates something beyond her words. In casting down her eyes, she offers the
Trojans a further favor. Servius auctus is certainly correct to interpret Virgil's
use of *officium* as "favor." Nevertheless, though Dido has a general obligation
of guest friendship, it is not clear how there would be another such obligation.[6] With *aliud*, he implies that a previous favor has been given by Dido
to the Trojans, one of a type (*genus*) entirely different from this.[7] What is the
previous favor to which Servius auctus refers?

To answer this question, an examination of the context of the first meeting of Dido and Aeneas can provide some clues. Aeneas and Achates have
arrived in Carthage, where they enjoy the privacy of the cloud sent by Venus.
From this vantage point, Achates and Aeneas observe that Ilioneus and the
others have come to seek aid from Dido:

dissimulant et nube caua speculantur amicti
quae fortuna uiris, classem quo litore linquant,
quid ueniant; cunctis nam lecti nauibus ibant

orantes ueniam et templum clamore petebant.
    Postquam introgressi et coram data copia fandi,
maximus Ilioneus placido sic pectore coepit. . . .   *Aen.* 1.516–521

[They stay in hiding, screened by folds of fog,
and wait to see what fortune found their friends,
on what beach they have left the fleet, and why
they come; for these were men who had been chosen
from all the ships to ask for grace, who now
made for the temple door with loud outcries.
When they had entered and received their leave
to speak in Dido's presence, then the eldest,
Ilioneus, calmly began. . . . (M. 1.727–735)]

In allowing the embassy to approach, Dido has fulfilled any possible obligation of a host.[8] Once received, Ilioneus and the Trojans (519) seek the opportunity to request some favor beyond a mere explanation of their presence in Carthage (520).[9] The men entreat Dido for *copia fandi* (520), an expression used elsewhere only twice in the poem: the debate between Turnus and Drances (11.378) and the embassy report sent by Latinus to Diomedes (11.248). Dido humanely grants them both permission to explain their situation in detail and the right to seek aid.

    The queen responds to their tale with a downward glance that Austin interprets as an indication of her "modesty and emotion."[10] But why would Dido, a monarch and city builder, seek to appear modest before outsiders? As ruler, she adopts the role of one who governs and directs men's labor, not the role of modest woman who defers to the wishes of men.[11] Not surprisingly, Virgil compares her to a goddess during her first appearance before Aeneas:

. . . dum stupet obtutuque haeret defixus in uno,
regina ad templum, forma pulcherrima Dido,
incessit magna iuuenum stipante caterua.
qualis in Eurotae ripis aut per iuga Cynthi
exercet Diana choros, quam mille secutae
hinc atque hinc glomerantur Oreades; illa pharetram
fert umero gradiensque deas supereminet omnis
(Latonae tacitum pertemptant gaudia pectus):
talis erat Dido. . . .   *Aen.* 1.495–503

[But while the Dardan watched these scenes in wonder,
while he was fastened in a stare, astonished,
the lovely-bodied Dido neared the temple,
a crowding company of youths around her.
And just as, on the banks of the Eurotas
or though the heights of Cynthus, when Diana
incites her dancers, and her followers,
a thousand mountain-nymphs, press in behind her,
. . .

       . . . gladness excites
Latona's silent breast: even so, Dido. . . . (M. 1.698–705, 708–709)]

Virgil uses language associated with Diana, the prototypical modest deity.
Aeneas would seem first to perceive her as an august Diana-figure,[12] a perspective important to Virgil's construction of Dido as the fulfillment of
Aeneas' encounter with Venus.[13] Gordon Williams supports such a reading, stating that the paradox of a female Carthaginian leader partially resolves itself as "Aeneas lifts his eyes from her [Penthesilea] and sees Dido,
whose beauty is taken up in a simile comparing her to the warrior-queen
Diana."[14] As Dido enters Aeneas' field of vision, she appears as the powerful
virgin-goddess.

Virgil's description of Dido involves Diana's appearance and her looming
presence. Like Diana, Dido walks in a stately procession, surrounded by her
retainers.[15] Clearly Virgil models his description of Diana on the Homeric
depiction of Artemis in *Odyssey* 6:

οἵη δ' Ἄρτεμις εἶσι κατ' οὔρεα ἰοχέαιρα,
ἢ κατὰ Τηΰγετον περιμήκετον ἢ Ἐρύμανθον,
τερπομένη κάπροισι καὶ ὠκείης ἐλάφοισι·
τῇ δέ θ' ἅμα νύμφαι, κοῦραι Διὸς αἰγιόχοιο,
ἀγρονόμοι παίζουσι· γέγηθε δέ τε φρένα Λητώ·
πασάων δ' ὑπὲρ ἥ γε κάρη ἔχει ἠδὲ μέτωπα,
ῥεῖά τ' ἀριγνώτη πέλεται, καλαὶ δέ πᾶσαι·
ὣς ἥ γ' ἀμφιπόλοισι μετέπρεπε παρθένος ἀδμής.   Od. 6.102–109

[. . . and as Artemis, who showers arrows, moves on the mountains
either along Taÿgetos or on high-towering
Erymanthos, delighting in boars and deer in their running,
and along with her the nymphs daughters of Zeus of the aegis,

range in the wilds and play, and the heart of Leto is gladdened,
for the head and brows of Artemis are above all the others,
and she is easily marked among them, though all are lovely,
so this one shone among the handmaidens, a virgin unwedded.]

Like Dido, the Artemis of Homer moves proudly amidst her company. Virgil increases the power of the image by including a quiver on Dido's shoulder (*illa pharetram / fert umero gradiensque deas supereminet omnis*, 500–501).[16] Both Homer and Virgil describe Diana to be a source of pride for Leto,[17] and both poets portray Diana as towering head and shoulders above her retinue and, therefore, easy to see.[18] Ovid will use Virgil's very description to portray Diana in her bath, when viewed by Actaeon (*Met.* 3.181–182). Gordon Williams associates Leto's view of Diana and Dido's perceptibility in his consideration of vision in Virgil's passage:

> The detail of Diana's mother and her pleasure at the sight of her daughter seems non-functional in the context. . . . But it is exactly this pleasure in the onlooker at the sight of Dido that needs to be read into the context, and especially in Aeneas, an onlooker whose name opened the description of Dido's approach (494) and who is named again.[19]

Aeneas' clandestine surveillance of Dido and his delight in her appearance approximate the encounter of Diana and the voyeur Actaeon. For both Actaeon and Aeneas, vision of Diana does not occur without consequence. Yet, Dido's charitable reaction to her visitor presents a distinct contrast to the violence of Diana toward Actaeon, even though Aeneas, as an Actaeon-like voyeur, looks upon the scene from a hidden location.

While Virgil's portrayal may echo the interaction of Diana and Actaeon, his Homeric description of Diana as treading the Cynthian heights or Eurotas' banks[20] does not evoke the response of the Actaeon-transforming Diana.[21] Instead, the queen treats Aeneas' men humanely, granting Ilioneus the "first favor" of a warm reception and the right to speak. But what of the further type of favor to which Servius refers? The answer is contained perhaps in the words of the queen herself. As Aeneas watches from his protective cloud, Dido finishes her welcoming speech to the Trojan strangers with the following sentiments:

'urbem quam statuo, uestra est; subducite nauis;
Tros Tyriusque mihi nullo discrimine agetur.
atque utinam rex ipse Noto compulsus eodem

adforet Aeneas! equidem per litora certos
dimittam et Libyae lustrare extrema iubebo,
si quibus eiectus siluis aut urbibus errat.'   *Aen.* 1.573–578

["... the city
I am building now is yours. Draw up your ships.
I shall allow no difference between
the Tyrian and the Trojan. Would your king,
Aeneas, too, were present, driven here
by that same south wind. I, in fact, shall send
my trusted riders out along the shores,
to comb the farthest coasts of Libya and
to see if, cast out of the waters, he
is wandering through the forests or the cities." (M. 1.806–815)]

This striking display of hospitality shows that Dido is a compassionate and caring ruler, and this offer would seem to be the second favor of which Servius speaks: she looks upon this embassy with compassion, granting its request. Having welcomed them with a gentle downward gaze (*uultum demissa,* 561), Dido now warmly offers them her city and the possibility of cultural merger.[22]

Within a few lines, Dido's prayer for Aeneas' safe arrival is expeditiously answered as Aeneas steps forth from the cloud that encompassed him and Achates. Dido's reaction to his arrival is characterized first in terms of her vision, then her speech:

Obstipuit primo aspectu Sidonia Dido,
casu deinde uiri tanto, et sic ore locuta est:
'quis te, nate dea, per tanta pericula casus
insequitur? quae uis immanibus applicat oris?'   *Aen.* 1.613–616

[First at the very sight of him, and then
at all he had endured, Sidonian Dido
was startled. And she told the Trojan this:
"You, goddess-born, what fortune hunts you down
through such tremendous trials? What violence
has forced you onto these ferocious shores?" (M. 1.859–864)]

Austin denies that *primo* has adverbial force within the phrase *primo aspectu;* instead, he considers *primo* a causal adjective of *aspectu.*[23] Such a rendering heightens the force of *obstipuit*, for Dido's amazement is *caused by* her first sight of Aeneas. At the moment he appears, Aeneas transforms into *voyant-visible* and abandons his role of invisible voyeur. The immediate, mutual gaze between him and Dido leads to the queen's empathetic words and marks the beginning of their relationship.

Virgil clearly models a portion of the visual aspects of the Aeneas and Dido encounter on Apollonius' account of the meeting of Jason and Medea.[24] Apollonius' description of Medea's longing eyes, however, goes far beyond Virgil's *primo aspectu:*[25]

> αὐτὰρ ὅγ' οὐ μετὰ δηρὸν ἐελδομένῃ ἐφαάνθη,
> ὑψόσ' ἀναθρῴσκων ἅ τε Σείριος Ὠκεανοῖο,
> ὃς δή τοι καλὸς μὲν ἀρίζηλός τ' ἐσιδέσθαι
> ἀντέλλει, μήλοισι δ' ἐν ἄσπετον ἧκεν ὀιζύν—
> ὣς ἄρα τῇ καλὸς μὲν ἐπήλυθεν εἰσοράασθαι
> Αἰσονίδης, κάματον δὲ δυσίμερον ὦρσε φαανθείς.
> ἐκ δ' ἄρα οἱ κραδίη στηθέων πέσεν, ὄμματα δ' αὔτως
> ἤχλυσαν, θερμὸν δὲ παρηίδας εἷλεν ἔρευθος·
>
> APOLLONIUS RHODIUS, *Arg.* 3.956–963

[But soon he appeared to her longing eyes, striding along loftily, like Sirius coming from ocean, which rises fair and clear to see, but brings unspeakable mischief to flocks; thus then did Aeson's son come to her, fair to see, but the sight of him brought love-sick care. Her heart fell from out her bosom, and a dark mist came over her eyes, and a hot blush covered her cheeks.[26]]

While Virgil describes Dido's initial vision of Aeneas as a momentary glance,[27] Apollonius refers repeatedly to Medea's vision. The eyes of Jason and Medea project and receive the loving glances that express the unspoken love of their nascent relationship. Apollonius goes on to describe Jason's love as a flame that enters Medea's eyes and warms her heart:

> . . . ἡ δ' ἐγκλιδὸν ὄσσε βαλοῦσα
> νεκτάρεον μείδησε, χύθη δέ οἱ ἔνδοθι θυμὸς
> αἴνῳ ἀειρομένης· καὶ ἀνέδρακεν ὄμμασιν ἄντην, . . .
> . . .
> τοῖος ἀπὸ ξανθοῖο καρήατος Αἰσονίδαο
> στράπτεν ἔρως ἡδεῖαν †ἀπὸ φλόγα, τῆς δ' ἀμαρυγάς
> ὀφθαλμῶν ἥρπαζεν, ἰαίνετο δὲ φρένας εἴσω

τηκομένη, οἷόν τε περὶ ῥοδέῃσιν ἐέρση
τήκεται ἠῴοισιν ἰαινομένη φαέεσσιν.
ἄμφω δ' ἄλλοτε μέν τε κατ' οὔδεος ὄμματ' ἔρειδον
αἰδόμενοι, ὁτὲ δ' αὖτις ἐπὶ σφίσι βάλλον ὀπωπάς
ἱμερόεν φαιδρῇσιν ὑπ' ὀφρύσι μειδιόωντες.

Arg. 3.1008–1010, 1017–1024

[. . . she cast her eyes down with a smile divinely sweet; and her soul
melted within her, uplifted by his praise, and she gazed upon him face
to face; . . . so wonderfully did love flash forth a sweet flame from the
golden head of Aeson's son; and he captivated her gleaming eyes; and
her heart within grew warm, melting away as the dew melts away
round roses when warmed by the morning's light. And now both were
fixing their eyes on the ground abashed, and again were throwing
glances at each other, smiling with the light of love beneath their
radiant brows.]

Apollonius' descriptive language and sustained emphasis of the visual aspects of the encounter portraying the psychological aspects of the lovers'
interaction is typical of Hellenistic baroque.[28] Apollonius is chiefly inter-
ested in emotion; his lovers' visions of each other stir feelings, but those
feelings are strictly amatory.

These lines from the *Argonautica* contrast with Virgil's simpler and less
erotic treatment of Dido's first view of Aeneas. Although Virgil does not
here practice *oppositio in imitando*, there is an obvious tension between
the Apollonian model and Virgil's more delicate treatment.[29] Virgil's careful attention to the gaze of Dido, while generally indebted to the Apollonian description of the heroine, differs significantly. Virgil passes beyond
Apollonius' "pervasive, learned and subtle imitations of earlier poetry"[30] to
construct a heroine with a gaze that mingles attraction and concern for her
partner. Despite her interest in Aeneas, at least at the beginning of their relationship, Dido also manages to attend to her public duties and, in contrast
to Medea's passionate glances, uses her vision and words to display compassion.[31] Virgil's inclusion of the detail of Dido's downward glance suggests,
therefore, that he wants his reader to learn about her character not only from
her words but also from her vision and gestures.

This last idea gains significance not only because recent work by Licinia
Ricottilli has demonstrated well the importance of gesture in the *Aeneid*[32]
but also because similar ideas were in the air in Virgil's lifetime. In one of his
many discussions of rhetorical technique in the *De oratore*, Cicero writes,

sed in ore sunt omnia, in eo autem ipso dominatus est omnis oculorum,[33] (3.59.221). Cicero's quip sheds light on the force of the sequence of *primo* (613) followed by *deinde* (614). First, the vision of Aeneas, and second, his "sufferings" (*casu*[34]), cause Dido to speak with her mouth—however pleonastic this may be—and, by extension, with her amazed (as *obstipuit* reveals, 613) yet compassionate visage.

Unlike that of Apollonius, Virgil's theme is not "love at first sight." In Virgil's account, the articulate and visionary Dido is both *dux* and *femina*. Qua *femina*, she emerges as a demonstrably sensual person, struck by and responsive to the hero's handsome bearing. She also emerges as a true leader who will soon articulately proclaim *non ignara mali miseris succurrere disco* (630) ["Not ignorant of trials, / I now can learn to help the miserable." (M. 1.881–882)], a phrase that succinctly summarizes the second favor that her downward glance suggested to Servius.

VIEWPOINTS OF DEPARTURE: DECEPTION, VISION, AND THE SEPARATION OF DIDO AND AENEAS

As the relationship of Dido and Aeneas begins to come to a close, vision is both an aspect of their gestures and a part of their discussion. Their vision of each other corroborates, through personal examination, the end of their affair. Dido's perception of the relationship's end brings desperate attempts to recover it; for Aeneas, the vision of Mercury replaces his focus on Dido and points toward the validation of his mission.

When Aeneas looks upon Dido for the last time in Carthage (4.389), he is shaken by great love (395). Conversely, as Dido looks upon Aeneas, she sees an unfaithful lover. Dido's final, distant view of Aeneas should be contrasted with her initial, proximate view of him (1.613). There, the compassionate response that her initial vision of him engendered betokened the closeness of their relationship as it would develop over the first four books. Now, her distant view of her departing lover symbolizes the distance in their relationship, both psychological and, as Aeneas will soon depart and she will commit suicide, physical as well. Vision prompts Dido to take such a drastic measure to find a final solution to her problems, whereas Aeneas will appeal to the formula "I have seen the god and heed his commands" (4.357–359). In Dido focusing on her own view of Aeneas' departure, Dido resolves to die because she now sees Aeneas as a different hero, namely, Theseus. Though vision was a striking feature of their union, Aeneas' vision of Mercury and fear of Dido's love, combined with Dido's appropriation of Ariadne's point of view, will ultimately drive them apart.[35] Dido's and Aeneas' divergent visions effect separation, and their words fail to suture their fraying relationship.

Aeneas' and Dido's divergent visions begin midway through Book 4 with Aeneas' attempt to reason with Dido. Having suggested already that their primary relationship has been that of host and guest (433–436),[36] he explains to her that a vision of his promised land compels him to leave:

sed nunc Italiam magnam Gryneus Apollo,
Italiam Lyciae iussere capessere sortes;
hic amor, haec patria est. si te Karthaginis arces
Phoenissam Libycaeque *aspectus* detinet urbis,
quae tandem Ausonia Teucros considere terra
inuidia est? et nos fas extera quaerere regna.   *Aen.* 4.345–350

        [But now Grynean
Apollo's oracles would have me seize
great Italy, the Lycian prophecies
tell me of Italy: there is my love,
there is my homeland. If the fortresses
of Carthage and the vision of a city
in Libya can hold you, who are Phoenician,
why, then, begrudge the Trojans' settling on
Ausonian soil? There is no harm: it is
right that we, too, seek out a foreign kingdom. (M. 4.467–476)]

Whatever his "real feeling" about the affair may be,[37] for Aeneas, Italy replaces both Dido (*amor*) and Carthage (*patria*).[38] Virgil includes in Aeneas' speech a conceptual play on words associated with sight: if the beholding (*aspectus*) of Carthage grips Dido, Aeneas argues, why then does she begrudge him the settlement of Ausonia (literally, why is the Trojan settlement in Ausonian land something "to be looked askance upon" [*inuidia*, 350[39]]? The tension between these positive and negative expressions involving visual concepts implicitly parallels the contrast between Aeneas, who goes to the land that he is ordered to seek (346), and Dido, whose vision detains her in her own land (348). This contrast culminates with Aeneas' stingingly blunt suggestion that the Trojans are merely doing what is right in seeking "foreign realms" (350).[40]

As he continues his speech, Aeneas again returns to arguments based on vision to establish his position:

'me patris Anchisae, quotiens umentibus umbris
nox operit terras, quotiens astra ignea surgunt,
admonet in somnis et turbida terret *imago;*
me puer Ascanius capitisque iniuria cari,
quem regno Hesperiae fraudo et fatalibus aruis.'   *Aen.* 4.351–355

["For often as the night conceals the earth
with dew and shadows, often as the stars
ascend, afire, my father's anxious image
approaches me in dreams. Anchises warns
and terrifies; I see the wrong I have done
to one so dear, my boy Ascanius,
whom I am cheating of Hesperia,
the fields assigned by fate." (M. 4.477–484)]

The troubled vision that Aeneas speaks of here (353) comes always at night, an appropriate time for the kind of dreamlike vision to which Aeneas refers.[41] In particular, he mentions how his father's apparition had warned him not to defraud Ascanius of the fated land of Hesperia. The distance between the possessive genitive (*patris*) and its noun (*imago*) frames the sentence, putting emphasis on the latter word. In addition, the contrast between fathers and sons is poignant here, as lines 351 (*me patris Anchisae*) and 354 (*me puer Ascanius*) both begin with similar sequences and cadences signaling the noble past and rich future toward which Anchises urges his son. The next generation's heritage could be less seemly if Aeneas does not heed his father's admonition (354–355).

Aeneas will move from this argument about Ascanius' inheritance to a further explanation that involves a clearly visual stimulus:

'nunc etiam interpres diuum Ioue missus ab ipso
(testor utrumque caput) celeris mandata per auras
detulit: ipse deum manifesto in lumine uidi
intrantem muros uocemque his auribus hausi.
desine meque tuis incendere teque querelis;
Italiam non sponte sequor.'   *Aen.* 4.356–361

["And now the gods'
own messenger, sent down by Jove himself—
I call as witness both our lives—has brought
his orders through the swift air. My own eyes

have seen the god as he was entering
our walls—in broad daylight. My ears have drunk
his words. No longer set yourself and me
afire. Stop your quarrel. It is not
my own free will that leads to Italy." [M. 4.484–492)]

Visual perception surrounds Aeneas' description of Ascanius' proper inheritance (355). On one side of that description, Aeneas delineates the vision of his father; on the other side, he comments on the vision of the messenger god whom, Aeneas explains, he saw plainly (*manifesto in lumine uidi*) and whose message he "drank in" (*uocem . . . auribus hausi,* 359). This new vision gives Aeneas religious locus standi. While he has seen Dido's compassion and has known her love, vision of the divine now calls him away from his private affair and the diversion that Dido and Carthage represent.

When Virgil describes Dido's response to Aeneas, he carefully calls particular attention to her eyes:

> Talia dicentem iamdudum auersa tuetur
> huc illuc *uoluens oculos* totumque pererrat
> *luminibus tacitis* et sic accensa profatur. . . .   *Aen.* 4.362–364

[But all the while Aeneas spoke, she stared
askance at him, her glance ran this way, that.
She scans his body with her silent eyes.
Then Dido thus, inflamed, denounces him. . . . [M. 4.493–496)]

Her extended gaze precedes her rolling eyes that wander over all of him (363). This attention to Dido's vision beckons the reader's involvement, an aspect of Virgil's subjective style.[42] Furthermore, the use of the adjective *tacitis* to describe Dido's gaze is an interesting choice and would seem to suggest that her eyes restrain her pain and anger, if only for a moment. Michael Putnam rightly compares Dido's rolling eyes to those of Aeneas in the poem's final scene.[43] In each description, Putnam suggests, rolling eyes indicate irrational behavior and show that a decision has not yet been made by the character.[44] This is especially striking when placed, as it is, within four lines of *hausi* (359), a verb also used metaphorically to describe perception in the poem's final scene. Yet it seems likely that more than a mere prefiguring of the poem's close is going on here. Virgil carefully positions his participial phrase (*uoluens oculos*) between adverbs (*huc illuc*) at the beginning of the line and the main verb at the line's end (*pererrat*). Dido scans Aeneas completely and, though preventing her eyes from revealing her emotional state (*luminibus tacitis*), becomes angry only after looking at him. The verbal parallelism to *Aeneid* 12 suggests that Dido's reaction to the very sight of Aeneas is comparable to the way Aeneas responds to seeing the spoils of Pallas in Book 12, a vision that provokes Aeneas to kill Turnus.[45]

After so beholding Aeneas, Dido responds with feigned indifference by using, for at least part of her speech, the third person to refer to Aeneas:

'nec tibi diua parens generis nec Dardanus auctor,
perfide, sed duris genuit te cautibus horrens
Caucasus Hyrcanaeque admorunt ubera tigres.
nam quid dissimulo aut quae me ad maiora reseruo?
num fletu ingemuit nostro? num lumina flexit?
num lacrimas uictus dedit aut miseratus amantem est?' *Aen.* 4.365–370

["No goddess was your mother, false Aeneas,
and Dardanus no author of your race;
the bristling Caucasus was father to you
on his harsh crags; Hyrcanian tigresses
gave you their teats. And why must I dissemble?
Why hold myself in check? For greater wrongs?
For did Aeneas groan when I was weeping?
Did he once turn his eyes or, overcome,
shed tears or pity me, who was his loved one?" (M. 4.497–505)]

Dido uses a resonating near-anaphora of *nam . . . num . . . num* (368–370) to suggest that deception on her part, even a kind of surreptitious restraint in the name of civility, is not within her purview (368).[46] The obvious reference to the Ariadne of Catullus 64 in Dido's characterization of Aeneas as *perfide* amounts to an allusion to the locus classicus of the abandoned lover who gazes upon her beloved as he departs.[47] Such allusion shows that Dido now realizes that she must assume the role of the abandoned heroine (365–368). Dido's emotional response is based on what she has herself seen; she characterizes Aeneas as deceptive like Theseus.

Now, having come to that portion of her speech in which she relegates Aeneas to third-person narrative, Dido mentions Aeneas' vision directly. Dido alludes to Aeneas' steady gaze, described thirty-eight lines earlier, borne out of his deference to Jupiter's admonitions (*ille Iouis monitis immota tenebat / lumina*,[48] 4.331–332). As Servius notes ad loc., Dido's agitated words now refer precisely to that moment (331) as she asks whether his vision wavers (*lumina flexit*, 369) and whether he has wept for her (369).

Aeneas never replies to Dido, who breaks off in the middle of her speech (388) and flees. Virgil notes specifically that she removes herself from his line of sight:

> his medium dictis sermonem abrumpit et auras
> aegra fugit *seque ex oculis auertit* et aufert,
> linquens multa metu cunctantem et multa parantem
> dicere.   *Aen.* 4.388–391

> [Her speech is broken off; heartsick, she shuns
> the light of day, deserts his eyes; she turns
> away, leaves him in fear and hesitation,
> Aeneas longing still to say so much. (M. 4.533–536)]

By taking herself out of Aeneas' line of vision, Dido is able to avoid the penetrating and resolute gaze alluded to in her previous question (*num lumina flexit?*, 369). Dido thus prevents herself from having to look upon him at close quarters. Any sense of an amiable gaze between them has been completely removed as Dido leaves Aeneas both speechless and hesitating.[49]

Once Aeneas and his men have returned to their ships, Dido sees him only from a great distance. This physical separation obviously reflects the spiritual distance between them. As viewed from her tower, Aeneas and his men appear as ants:

> migrantis cernas totaque ex urbe ruentis:
> ac uelut ingentem formicae farris aceruum
> cum populant hiemis memores tectoque reponunt,
> it nigrum campis agmen praedamque per herbas
> conuectant calle angusto; pars grandia trudunt
> obnixae frumenta umeris, pars agmina cogunt
> castigantque moras, opere omnis semita feruet.   *Aen.* 4.401–407

> [And one could see them
> as, streaming, they rushed down from all the city:
> even as ants, remembering the winter,
> when they attack a giant stack of spelt
> to store it in their homes; the black file swarms

across the fields; they haul their plunder through
the grass on narrow tracks; some strain against
the great grains with their shoulders, heaving hard;
some keep the columns orderly and chide
the loiterers; the whole trail boils with work. (M. 4.551–560)]

This description compares to other insect similes from elsewhere in Virgil,[50] with precedents in Homer (e.g., *Il.* 2.469–470) and in Apollonius (*Arg.* 4.1452–1453); one even finds a possible echo of Accius here.[51] Virgil's emphasis, however, differs, for he gives attention not only to the reader's point of view, as his apostrophe at 401 indicates, but also to Dido's vision of this very scene.[52] Specifically, Virgil shows the depth of his own subjective style by addressing her directly.[53] This style is borne out also in the lines that follow:

quis tibi tum, Dido, *cernenti* talia sensus,
quosue dabas gemitus, cum litora feruere late
prospiceres arce ex summa, totumque *uideres*
misceri ante oculos tantis clamoribus aequor!   *Aen.* 4.408–411

[What were your feelings, Dido, then? What were
the sighs you uttered at that sight, when far
and wide, from your high citadel, you saw
the beaches boil and turmoil take the waters,
with such a vast uproar before your eyes? (M. 4.561–565)]

"The apostrophe," Williams writes, "is enormously effective; the personal involvement of the poet with Dido's tragic plight is such that his direct address to her seems natural and real rather than rhetorical."[54] This apostrophe also connects the reader, who was only moments ago the subject of such an apostrophe, with Dido, for, in the same passage, Virgil addresses both the heroine and the reader as viewers of the same event.[55] Virgil employs a visual *tour de force* here to emphasize Dido's perception; she sees Aeneas departing (408) as she looks forth from the citadel's summit (410), beholding the entire sea before her eyes (411).[56]

In the final stages of Aeneas and Dido's relationship, vision is still a vital aspect of their interaction, but the view has changed from Dido's initial amazement (*obstipuit primo aspectu*, 1.613) and sympathetic response (*non ignara mali miseris succurrere disco*, 1.630) to a final, distant view, suggesting the new spiritual breach that Aeneas' fear of commitment has helped

create (*magnoque animum labefactus amore*, 4.395). Virgil's introduction of
Aeneas portrayed him as the opposite of the isolated gazer described in Lucretius' prologue to his second book.[57] Lucretius' removed viewer, one recalls, looks down from the *templa serena* (*DRN* 2.8), at a safe distance from
harm. Now, at Aeneas' departure, Dido similarly views Aeneas' men at a
great distance, for they appear as ants. Yet Dido cannot achieve, through her
vision, the state of *ataraxia* that Lucretius advocates.[58] Instead, the distant
view prepares Dido for suicide, while allowing Aeneas to have the spiritual
distance sufficient to obey the admonition that he will receive during the
second vision of Mercury.

Though the first vision of the messenger god had a dramatic effect on
Aeneas, it was not adequate in and of itself. That the second vision of Mercury has a powerful effect is clear because Virgil emphasizes Aeneas' silence
at the god's epiphany:

> tali Cyllenius ore locutus
> mortalis uisus medio sermone reliquit
> et procul in tenuem ex oculis euanuit auram.
>   At uero Aeneas aspectu obmutuit amens,
> arrectaeque horrore comae et uox faucibus haesit.   *Aen.* 4.276–280

[So did Cyllene's god speak out. He left
the sight of mortals even as he spoke
and vanished into the transparent air.
This vision stunned Aeneas, struck him dumb;
his terror held his hair erect; his voice
held fast within his jaws. (M. 4.370–375)]

Though Virgil emphasizes this vision three times, it is rather the vision of
the future land that will have a more lasting effect on the hero:

> 'Ascanium surgentem et spes heredis Iuli
> *respice*, cui regnum Italiae Romanaque tellus
> debetur.'   *Aen.* 4.274–276

        ["... remember
Ascanius growing up, the hopes you hold
for Iülus, your own heir, to whom are owed
the realm of Italy and land of Rome." (M. 4.366–369)][59]

Mercury's words suggest a tangible future vision, for he has reminded Aeneas to have regard for the future and specifically for Ascanius' race. The "hope" that Mercury has in mind turns out to be Italy and the Roman land, where the foundation of the city (*dum conderet urbem*, 1.5) is the telos of the narrative. The internal conception—vision in a more encompassing sense—of that land and its potential motivates Aeneas to make the harsh decision to leave Dido and Carthage.

In contrast to the admonishing vision of Mercury, Dido's messages, conveyed through her sister, utterly fail:

> sed nullis ille mouetur
> fletibus aut uoces ullas tractabilis audit;
> fata obstant placidasque uiri deus obstruit auris.　　　*Aen.* 4.438–440

[For lamentation cannot move Aeneas;
his graciousness toward any plea is gone.
Fate is opposed, the god makes deaf the hero's
kind ears. (M. 4.604–607)]

Dido has arranged for her sister to covey a verbal plea, and thus Dido's request is made by proxy: Aeneas does not again have to see the woman whom he rejects. This verbal request is, strikingly, prevented from reaching fruition by the blocking of Aeneas' ears. The vision of the promised land, prompted by Aeneas' vision of Mercury, has effected a victory over words, secured, not inconsequentially, by the physical absence of Dido.

For Dido, the vision of Aeneas as a fleeing Theseus has supplanted all previous sight of him. For Aeneas, a new vision and a new love have captured his attention (*hic amor, haec patria est*, 4.347). By contrast, Dido desperately attempts to cling to her vision of Aeneas by taking an effigy of him with her upon the pyre (508).[60] This false image is symbolic of the false image of a husband that other heroines, such as Laodamia or Evadne—women who accompany Dido in the Underworld (6.442)—take to their own funeral pyres.[61] Dido's vision has become fixed upon false visions, much like Andromache of *Aeneid* 3, whereas Aeneas, by contrast, remains future-oriented, focused on a land that, though still unseen, can be visualized by him, through Mercury's admonition (*spes heridis Iuli / respice, cui regnum*, 4.274–275).[62] Though their amatory relationship has come to a close, these two will encounter each other one last time in the Underworld, when Dido's sharp and memorable gaze conclusively vanquishes Aeneas' final words to her.

FIXOS OCULOS

Virgil uses vision in Dido's final encounter with Aeneas to offer closing observations about Dido's character and especially to delineate how the queen
views Aeneas and the love they shared. Virgil also allows the reader to see
Dido through Aeneas' eyes, which offers insight into how Aeneas perceives
her. Vision in this final encounter therefore brings the episode to a close, revealing, in a final rendezvous of this kind, the ineffectiveness of speech[63]
and the lasting impression of a final glance. Aeneas only discovers reports of
Dido's death to be true when he sees her in the Underworld. He comes upon
her in the *campi lugentes*, where he looks upon those whom harsh love has
gnawed:

> hic quos durus amor crudeli tabe peredit
> secreti celant calles et myrtea circum
> silua tegit; curae non ipsa in morte relinquunt.
> his Phaedram Procrinque locis maestamque Eriphylen
> crudelis nati monstrantem uulnera cernit,
> Euadnenque et Pasiphaen; his Laodamia
> it comes et iuuenis quondam, nunc femina, Caeneus
> rursus et in ueterem fato reuoluta figuram.
> inter quas Phoenissa recens a uulnere Dido
> errabat silua in magna. . . .   *Aen.* 6.442–451

[And here, concealed by secret paths, are those
whom bitter love consumed with brutal waste;
a myrtle grove encloses them; their pains
remain with them in death. Aeneas sees
Phaedra and Procris and sad Eriphyle,
who pointed to the wounds inflicted by
her savage son; he sees Pasiphaë
and then Evadne; and Laodamia
and Caeneus, once a youth and now a woman,
changed back again by fate to her first shape.
Among them, wandering in that great forest,
and with her wounds still fresh: Phoenician Dido. (M. 6.583–594)]

Commentators have regarded this retinue with varying degrees of acceptance. The women are alternately viewed as either unsuited to the context[64]
of the passage or as acceptable for full[65] or at least partial inclusion.[66] In his

analysis of the passage, Owen Lee posits an interesting correlation between these heroines and the ecphrasis describing the contents of the temple doors (6.20–30) with which Book 6 opens.[67] Lee emphasizes the clear connection between the Cretan theme of the doors and the presence of Pasiphaë among these tragic lovers. As had Kraggerud before him, Lee sees the heroines here depicted as telling Dido's story.

Moved to tears at the sight of her, Aeneas soon recognizes Dido among these women:

> ... errabat silua in magna; quam Troius heros
> ut primum iuxta stetit agnouitque per umbras
> obscuram, qualem primo qui surgere mense
> aut uidet aut uidisse putat per nubila lunam. ... *Aen.* 6.451–454

> [Among them, wandering in that great forest,
> and with her wounds still fresh: Phoenician Dido.
> And when the Trojan hero recognized her
> dim shape among the shadows (just as one
> who either sees or thinks he sees among
> the cloud banks, when the month is young, the moon
> rising). ... (M. 6.593–599)]

Virgil begins by portraying Aeneas' point of view, and he does so with a subtle psychological portrait. Ralph Johnson has observed that the phrase *uidet aut uidisse putat* (454) "reflects the obscure complex of emotions that suddenly besets him on realizing that indeed this is she, Dido. ... He fears seeing her; he wants to see her; he feels guilt in seeing her."[68] Dido appears as a faint figure (*obscuram*), suited to the Underworld and specifically likened to the moon (454). This lunar comparison is apposite, for, among her last acts on earth, Dido had evoked the goddess Hecate/Diana:

> stant arae circum et crinis effusa sacerdos
> ter centum tonat ore deos, Erebumque Chaosque
> tergeminamque Hecaten, tria uirginis ora Dianae. *Aen.* 4.509–511

> [Before the circling altars the enchantress,
> her hair disheveled, stands as she invokes
> aloud three hundred gods, especially
> Chaos and Erebus and Hecate,
> the triple-shaped Diana, three-faced virgin. (M. 4.704–708)]

In a recent article, William DeGrummond has aptly emphasized Hecate's connection with Diana, a connection made explicit by Virgil in this passage.[69] About the last of these lines, Servius Danielis writes:

> et cum super terras est, creditur esse Luna; cum in terris, Diana; cum sub terris, Proserpina. quibusdam ideo triplicem placet, quia Luna tres figuras habet . . .   Servius ad 511

> [And when she is above the earth, she is believed to be Luna; when on the earth, Diana; when beneath the earth, Proserpina. Therefore it is pleasing to some that she be threefold, because Luna has three figures . . .'[70]]

The comparison of Dido with Diana is evident not only when she enters to take her throne (1.496–504) but also in the fourth book when she accompanies Aeneas in the hunt.[71] Because Dido becomes Aeneas' lover during a hunt, one might regard Dido as having donned one aspect of the threefold Diana, namely, that of the huntress.[72] As they set out in Book 4, Dido bears the quiver and sports the hairstyle of Diana (*crines nodantur in aurum*, 4.138). She is crowded by her followers (*Aen.* 4.136–138)[73] in the way that Diana had been described as surrounded by her retinue in Book 1 (500–501).[74]

In this final meeting, Aeneas perceives Dido as the moon, another aspect of the goddess Diana.[75] In the first book, Aeneas was prevented from breaking through the cloud that surrounded him (1.580–581), even though the notion to do so "rises" in his mind (1.582). At the close of their relationship, Dido is like a moon "rising" ironically beneath the earth while still obscured in mist (4.453). Aeneas therefore thrice perceives Dido as Diana: in the simile of Book 1, in the striking description of her as they embark on the hunt of Book 4 (*infert se socium Aeneas*, 4.142), and in their final rendezvous. For Dido, this threefold repetition is fitting, as she is identified with Diana, the goddess of three manifestations. Dido has become the visual counterpart to Aeneas in Book 1 when he was first introduced to her. She could not see him clearly then; he cannot quite see her now.[76] She imagined him to have been the one likely to have been wandering in the woods (1.578); now he sees her as that very sylvan wanderer. Their visions of each other reverse, as do their roles as *voyants-visibles*.[77]

Dido is therefore only a pale reflection of the *voyant-visible* that she once was in Book 1, for though she is visible among those whom love has gnawed, she by no means beholds Aeneas. While Dido was attracted by the sight of Aeneas at their first meeting (1.613), her vision of him has changed:

'siste gradum teque *aspectu* ne subtrahe nostro.
quem fugis? extremum fato quod te adloquor hoc est.'
talibus Aeneas ardentem et torua *tuentem*
lenibat dictis animum lacrimasque ciebat.
illa solo *fixos oculos* auersa tenebat
nec magis incepto uultum sermone mouetur
quam si dura silex aut stet Marpesia cautes.   *Aen.* 6.465–471

        ["But stay your steps
Do not retreat from me. Whom do you flee?
This is the last time fate will let us speak."
These were the words Aeneas, weeping, used,
trying to soothe the burning, fierce-eyed Shade.
She turned away, eyes to the ground, her face
no more moved by his speech than if she stood
as stubborn flint or some Marpessan crag. (M. 6.612–619)]

Ironically, while in Book 4 Aeneas had fled from Dido's sight, Aeneas is now concerned lest Dido leave his vision (465). Dido's flight (*quem fugis?*, 466) also recalls the fleeing shades of Creusa (*Aen.* 2.793) and Eurydice (*G.* 4.500), as well as Dido's own words to Aeneas at 4.314.[78] Yet Dido's vision is differ-ent: it is, for the moment, that of a statue, a frozen gaze.[79] She does not look at Aeneas in amazement, as she had in Book 1 (613). Rather, gazing fiercely (468), Dido fixes her eyes upon the ground (469), unmoved by his attempted speech (470) and his appeal that she not withdraw from his sight (465). The woman who once cast down her gaze in compassion for Aeneas' men now resolutely fixes her vision on the ground (469), unwilling to acknowledge even the physical presence, let alone the words, of the epic's hero (470–471).

Her vision resists Aeneas' one-sided conversation in which, through an awkward allusion to Catullus' version of the *Coma Berenices* (*inuitus, regina, tuo de litore cessi*, 6.460),[80] Aeneas shows his remorse at having abandoned her.[81] As von Albrecht insightfully observes, "What Aeneas had known until now only at secondhand he now finds to be true, he experiences it painfully as reality. . . . The decisive thing is . . . objective recognition."[82] Dido presents herself by silent, visual gesture as a kind of Athena; her gaze recalls the rep-resentation of the goddess that Aeneas had seen on the temple of Juno in Carthage: *diua solo fixos oculos auersa tenebat* (*Aen.* 1.482).[83] This internal reference is, of course, well known, as is the allusion to the supplication of Athena at *Iliad* 6.311.[84] The goddess' downcast gaze is similar to that of a Medea[85] (Figure 4.1) or a Phaedra[86] (Figure 4.2), as depicted in examples of

Figure 4.1. *Medea Meditating on Killing Her Children.* Pompeian Fresco. Museo Archeologico Nazionale, Naples.

Pompeian wall painting. Yet, as Andrew Feldherr rightly warns in his analysis of the Underworld scene, we should not think of Dido as merely an art object, for "the *Aeneid* allows her to undergo a second metamorphosis that reveals the emptiness of such an image."[87] This metamorphosis reestablishes the queen's autonomy, as she now ignores Aeneas. As Putnam has observed, "Dido's mind gains its own powers of vision."[88] Aeneas looks upon her and attempts to speak, but she refuses even to acknowledge her former lover:

> tandem corripuit sese atque inimica refugit
> in nemus umbriferum, coniunx ubi pristinus illi
> respondet curis aequatque Sychaeus amorem.
> nec minus Aeneas casu percussus iniquo
> prosequitur lacrimis longe et miseratur euntem.   *Aen.* 6.472–476

Figure 4.2. *Phaedra and Maid Servant.* Pompeian Fresco. Museo Archeologico Nazionale, Naples.

[At last she tore herself away; she fled—
and still his enemy—into the forest
of shadows, where Sychaeus, once her husband,
answers her sorrows, gives her love for love.
Nevertheless, Aeneas, stunned by her
unkindly fate, still follows at a distance
with tears and pity for her as she goes. (M. 6.620–626)]

Here, through the use of the present tense (*respondet, aequat*), Virgil empha-sizes Dido's interaction with Sychaeus.[89] Virgil has left the reader with the lingering contrast between Aeneas, normally a rather reticent hero,[90] whose speech in this passage fails to persuade Dido or to redirect her vision, and the clearly heroic and perfectly reticent Dido. Aeneas, who once told Dido that he did not "follow" Italy of his own accord (4.361), can now only follow his former lover as he weeps, moved by her misfortune (475–476).

Dido is more than merely a woman scorned. She is a visual creature whose personal vision is as important to the narrative as the way she is seen. It is thus fitting that Aeneas' first and last encounters with the queen give special attention to her vision, an aspect that informs and enriches the way the lovers' relationship is portrayed in the narrative. Dido's vision is her final answer to Aeneas' failed entreaties.

LAUINIAQUE UENIT

Although she does not receive as much attention as Dido, Lavinia represents the new vision of Italy and provides a vital motive for the fighting that characterizes so much of the second half of the *Aeneid*. We never hear her voice or fully fathom her point of view, but we do "see" her. Indeed, beginning with the prophecy about her and Aeneas in Book 7, Virgil makes a point of visually incorporating Lavinia into the narrative, encompassing the description (Book 11) of her as having downcast eyes and culminating with her famous blush in Book 12.[91] Just as Dido's introduction in Book 1 and Aeneas' final view of her in Book 6 were cast in visual terms, so references to the manner in which Lavinia is beheld frame the second half of the *Aeneid*. If she is not a powerful figure in the epic, Lavinia is nevertheless a pivotal character, the vision of whom stimulates the action of the twelfth book.[92] Through her beauty and the influence of portents involving how she is beheld, Lavinia proves to be an impetus for Turnus' action against Aeneas.[93]

Just after the *uates* predicts, in distinctly visual terms (*cernimus*, 7.68), that she will wed a foreigner, Lavinia's hair catches fire. The flame burns her hair and the crown with its gemstones:

> praeterea, castis adolet dum altaria taedis,
> et iuxta genitorem astat Lauinia uirgo,
> uisa (nefas) longis comprendere crinibus ignem
> atque omnem ornatum flamma crepitante cremari,
> regalisque accensa comas, accensa coronam
> insignem gemmis. . . .   *Aen.* 7.71–76

> [More, while the virgin
> Lavinia with pure and fragrant torches
> kindled the altars, standing by her father,

she seemed—too terrible—to catch that fire
in her long tresses; all her ornaments
were burning in that crackling blaze, and burning. . . . (M. 7.90–95)]

At one level, this description parallels the portentous flame that had appeared over Iulus' head in the second book (2.682–684).[94] On another level, Virgil calls attention to Lavinia's "regal" hair (*regalisque . . . comas*, 75) to evoke an association with the *coma regia* of Catullus (66.93), which occurs in a poem that informs the final farewell of Dido and Aeneas in the Underworld.[95] Now, "regal hair" characterizes Aeneas' destined bride. This characterization is fitting, for, as Francis Cairns has shown, the term *rex* and its cognates are redeemed in the *Aeneid* and deployed in a way that befits Aeneas as sole ruler of his people, anticipating the monarchical character of the early principate.[96] Accordingly, the "regal" hair of Lavinia, now brought to center stage by the fire that kindles it, befits the future bride of Rome's first ruler.

The flame that encompasses her hair then spreads from the princess to the palace itself:

> . . . tum fumida lumine fuluo
> inuolui ac totis Volcanum spargere tectis.
> id uero horrendum ac uisu mirabile ferri:
> namque fore inlustrem fama fatisque canebant
> ipsam, sed populo magnum portendere bellum.   *Aen.* 7.76–80

[. . . then wrapped in smoke and yellow light, she scattered
her flames throughout the palace. This indeed
was taken as a sign of fear and wonder:[97]
they sang she would be glorious in fame
and fate but bring great war to her own people. (M. 7.97–101)]

The sight of the fire, whose leaping flames recall the fire that the Trojan women had lit in Book 5, is marvelous to look upon (78). The visual images of the flaming Lavinia will later become a subject of song (*canebant*, 79).

When we next see Lavinia, she is characterized specifically in terms of her eyes.[98] In the eleventh book, Lavinia accompanies a throng of matrons who bring gifts to the temple of Minerva:

> nec non ad templum summasque ad Palladis arces
> subuehitur magna matrum regina caterua

dona ferens, iuxtaque comes Lauinia uirgo,
causa mali tanti, *oculos deiecta decoros.*   *Aen.*11.477–480

[And Queen Amata, too,
With many women, bearing gifts, is carried
into the citadel, Minerva's temple
upon the heights; at her side walks the girl
Lavinia, the cause of all that trouble,
her lovely eyes held low. (M. 11.631–636)]

In this description, Lavinia directs her vision toward the ground in a manner that recalls Dido's similar gaze upon encountering Aeneas' men (4.561).

This gazing posture suggests Lavinia's attitude, for she seems to be aware that she is in fact the *causa mali.* Comparison with comparable gestures in wall painting bears this out. Bettina Bergmann has reconstructed the paintings of the Tragic Poet in Pompeii within this house, noting that the portrait of Helen (Figure 4.3) would have been in the same room as two other portraits of females[99] in which vision is also an important feature.[100]

Recently, Nancy Worman has suggested that Helen serves as an object of desire in Greek texts such as those of Gorgias, Euripides, and Sappho. Following Prier,[101] Worman suggests that vision is the conduit of seduction "through the love object's being seen by the lover and through the beloved as seeing subject attracting with her eyes."[102] The iconographic tradition surrounding Helen, Worman argues, corresponds to the ambiguous conception of Helen that one often finds in Greek literature, where she is both viewed object and viewing subject. Helen is the beholder of Paris in some representations of the couple, while in others she casts her vision toward the ground in a manner similar to that of Lavinia in our *Aeneid* 11 passage. This downcast look may partially reflect Helen's reaction to her decision to go with Paris, a despondency seen on a fifth-century kylix (Figure 4.4) or Fourth-style wall painting from the Vespasianic period.[103] Worman's consideration of the literary tradition involving Helen is not at odds with the interpretation, in the Tragic Poet fresco, of Helen's gaze as indicator of an introspective captive, a woman dishonored and aggrieved.

The portrayal of Helen's vision in the Tragic Poet Fresco parallels and illustrates the gaze of Lavinia at *Aeneid* 11.480. The vision of both these women suggests grief and perhaps even regret for having been the cause of the battle. Virgil's description of the downcast gaze of Lavinia (*oculos deiecta decoros,* 480) gives us insight into her state of mind, through her eyes: her

Figure 4.3. *Helen Embarking.* Fresco from the House of the Tragic Poet. Museo Archeologico Nazionale, Naples.

vision not only reveals her inner beauty but also suggests an awareness of her status as the reason for war. The grievous outcry of the Teucrian women that follows (482) represents an expansion of this realization, a scene that does more than merely repeat the Homeric description of women bringing the peplos to Athena (*Il.* 6.297–298). Their procession forges a connection with the *Iliad* passage and thereby with the representation of that same scene on the Juno temple (*Aen.* 1.479–482), itself allusively connected with Dido's goddesslike gaze in the Underworld (6.469). Goddesses and heroines are united through allusion to a single visual act.

Lavinia will appear for the last time in the poem at the beginning of Book 12. There, Amata enjoins Turnus to cease fighting. She seeks from Turnus a single favor, a refusal to fight on the Teucrians' behalf (*unum oro: desiste, Aen.* 12.60). Though Amata addresses Turnus directly, Virgil delays in describing Turnus' reaction. Instead, Virgil first depicts Lavinia's reaction to the words of her mother:

accepit uocem lacrimis Lauinia matris
flagrantis perfusa genas, cui plurimus ignem
subiecit rubor et calefacta per ora cucurrit.
Indum sanguineo ueluti uiolauerit ostro
si quis ebur, aut mixta rubent ubi lilia multa
alba rosa, talis uirgo dabat ore colores.
illum turbat amor figitque in uirgine uultus. . . .   *Aen.* 12.64–70

[Lavinia's
hot cheeks were bathed in tears; she heard her mother's
words; and her blush, a kindled fire, crossed
her burning face. And just as when a craftsman
stains Indian ivory with blood-red purple,
or when white lilies, mixed with many roses,
blush: even such, the colors of the virgin.
His love drives Turnus wild; he stares at his
Lavinia . . . (M. 12.88–96)]

Figure 4.4. *Helen in Her Boudoir.* Red-figured Attic drinking cup (kylix) from Nola, 450–440 BC. Side B. Berlin Staatlandes Museum.

Virgil's use of color in this passage is perhaps the most vivid example in the poem.[104] The simile describing Lavinia's blush is itself modeled on the description of the wound of Menelaus in *Iliad* 4.141–142, where the blood of that wound is compared to the stain of red dye on ivory.[105] Lavinia's blood-red blush suits the martial aspects of Turnus' soldierly response, and he pours forth words that show his determination to fight:

> . . . ardet in arma magis paucisque adfatur Amatam:
> 'ne, quaeso, ne me lacrimis neue omine tanto
> prosequere in duri certamina Martis euntem,
> o mater; neque enim Turno mora libera mortis.'   *Aen.* 12.71–74

> [. . . even keener now for battle,
> he answers Queen Amata with few words:
> "I pray you, Mother, as I go to face
> so hard a duel, do not send me off with
> weeping, with such dreary omens. Turnus
> cannot delay his death, if it must come." (M. 12.96–101)]

The opening words of his response recall Hector's speech to Andromache from the sixth book of the *Iliad*.[106] While Turnus does not have much to say (*paucis*, 71), Lavinia's blush motivates him to fight (*ardet in arma*, 71), driving him to single combat with Aeneas and to the wounds produced by such combat. Vision of Lavinia, to a certain extent, therefore inspires him to a course of action, although he himself will retreat to rhetoric when confronted with Aeneas' wrath.

Lavinia's vision and her blush are important elements in her characterization. Her blazing hair foretells an ambivalent destiny; although she is ordained to be Aeneas' bride, Lavinia is nevertheless the woman who will precipitate war. Her downcast gaze confirms her feeling of shame in a role comparable to the way Helen is often characterized, as the wall painting from the House of the Tragic Poet aptly shows. Finally, Turnus' vision of Lavinia will provide an impetus for his final push toward defeating Aeneas. Virgil's treatment of Lavinia as a markedly visual character may not fully define her personality but nevertheless suggests that she is to be a motivational character in the poem.

CONCLUSION

Vision in the amatory scenes of the *Aeneid* frames both the first and second halves of the poem (Dido in Books 1 and 6 and Lavinia in Books 7 and 12).

Vision anticipates and stimulates a series of events that causes the poem to work toward its telos. In several instances of the gaze between Aeneas and Dido, glances detail the development of their love affair: from Dido's initial downcast gaze (1.561), to their exchange of vision in the departure scene (4.347–350), to their final encounter in the Underworld (6.469) in which Aeneas' words fail while Dido's vision abides. Virgil's use of vision in the episode emphasizes the deterioration of the relationship and anticipates the ultimate goal of Rome's foundation. This process begins as early as Aeneas' explanation to Dido that his love and his country are to be found by obeying the Lycian lots' prophecy about Italy: he relies on her vision of Carthage to explain his vision for his own land.[107] The foundation of Rome will be achieved through Aeneas' victory at the poem's close, a victory realized in part because Turnus' vision of Lavinia's blush has steeled Turnus' resolve to continue his fated course of action.

CHAPTER 5

Vidi, Vici

VISION'S VICTORY AND THE TELOS OF NARRATIVE

❧

Pontico triumpho inter pompae fercula trium uerborum praetulit
titulum veni : vidi : vici . . .   SUETONIUS, *Vita Divi Iulii*, 37 [1]

The first half of the *Aeneid*, which showcases Aeneas and Dido's love affair, flows into a treatment of primarily martial themes in the second half;
these themes point toward Aeneas' killing of Turnus, the act that will lead
ultimately to establishing the Roman nation. In the *Aeneid*'s second half,
there emerges an increase in the importance of visual stimuli and a waning
in the influence of rhetorical persuasion. This shift toward vision's predomi-
nance quietly but pointedly reflects the building program of Julius Caesar
and Augustus.

At the time of the writing of the *Aeneid*, Rome's first emperor was ar-
ranging a monumental progression of visual signals in the form of statues
lining the flanking of colonnades of the Forum Augustum, a structure that,
as Carole Newlands has argued, was all Augustus' own.[2] In about 25 BC,
the first emperor began construction of the Forum Augustum contiguous
with and perpendicular to Julius Caesar's forum, which was itself connected
to the Forum Romanum.[3] From the visually striking Forum of Caesar, one
could easily pass into the Forum Augustum, which was undergoing construction at the time of Virgil's death. Slow as the completion apparently was,[4]
Virgil would likely have known the lines along which the forum, marvelous
even a hundred years later,[5] was being developed.

The Forum of Augustus enhances the two major themes of love and war
by associating them with the *gens Iulia* and Rome's *summi uiri:* on the north-

west side of this forum was the colonnade for Caesar's family, connected with Venus through Aeneas, while the southeast colonnade was dedicated to the descendants of Mars' son Romulus. Concerning the connection between the Forum of Caesar and the Forum of Augustus, Diane Favro comments:

> A complicated iconographical program linked the two complexes. The Augustan temple honored Mars Ultor who helped Octavian avenge the murder of Caesar. Equally important, Mars was both the consort of Venus, who was worshipped in the Forum Julium, as well as the father of Romulus, distant ancestor of the Julii. The elaborate sculptural program of the new Augustan forum clarified and celebrated these interconnections. For example, the sculpture group in the temple represented Venus Genetrix, Mars Ultor, and Divus Julius.[6]

Whether the forum reversed the *Aeneid*'s arrangement of ideas, as Zanker has suggested,[7] or the *Aeneid* responded to and exploited the emperor's iconographic program is not of great consequence. Rather, the common visual bond that the monumental structures and the *Aeneid* share is germane to my discussion of Virgil's treatment of vision in the first and second halves of the poem.

For these monumental structures, visual images were the primary means of communication.[8] Ovid portrays the confines of the forum in visual terms, but instead of describing how the forum appeared to the human viewer, with characteristic wit he presents it from the god's point of view:

> Ultor ad ipse suos caelo descendit honores
> templaque in Augusto *conspicienda* foro.
> et deus est ingens et opus: debebat in urbe
> non aliter nati Mars habitare sui.
>   . . .
> *prospicit* armipotens operis fastigia summi
> et probat inuictos summa tenere deos.
> *prospicit* in foribus diuersae tela figurae
> armaque terrarum milite uicta suo.
> hinc *uidet* Aenean oneratum pondere caro
> et tot Iuleae nobilitatis auos:
> hinc *uidet* Iliaden humeris ducis arma ferentem,
> claraque dispositis acta subesse uiris.
> *spectat* et Augusto praetextum nomine templum

et *uisum* lecto Caesare maius opus.
uouerat hoc iuuenis tunc, cum pia sustulit arma:
a tantis Princeps incipiendus erat.   *Fasti* 5.551–554, 559–570

[The Avenger himself is descending from heaven for his own festivities
to his eye-catching temple in the Forum of Augustus. The god and the
structure are both impressive, just the way Mars should dwell in his
son's city. . . . The patron of war surveys the gables of his tall structure
and approves the presence of Victories at the top. He surveys the
weapons of various shapes on the doors and armor of the world which
his troops have won. From here he sees Aeneas loaded with a priceless
burden and so many ancestors of the noble Julian line. From here he
sees Romulus shouldering spoils from a general, and exploits inscribed
beneath a row of statues. He examines the name of Augustus bordering
the temple. From reading "Caesar," he thinks the structure even greater.
The young man vowed this temple when he dutifully took up arms: he
had to make such a start as our leading citizen.[9]]

Ovid's description of Mars' vantage point is from the top down, as if the god
were descending upon his precinct from the sky, for one notices especially
the gable (*fastigia*, 559) of the building's top and the divinities represented
in the pediment (560).[10] Once on the ground, the god seems to look from the
temple's pronaos toward the northwest, first noticing the statue of Aeneas in
the northern exedra, then scanning the colonnade as it runs toward the west-
ernmost entrance from the Julian forum (*tot Iuleae nobilitatis auos*, 564).
Mars then hones in on Romulus in the southern exedra, running his eye
along the southeastern colonnade with its repertoire of great men of Republican history. Finally, Mars sees the temple adorned with Augustus' name,
from a perspective that would have required him to descend the staircase
connecting the pronaos with the forum proper and revert his eyes to the inscription on the architrave. Zanker has argued that Ovid's playfulness results
from the heavy use of political messages in Augustus' program of artistic and
architectural renewal, an agenda so programmatically charged that "to the
more perceptive observer, even then, it all became too much."[11]

This new structure's visible symbolism contrasts sharply with the rostra
and the comitium of the old Forum Romanum, where rhetorical exhibition
was at least as integral an aspect of the forum as the physical hodgepodge of
images and buildings that peppered that zone. The Forum Romanum was old
Rome: it was a place for legal business, politics, triumphal processions, and,

on a more mundane level, for meeting associates, shopping, and, Ovid says, even romantic encounters.[12] It was also, notably, the place of old Republican rhetoric where Hortensius, Cato, and Cicero had all delivered speeches.

In comparison to the original Roman Forum, the first two imperial fora were designed more programmatically. Newlands puts it this way:

> Unlike the old Roman Forum, this new forum was not a busy marketplace and legal center crisscrossed by streets and filled with a variety of public monuments. The new forum consisted only of the temple, the exedras, and the porticoes; it had no basilica, a building which Vitruvius (5.1.4) describes as the center of commercial activity. The Forum Augustum, separated from the bustling life of the city by a high surrounding wall, was conceived as a historical monument that expressed a unified political and architectural program."[13]

These new imperial structures were clearly meant to communicate visual information about the new regime and, as a corollary, the nascent Roman empire. In the *Aeneid*, vision also emerges as an important means of communication and, by the epic's conclusion, has become the vital means of communication. En route to that conclusion, the reader discovers how vision is used to point toward the poem's telos, both in the relationship between Dido and Aeneas and in numerous other vignettes.

In this chapter, I will argue that Virgil links his *Aeneid* to the Augustan monuments through vision in three ways. First, the manner in which human characters in the poem use the verb *orare* and its close cognates shows a decline in the effectiveness of rhetoric that clears space for vision to be the successor of speech, even as the visual qualities of the Forum Augustum supplant the orality of the rostra of the Forum Romanum. A decline in rhetoric's effectiveness is particularly clear in the second half of the poem: embassies tend to fall short or at best to achieve mixed results, and the pleas of warriors for their own lives (also expressed with the verb *orare*) do not succeed.

Second, in the Hercules-Cacus tale, an episode long recognized as emblematic of Aeneas' triumph over Turnus,[14] Virgil manipulates light and darkness to anticipate the poem's final duel in which a glittering *balteus* (12.941–942) will lead to the deprivation of light for Turnus[15] and his relegation to the dark regions (*umbras*, 952).

Third, the final scene itself, read in light of both the Hercules-Cacus episode and the verb *orare*'s increasing ineffectiveness, suggests a final victory of vision over words, a feature not unrelated to parallel developments in the iconography of the nascent Roman empire. The fulfillment of this victory of vision comes at the poem's close.

This fulfillment is foreshadowed even in the initial passages of the poem. As the *Aeneid* opens, descriptions of orators are mainly favorable. The first description occurs in a simile applied to Neptune, whose words have sway over the out-of-control winds (*Aen.* 1.148–153).[16] Yet even in that passage, the presence and outward appearance of the leader command the attention of the crowd before he begins to speak (*conspexere, silent arrectisque auribus astant*, 152 ["They are silent / and stand attentively" (M. 1.214–215)]). The speaker of Book 1 is described as a man "weighty in devotion and merits" (*pietate grauem ac meritis*, 151), who rules the crowd's high spirits by his words (*regit dictis animos*, 153). While this type of description could easily be applied to a ruler such as Octavian and not simply to an orator, the person depicted clearly demands respect in part because of his words. His appearance and words work harmoniously.[17]

Elsewhere in Book 1, Ilioneus speaks on behalf of the first Trojan embassy in the poem.[18] In each of the poem's two halves, Ilioneus has some success as ambassador. But despite each initial success, embassies, most often referred to as *oratores*, become less successful as the poem proceeds. Moreover, oratory in general becomes increasingly suspect and devalued. Laocoon, for example, has been interpreted as representing the failure of old Republican rhetoric.[19] In the sixth book, Anchises tells his son that others will outstrip the Romans in rhetorical ability (*orabunt causas melius*, 6.849). Roman oratory fails to bring the peace that Anchises speaks about in the lines that follow (*tu regere imperio populos, Romane, memento / (hae tibi erunt artes), pacique imponere morem . . .* , *Aen.* 6.851–852).[20]

Not without reason Gilbert Highet concludes, at the end of his monumental study of speeches in Virgil's work, that Virgil did not trust oratory;[21] James O'Hara compares oratory and prophecy in the poem: "Like the orator, the speaker of a prophecy need not hesitate to deceive, especially when the deception can be cleverly worded."[22] Denis Feeney has also devoted attention to the study of Aeneas' taciturnity, suggesting that Aeneas is the only trustworthy character in the poem.[23] Sarah Spence advanced this discussion, noting that, because the rhetorical paradigm of the Republic has begun to break down, the *Aeneid* looks toward "a new system—a new Roman rhetoric or art."[24] That new system is visual communication. Let us begin this discussion of vision with a consideration of *oratores*, the first aspect of the argument for the decline of rhetoric in the *Aeneid*.

FAILURE OF RHETORIC (PART I): EFFETE *ORATORES*

Virgil refers to the members of an embassy as *orantes* and *legati* and explains their function, on occasion, with a relative clause of purpose and the verb *petere*. Most often, however, he calls them *oratores*. Indeed, passages involving ambassadors occur frequently enough in the *Aeneid* to merit an entry in the *Enciclopedia Virgiliana* (s.v. "oratores"[25]). Gualtiero Calboli, the author of the lemma, details the number of times embassies occur and specifies whether or not the word *orator* is applied to a member of an embassy. Calboli follows Walter Neuhauser[26] in believing that the term *orator*, qua legate, probably has a vaguely archaizing tone,[27] a throwback to authors such as Cato (*Orig.* 1.21). If Calboli's assertion is true, Virgil's use of *orator* or cognate terms such as *orantes* to indicate an embassy would seem to be deliberate, evidence that Neuhauser, too, has noted.[28]

The first passage concerning embassies in the *Aeneid* is that of the Trojan delegation led by Ilioneus to Carthage (1.518–558), a passage referred to in the introduction of this chapter and discussed in the previous chapter in reference to Dido's kind response.[29] One recalls that, in addition to explaining the Trojan situation well, Ilioneus used visible proofs to strengthen his arguments (*propius res aspice nostras*, 526). This embassy's request was granted, ratified by Dido's reassuring words, *soluite corde metum, Teucri, secludite curas* (562). As the poem proceeds, however, the appeals offered by embassies become increasingly less successful. The next example of an embassy occurs in Book 7, where Aeneas sends a delegation of one hundred *oratores*, also led by Ilioneus, to King Latinus:

> tum satus Anchisa delectos ordine ab omni
> centum oratores augusta ad moenia regis
> ire iubet, ramis uelatos Palladis omnis,
> donaque ferre uiro pacemque exposcere Teucris.   *Aen.* 7.152–155

> [Then Anchises' son
> gives orders that a hundred emissaries,
> men chosen from each rank, be sent—to go
> before the king's majestic walls; all should
> be shaded by Minerva's boughs and bring
> gifts to the king and ask peace for the Trojans. (M. 7.196–201)]

There is an important contrast between the success of the first embassy of Book 1 and the outcome of this encounter. After King Latinus asks the Trojan embassy about the object of their mission (*quid petitis?* 7.197), Ilioneus presents the Trojan cause. He begins by explaining the situation in a lengthy *narratio* (213–227) leading up to a *propositio* (229–230), followed by an *argumentum* founded on that which is *utile* (231–233) and *honestum* (234–238), with a religious flavor suited to epic (239–241).[30] These elements of oratory justify Virgil's use of the term *oratores* to signify ambassadors, for Ilioneus speaks in the manner of an orator presenting a brief rhetorical set piece. The rhetorical aspects of his narrative also indicate that the request of the embassy is to be taken most seriously, much as the speech of a true orator would have been received in Republican Rome. Through his skill and effort, Ilioneus does obtain the verbal assent of Latinus, though this is achieved at least partly through the oracle of Faunus (81–82). Ultimately, however, Ilioneus' embassy fails as the temporary peace between the two peoples rapidly erodes.

The next embassy occurs when Turnus dispatches Venulus to Diomedes in Book 8. Though Virgil never qualifies this Venulus as an *orator*—instead simply stating in the passive voice that Venulus "is sent" (*mittitur*, 8.9)—it is clear from a subsequent relative clause of purpose that Turnus desires him to act as an ambassador:

> . . . qui petat auxilium, et Latio consistere Teucros,
> aduectum Aenean classi uictosque penatis
> inferre et fatis *regem* se dicere posci
> edoceat, multasque uiro se adiungere gentis
> Dardanio et late Latio increbrescere nomen:
> quid struat his coeptis, quem, si fortuna sequatur,
> euentum pugnae cupiat, manifestius ipsi
> quam Turno *regi aut regi* apparere Latino.   *Aen.* 8.10–17

> [. . . to ask help, to tell him that
> the Teucrians have come to Latium—
> Trojan Aeneas with his fleet, who brings
> defeated household gods, declaring he
> is called by fates to be a king; that many
> nations now have joined the Dardan chieftain,
> his name gains ground in Latium. What end
> Aeneas means with these beginnings, wants
> as outcome of the quarrel if fortune favors,
> will surely be more clear to Diomedes
> than to King Turnus or to King Latinus. (M. 8.12–22)]

Although Turnus' injunction to the embassy is here reported indirectly, Virgil makes it clear that Turnus issues the orders. The ambassadors are to explain that the Trojans have arrived and that they are bringing with them conquered household gods, a detail that may be an attempt on Turnus' part to arouse the pride of Diomedes as conquerer of the Trojans. Further, they are to make clear that Aeneas claims he is fated to be king. Turnus again shows deference to Diomedes when he mentions that Diomedes is more likely to know what to expect than either he or Latinus, calling himself and Latinus each "king" but notably excluding Aeneas.[31]

The manner in which Venulus and his fellow emissaries were received is deduced from their report on the response of the Greek hero:

> Hos inter motus, medio in flagrante tumultu,
> ecce super maesti magna Diomedis ab urbe
> legati responsa ferunt: nihil omnibus actum
> tantorum impensis operum, nil dona neque aurum
> nec magnas ualuisse preces, alia arma Latinis
> quaerenda, aut pacem Troiano ab *rege* petendum.　　*Aen.* 11.225–230

> [But in the middle of this heated brawl,
> this angry fracas, the ambassadors
> come back from Diomedes' city; sadly
> they carry this reply: that all their work
> has gone for nothing; gifts were of no help,
> nor gold, nor their entreaties; Latium
> must seek out other arms or else must sue
> the Trojan chief [king][32] for peace. (M. 11.295–302)]

The term *legati* (227) refers to the embassy led by Venulus, sent out by Turnus at the opening of Book 8. The purpose clause there explained specifically what was sought (*auxilium*, 8.10); one sees in the passage from Book 11 that the embassy clearly fails to receive such aid from Diomedes. Whereas Turnus' request had qualified himself and Latinus as kings with the formal phrase "regi aut regi,"[33] Diomedes' advice refers only to Aeneas as king, not Latinus or Turnus. Turnus then refuses to heed the advice of the very embassy he commissioned.

This delegation of Venulus is one in a series of diplomatic failures in the second half of the *Aeneid*. Elsewhere in Book 8, we learn that Evander tells of an embassy that had come to request that he rule as the "foreign leader" predicted by their haruspex to marshal the Etruscans (*nulli fas Italo tantam subiungere gentem: / externos optate duces,* 8.502–503).[34] This prediction, Evander reports, causes the Etruscan armies to fear the gods' warning—ironically, inasmuch as their principal fighter Mezentius is *contemptor diuum* (7.648, 8.7)—and to send an embassy:

> ipse oratores ad me regnique coronam
> cum sceptro misit mandatque insignia Tarchon,
> succedam castris Tyrrhenaque regna capessam.
> sed mihi tarda gelu saeclisque effeta senectus
> inuidet imperium seraeque ad fortia uires.   *Aen.* 8.505–509

> [Tarchon himself
> has sent me envoys with the royal crown
> and scepter, offering these emblems to me,
> that I might join their camp and take the throne
> of Tuscany. But I am held in check
> by age, made weak by time; its sluggish frost
> begrudges me that kingdom; it is late
> for bravery. (M. 8.656–663)]

Evander maintains that his old age prevents him from such a command, and instead he encourages Aeneas to view himself as the fulfillment of the soothsayer's prediction[35] (*ingredere, o Teucrum atque Italum fortissime ductor,* 513).[36] Despite Evander's assurance of additional Arcadian troops to join Aeneas (518), Virgil implies that the embassy sent to Evander has gone away unfulfilled, having failed to gain Evander's leadership. At this point in the second half of the poem, even the most earnest embassies have failed. Ilioneus has not achieved a lasting peace, Turnus has refused his embassy's advice, and Evander will not become the Etruscan's leader as requested.

This pattern of the embassies' lack of success is somewhat broken in the eleventh book when a group of *oratores* comes to Aeneas:

> Iamque oratores aderant ex urbe Latina
> uelati ramis oleae ueniamque rogantes:
> corpora, per campos ferro quae fusa iacebant,
> redderet ac tumulo sineret succedere terrae;
> nullum cum uictis certamen et aethere cassis;
> parceret hospitibus quondam socerisque uocatis.   *Aen.* 11.100–105

[Now from the Latin city envoys came,
shaded with olive branches, asking grace:
they beg Aeneas for the bodies scattered
by sword across the plain, to bury them
in mounds of earth. One cannot war, they plead,
against the dead or the defeated; let him
spare men who once had welcomed him, the kinsmen
of his own bride-to-be. (M. 11.130–137)]

In this passage, the emissaries do obtain a temporary truce so they may bury their dead. Yet while Aeneas does not hesitate to cede what they have requested, he concludes with somber words that cast doubt on the fundamental premise of their request:[37]

quos bonus Aeneas haud aspernanda precantis
prosequitur uenia et uerbis haec insuper addit:
'quaenam uos tanto fortuna indigna, Latini,
implicuit bello, qui nos fugiatis amicos?
pacem me exanimis et Martis sorte peremptis
oratis? equidem et uiuis concedere uellem.'   *Aen.* 11.106–111

[And good Aeneas—
to those who ask what cannot be denied—
replies with kindness, and he adds these words:
"Latins, what shameful fate so tangled you
in such a war that now you fly from us,
who are your friends? You seek peace for the dead
and those cut down beneath the chance of battle?
But I would give that to the living, too." (M. 11.137–144)]

The gerundive phrase *haud aspernanda precantis* (106) explains why, to some extent, the embassy simply cannot fail. Aeneas suggests, however, that this embassy, like that of Venulus, falls short. Aeneas then indicates at 11.230 (cf. 11.110–111) that he would rather grant a lasting peace (*pacem*, 110), a word emphasized by its position as well as its obvious import[38] for not only the dead but also the living. This peace is the very thing that, as we learn later, Diomedes has urged the Rutulians to obtain from Aeneas (*pacem Troiano ab rege petendum*, 11.230[39]).

While the embassy's temporary truce allows for burial of the dead, the incident ultimately becomes a reminder to the Rutulians that real peace would have been obtainable had the correct objectives been sought. The embassy's success, therefore, is muted, for they fail to achieve real peace, an irony underscored at line 133 by the manner in which Virgil describes the forging of the peace as *sequestra*.

The final instance of unsuccessful *oratores* occurs in the eleventh book with Latinus' proposal to send an embassy to Aeneas. As had Aeneas in Book 7, so Latinus says that this embassy should consist of one hundred *oratores*:[40]

'praeterea, qui dicta ferant et foedera firment
centum oratores prima de gente Latinos
ire placet pacisque manu praetendere ramos,
munera portantis aurique eborisque talenta
et sellam regni trabeamque insignia nostri.
consulite in medium et rebus succurrite fessis.'   *Aen.* 11.330–335

["And in addition I should have this message
brought to them by a hundred Latin envoys,
men chosen from our nobles, to confirm
this treaty. They must carry with them gifts
of ivory, golden talents, and my chair
and robe—the emblems of my sovereignty.
Now counsel frankly, help our troubled state." (M. 11.437–443)]

The ambassadors are to extend the boughs of peace and to bring gifts and tokens of Latinus' realm. Yet it is too little, too late, and indeed this proposal never comes to pass. The magnitude of the failure is borne out by the consequent action of the final book of the poem. Aeneas speaks of the fact that he was forced to fight:

ipse inter primos dextram sub moenia tendit
Aeneas, magnaque incusat uoce Latinum
testaturque deos iterum se ad proelia cogi,
bis iam Italos hostis, haec altera foedera rumpi.
exoritur trepidos inter discordia ciuis. . . .   *Aen.* 12.579–583

[Aeneas
himself is in the vanguard, stretching out
his hand beneath the ramparts; and he shouts

his accusations at Latinus, calls
the gods to witness that he had been forced
to battle; twice the Latins have become
his enemies; twice they have broken treaties.
Dissension takes the panicked citizens. . . . [M. 12.777–784)]

Aeneas calls heaven to witness a second time (*iterum*, 581) that he was com-
pelled to fight because the pacts, originally established by Ilioneus' embassy
in Book 7, have been broken. Discord follows as broken pledges presage the
epic's resolution in the final scene.

The inefficacy of embassies, whether Trojan or Rutulian, is a feature especially evident in the poem's second half. This failure can also be seen in the
interchanges between Turnus and the senior statesman of the Rutulians,
Drances. Let us now turn our attention to this character, a rhetorician[41] who,
whether from his hatred for Turnus or respect for Aeneas, does prove to be a
somewhat successful speaker.[42] His success, however, seems to be partially
owed to his reliance on vision.

DRANCES AND TURNUS: OPPOSING VISIONS

Drances speaks with rhetorical flair on two distinct occasions in Book 11:
in his encounter with Aeneas and in his debate with Turnus in the Latin
war council. Unlike other *oratores*, Drances goes beyond the minimum requirements of his position and relies on sight in making his arguments. The
only other "orator" who previously used vision thus is Ilioneus, in his urg-
ing of Dido "to behold" the Trojan misfortunes (1.526). Such use of sight to
strengthen an argument, as we see in the case of Drances or Ilioneus, would
seem to make the argument generally quite effective.

We first encounter Drances in the eleventh book of the poem. Before
he speaks, we learn something interesting about the embassy he leads, for
though they are *oratores* (100), they react to Aeneas with silence:[43]

> illi obstipuere silentes
> conuersique oculos inter se atque ora tenebant.
> Tum senior semperque odiis et crimine Drances
> infensus iuueni Turno sic ore uicissim
> orsa refert. . . .   *Aen.* 11.120–124

> [. . . they stood amazed
> and silent, searching out each other's eyes.

But then the aged Drances, one who hated
young Turnus with a festering bitterness,
replies. . . . (M. 11.157–161)]

Virgil notes that the members of this delegation look silently into each
other's eyes. Their voices have temporarily been silenced, and Drances
speaks on their behalf. Drances is older than the rest (122) and, possibly as a
result of his senior status, appears especially hostile to youthful Turnus (123).
He represents both the other ambassadors and King Latinus in his speech,
which begins with praise and admiration for Aeneas:

> . . . 'o fama ingens, ingentior armis,
> uir Troiane, quibus caelo te laudibus aequem?
> iustitiaene prius mirer belline laborum?
> nos uero haec patriam grati referemus ad urbem
> et te, si qua uiam dederit Fortuna, Latino
> iungemus regi. quaerat sibi foedera Turnus.
> quin et fatalis murorum attollere moles
> saxaque subuectare umeris Troiana iuuabit.'   *Aen.* 11.124–131

> ["O Trojan, great in glory but
> far greater still in battle, how can my
> words praise you heaven-high? Shall I admire
> your justice first, or else your work in war?
> But, grateful, we shall carry what you have said
> back to our native city; and if fortune
> helps us, then we shall join you to Latinus.
> Let Turnus seek out treaties for himself.
> And more, we even shall be glad to raise
> your massive walls decreed by fate, to carry
> the stones of Ilium upon our shoulders." (M. 11.161–171)]

Drances' words suggest that he and his fellow ambassadors wish to assist Aeneas in achieving his destiny. Drances evokes the *Aeneid*'s prologue
through his allusion to wall building, an activity evocative of the entire mission.[44] The synecdoche of walls for the city of Rome indicates the extent of
Drances' desire for his people to be among those who lay the very founda-
tions of Aeneas' new empire.

Later in Book 11, Virgil describes the Latin war council and Drances' emergence within that council. Before Drances steps forward to speak, Virgil offers additional descriptive information on his character: *largus opum et lingua melior, sed frigida bello / dextera* (338–339).[45] Though he may not be much of a warrior, Drances is described as an adept speaker, not unlike orators later described by Tacitus.[46]

With rhetorical flair appropriate to the occasion, Drances opens his speech by emphasizing the obvious nature of the request:

> 'rem nulli obscuram nostrae nec *uocis* egentem
> consulis, o bone rex: cuncti se scire *fatentur*
> quid fortuna ferat populi, sed *dicere* mussant.
> det libertatem *fandi* flatusque remittat,
> cuius ob auspicium infaustum moresque sinistros
> (*dicam* equidem, licet arma mihi mortemque minetur). . . .'
>
> *Aen.* 11.343–348

> ["Good king, you ask for counsel about things
> that are not hid from anyone, that need
> no words of ours. For all confess they know
> the way our people's fortune has to go,
> and yet they hesitate to speak aloud.
> Just let him grant us liberty to speak,
> relax his arrogance; his stubborn ways
> and his unhappy auspices (yes, I
> shall speak, although he menace me with arms
> and death). . . ." (M. 11.452–461)]

Virtually every line of this section of Drances' speech refers to the spoken word, yet he asserts that there is no need for words, for the matter is obscure to none (343). Drances explains that, if hesitant to speak about their nation's prophesied downfall, the people are no less cognizant of coming events (345) and would be wise simply to acknowledge Aeneas' foretold triumph. Drances' boldness stands out here.[47] Though he duly asks for the right to speak (*det libertatem fandi,* 346), he is clearly also prepared to appropriate that right if no one else will speak against Turnus (*dicam equidem,* 348).[48]

Immediately afterward, Drances establishes a contrast between the spoken word and the veracity that vision affords. He emphasizes that his argument against Turnus will be based on what the Rutulians see:

'. . . lumina tot cecidisse ducum totamque *uidemus*
consedisse urbem luctu, dum Troia temptat
castra fugae fidens et caelum territat armis.'   *Aen.* 11.349–351

["... his stubborn ways

. . .

. . . have led to ruin for so many
bright chieftains, a whole city sunk in mourning,
while he, when sure of flight, provokes the Trojans' camp, frightening
   the heavens with his weapons." (M. 11.458, 461–464)]

The Rutulians have witnessed the "lights"—*id est proceres*, says Servius, ad
loc.—of the leaders fallen and the entire city settled into grief, while Turnus
has personally avoided battle. Drances, unlike most *oratores* in the poem,[49]
uses vision as a basis for his words and informs and invigorates his speech
by describing what he and others see (349).
   Drances soon suggests that Latinus add his daughter to the gifts for
Aeneas, as other heroines such as Helen had once been offered as war booty.[50]
Realizing that Latinus may fear to do so, Drances boldly calls upon Turnus
to cede her to the king:

'. . . quin natam egregio genero dignisque hymenaeis
des pater, et pacem hanc aeterno foedere iungas.
quod si tantus habet mentes et pectora terror,
ipsum obtestemur ueniamque *oremus* ab ipso:
cedat, ius proprium regi patriaeque remittat.
quid miseros totiens in aperta pericula ciuis
proicis, o Latio caput horum et causa malorum?
nulla salus bello, pacem te poscimus omnes,
Turne, simul pacis solum inuiolabile pignus.'   *Aen.* 11.355–363

["... do not let violence by any man
prevent you, as a father can, from giving
your daughter to a famous son-in-law
in worthy wedding that would seal this peace
by an eternal pact. But if our minds
and our hearts are so afraid, let us beseech
Turnus, and beg his favor, that he may
give way, forego his own right for the sake
of king and homeland. Why have you so often

driven your luckless countrymen to open
dangers: you who are source and cause of all
these trials of Latium? There is no safety
in war. What all of us are asking you,
Turnus, is peace—peace and the only thing
that is the inviolable pledge of peace." (M. 11.467–481)]

The king that Drances refers to in line 359 is not Latinus but rather Aeneas, as commentators since Servius have observed.[51] Drances proposes that the Rutulians beg clemency from Aeneas (358) and accuses Turnus of putting his fellow citizens in harm's way (360).[52] The marriage of Lavinia to Aeneas would be the inviolable pledge of which Drances speaks (363). Such an arrangement would surely have allowed the Latin appeal (*oremus*, 358) to prevail and would have prevented further bloodshed—something we know Aeneas was eager to grant (11.111) when he spoke with the embassy that came to request burial for the dead.

Drances had been part of that embassy, and he alludes to the "fruits" of the embassy's appeal as he continues to utilize visual aspects to portray his intentions. First, he states that Turnus has regarded him scornfully (*inuisum*, 364). "Behold," he goes on to add, "I came to you as a suppliant."[53] Drances then states that the Rutulians have "seen" enough funerals (*sat funera fusi / <u>uidimus</u> ingentis et desolauimus agros*, 366–367) before closing his speech with yet another powerful visual challenge to Turnus:

> 'etiam tu, si qua tibi uis,
> si patrii quid Martis habes, illum *aspice* contra
> qui uocat.'   *Aen.* 11.373–375

> ["Now you: if any
> force is in you, or any of your fathers'
> old fight, go out to face your challenger!" (M. 11.495–497)]

Mandelbaum's translation hardly does justice to the Latin here, for, more literally rendered, Drances calls upon Turnus to "look face to face at the opponent who calls you."[54] No other *orator*—whether among the Trojan ambassadors of Book 7 or the envoys with Venulus, as instructed in Book 8 or when reporting in Book 11, or among the *oratores* sent to Evander in Book 8 or the large embassy proposed by Latinus to bring gifts to the Trojans—has used so much visual imagery and laced his words with so many references to the corroboration that vision provides. For Drances, vision would seem to be the vital ingredient of credibility; he and others have witnessed the very things of which he speaks, and their view of the situation gives his words power and distinction, along with a believability that would not otherwise exist. Drances proves to be "wisest in a critical situation"[55] because he relies on visual stimuli as well as rhetorical flair.

Turnus' response mimics Drances' speech, often quoting his very words. This feature of *refutatio* begins in the first line, a placement that technically violates the rules of good oratory found in the *ad Herennium* (1.5).[56] Nevertheless, Turnus begins by citing and immediately refuting Drances' claims:

> 'larga quidem semper, Drance, tibi *copia fandi*
> tum cum bella manus poscunt, patribusque uocatis
> primus ades. *sed non replenda est curia uerbis,*
> quae tuto tibi magna uolant, dum distinet hostem
> agger murorum nec inundant sanguine fossae.
> *proinde tona eloquio (solitum tibi) meque timoris*
> *argue* tu, Drance, quando tot stragis aceruos
> Teucrorum *tua dextra* dedit, passimque tropaeis
> insignis agros.'   *Aen.* 11.378–386

> ["O Drances, you are always rich in words,
> even when war has asked for swords; and when
> the elders are assembled, you are first.
> There is no need to fill the senate house
> with speeches, all the blustering that you
> let fly in safety, while the enemy
> is still beyond the battlements and no
> blood floods our trenches. Therefore, Drances, thunder
> eloquently—as you always do—
> accusing me of fear, since your right hand
> has made so many heaps of slaughtered Trojans,
> and everywhere your trophies mark the fields." (M. 11.500–511)]

Turnus opens by using the same word (*fandi*) for speaking that Drances used in line 346, followed by a reversal of "hands": Drances had referred to Turnus' character as "left-handed" (*sinistros mores,* 347), whereas Turnus sarcastically accuses Drances' right hand of inactivity with respect to the fighting.[57] As noted above, this is a *refutatio,* which Turnus rushes into without a proper *exordium.*

He closely follows this mocking accusation with another allusion to Drances' words, namely, the reference to Mars:

'imus in aduersos—quid cessas? an tibi Mauors
uentosa in lingua pedibusque fugacibus istis
semper erit?'   *Aen.* 11.389–391

["Shall we
go out to meet them? Why do you draw back?
Will Mars be always in your windy tongue
and in your flying feet?" (M. 11.514–517)]

Turnus alleges that Mars is "upon [Drances'] windy tongue," an interesting claim for one who has, to this point, completed only one fifth of his own speech and whose speech reaches almost twice the length (67 lines) of Drances' address (33 lines). As Gransden points out, if one excludes the Hercules-Cacus tale, Turnus' speech is "the longest and grandest oration in the second half of the poem."[58]

In the words that follow, Turnus again imitates Drances by juxtaposing implied ineffectiveness of verbal communication (390, cited above, and 393) and the convincing aspects of vision (394):

'pulsus ego? aut quisquam merito, foedissime, pulsum
arguet, Iliaco tumidum qui crescere Thybrim
sanguine et Euandri totam cum stirpe *uidebit*
procubuisse domum atque exutos Arcadas armis?'   *Aen.* 11.392–395

["Have I been beaten?
Will anyone, you faithless liar, rightly
call me defeated, who can see the swollen
Tiber rising with the blood of Ilium
and all Evander's house and race in ruin
and his Arcadians stripped of arms?" (M. 11.517–522)]

Turnus' vision, however, does not parallel the present (so Drances' reference to sight at line 349) or past vision (cf. Drances' reference to past vision at line 367) of the Rutulians; by contrast, Turnus looks to the future, which he characterizes in terms of bloodshed and ruin (394).[59] This "future" is founded not only on the reality of battle[60] but also on past epic prowess, given heightened vividness by poetic reference to Greek epic[61] and by the emotional force with which Turnus delivers these lines.[62] This process, which Longinus[63] calls *phantasia* ("visualization"), is here achieved through a third-person reference (*quisquam . . . uidebit*, 392–394).[64]

As he persists in deriding Drances, Turnus continues to spout back the orator's own words through several allusions to Drances' speech. For example, he questions Drances' statement that there is no safety in war (362). Having cited epic examples of those who "feared" Phrygian weapons (403–405), Turnus continues to refute Drances' claims about the leaders' apprehension, stating that Drances rather projects his own fear onto others (406–409). Turnus then addresses Drances' statement (370–375) that Turnus should confront Aeneas alone in battle rather than allow the Rutulians to continue to be killed:

> 'si nullam nostris ultra spem ponis in armis,
> si tam deserti sumus et semel agmine uerso
> funditus occidimus neque habet Fortuna regressum,
> *oremus pacem* et dextras tendamus inertis.
> quamquam o si solitae quicquam uirtutis adesset!
> ille mihi ante alios fortunatusque laborum
> egregiusque animi, qui, *ne quid tale uideret*,
> procubuit moriens et humum semel ore momordit.'   *Aen.* 11.411–418

> ["If you have lost all hope in Latin arms,
> if we are so abandoned—so undone
> by one repulse—that fortune cannot change,
> then let us plead for peace, stretch out our hands,
> defenseless. But if something still remains
> of our old courage, then I should consider
> him happy in his trials and best of souls
> who—to avoid the sight of such a peace—
> would fall in death and gnaw the dust once and
> for all." (M. 11.546–555)]

Turnus here juxtaposes the people's appeal for peace (414) with the vision of the loyal soldier who will follow Turnus to death (417–418). Servius suggests that Turnus makes such a statement to avoid having to encounter Aeneas in single battle, while simultaneously commending those who, having persisted, would not want to see the surrender that Drances advocates.[65] Turnus' description at 414 of the final hopeless appeal vividly foreshadows his own final appeal in which he will use this very verb (*orare*) and perform the very action of supplication that he describes here (*dextras tendamus*, 414).[66]

Turnus' rhetorical flair is also evident in his *argumentum ab honesto*[67] when he proposes that the Rutulians should sue for peace only if their arms fail them. Turnus insists that the tide has turned (425–426) and that allies will come to their aid (428–433). He closes by boasting that he will go to meet "Aeneas' Achilles" (11.438–442). Turnus pleads for Aeneas to call him to single combat (*solum Aeneas uocat! et uocet oro*, 11.442).[68]

Turnus, as we have seen elsewhere,[69] uses the verb *orare* frequently.[70] He begs Allecto at 7.446, weighs heaven down with prayers at 9.24, prays for winds at 10.677, beseeches Juturna for a fevered pitch of madness at 12.680, and, of course, appeals to Aeneas to spare him at 12.933. Though, as befits a warrior, Turnus speaks boldly in his refutation of Drances' speech, his use of *orare* reflects prior usage in the poem.[71] Ironically, Turnus' plea for Aeneas to call him to battle alone (442) will be granted, ultimately to Turnus' detriment, in the poem's closing scene.

HERCULES AND CACUS: LIGHT, DARKNESS, AND DICTION

When Evander meets Aeneas in Book 8, he expounds upon details of the local geography, the site of future Rome. Evander focuses his topographical narrative on the Ara Maxima, the etiology of which is the tale of Hercules and Cacus. Karl Galinsky[72] and R. O. A. M. Lyne[73] have noted that this episode anticipates the *Aeneid's* close. Galinsky sees Hercules as a prototype of Aeneas, whose victory over Turnus seals Rome's destined right to exist. Lyne acknowledges the parallel but likens Aeneas to the monster by suggesting that Cacus' vomiting of fire should be compared to the fiery "light beaming from Aeneas," a reference to Aeneas' appearance to his troops at 10.271.[74] In this section, I will consider afresh how the visual imagery of the Hercules-Cacus tale points toward the telos of the *Aeneid*. As the victor who symbolizes light conquering darkness, Hercules represents the first installment of vision's victory.

When Aeneas meets him, Evander focuses on how Aeneas appears, stating plainly that he can "recognize" the Trojan from his appearance. As Aeneas speaks, Evander examines his face, his eyes, and even his entire body: *dixerat Aeneas. ille os oculosque loquentis / iamdudum et totum lustrabat lumine corpus* (8.152–153).[75] After scrutinizing Aeneas' person with his eyes, Evander evokes the memory of Aeneas' father, drawing upon Anchises' visit to Arcadia, where they had met many years before. Evander specifically recalls Anchises' words, voice, and features (855–856). Evander's vision of Anchises made a lasting impression, for he clearly recollects the physical presence and stature of Anchises (*cunctis altior*,[76] 162). Their encounter thus begins with emphasis on the significance of appearance and its effect on the dialogue that follows.

Evander proceeds to tell the story of Hercules and Cacus in which the theme of light and darkness parallels visual themes already introduced. While casting his eyes over the site of future Rome, Aeneas learns the details about Cacus from Evander, who draws on a past that will inform the Augustan future. Evander launches this tale by enjoining Aeneas to behold the physical terrain of the hill and, specifically, the base of Cacus' cave. Evander explains how Cacus' cave should be seen in terms of the darkness (193) that encompasses the *Caci facies* (194), a darkness that Servius interprets as the general appearance of Cacus (*uniuersus uisus*).[77] The monster's cave is specifically cut off from the sun's rays (195), and the pale, ghastly faces of the dead dangle gruesomely.[78]

Cacus is a dark figure, characterized by Evander as belching[79] oxymoronic black fires (*illius atros / ore uomens ignis*[80] [198–199]). Having resolved to steal the cattle (207–208), the monster Cacus hides the animals in a place fittingly devoid of light (*saxo . . . opaco*, 211). Hercules' consequent pursuit of Cacus through the mountain slopes causes the monster to become a spectacle for the Arcadians to behold:

'tum primum nostri Cacum uidere timentem
turbatumque oculis; *fugit ilicet ocior Euro*
speluncamque petit, pedibus timor addidit alas.'   *Aen.* 8.222–224

["That was the first time that our shepherds ever
saw Cacus terrified, fear in his eyes.
He flies more swiftly than the east wind, seeking
the cave; and to his feet, fear added wings." (M. 8.290–293)]

Whether one accepts the *lectio difficilior* "oculis" at line 223 or the less awkward "oculi" (so Gransden), the emphasis is on the Arcadians' view of the fearful Cacus. Further, this is the first time that they have seen him so violently frightened. In such a state, Cacus seeks out the dark shadows of his cave (224). Cacus' flight will later be alluded to in the description of Turnus' flight in Book 12, where Turnus, too, is described as fleeing more swiftly than the East wind:

. . . arrectaeque amborum acies. at perfidus ensis
frangitur in medioque ardentem deserit ictu,

ni fuga subsidio subeat. *fugit ocior Euro*
ut capulum ignotum dextramque aspexit inermem.   *Aen.* 12.731–734

> [. . . the tension takes both ranks.
> But, treacherous, that blade breaks off, deserts
> fanatic Turnus at his blow's midstroke
> had flight not helped him then. As soon as he
> sees that strange hilt in his defenseless hand,
> he runs away, swifter than the east wind. (M. 12.968–973)]

The attempted escape of one soon to be vanquished and the viewing of this attempt by others appear in descriptions of both Cacus and Turnus. Virgil specifically associates the standoff between Aeneas and Turnus with that of Hercules and Cacus through comparing the flights of Turnus and Cacus to Eurus. Moreover, just as the Arcadians were said by Evander to have beheld Cacus, so in Book 12 during this encounter the eyes of both sides are trained on Turnus (*et Rutuli certatim et Troes et omnes / conuertere oculos Itali,* 12.704–705).[81]

As Evander describes the battle between Hercules and Cacus, Hercules emerges as a prototype of the *voyant-visible* that Aeneas will prove to be.[82] After Cacus confines himself to his cave (225), Hercules rages and seeks him out:

> '. . . ecce furens animis aderat Tirynthius omnemque
> accessum lustrans huc ora ferebat et illuc,
> dentibus infrendens. ter totum feruidus ira
> lustrat Auentini montem, ter saxea temptat
> limina nequiquam, ter fessus ualle resedit.'   *Aen.* 8.228–232

> ["... look
> Tirinthyus was come in frenzied anger
> and scanning every entry. Hercules,
> gnashing his teeth, turned this way, that. He tramps
> three times across the Aventine, in wrath;
> three times he tries in vain the gates of stone;
> three times he sinks, tired out, along the valley." (M. 8.298–304)]

In the role of pursuer, Hercules scans the territory carefully; at the same time, as the central character beheld by Evander and his people, Hercules is most assuredly the object of the spectators' gaze. Gnashing his teeth and unable to discover an access to Cacus' lair, Hercules finally comes upon a lofty pillar (*acuta silex / altissima uisu*, 233–234). The light/dark contrast is sustained, for the removal of this rock exposes the unlit palace of Cacus to the penetrating rays of the sun:

'at specus et Caci detecta apparuit ingens
regia, et umbrosae penitus patuere cauernae,
non secus ac si qua penitus ui terra dehiscens
infernas reseret sedes et regna recludat
pallida, dis inuisa, superque immane barathrum
cernatur, trepident immisso lumine Manes.'   *Aen*. 8.241–246

["The den of Cacus, his enormous palace,
lay bare and, deep inside, his shadowed caverns
were naked to the eye; as if the earth,
ripped open by some violence, unlocked
the house of hell and all its pallid kingdoms,
so hated by the gods, and one could see
deep down in that dread abyss, the Shades
trembling within as sunlight made its way." (M. 8.315–322)]

Cacus is appropriately tied to the chthonic nether realms. Even the vast depths (*immane barathrum*, 245) are made visible, and the spirits beneath the earth quake with fear. To explain this with full effect, Virgil uses a perhaps "over-adequate"[83] simile of the land splitting during an earthquake. R. D. Williams comments, "The viewpoint shifts first from above and then from below, as the ghosts tremble at the light let in (like Cacus)."[84] The direction of the viewers' eye movement is vertical, moving from the heights (234) to the subterranean cave (*super*[85] . . . / *cernatur*, 245–246), shadowy, deep, and suitably pallid.

Following this linear movement, Evander proceeds to describe Cacus in his lair, where the monster is ill-equipped to receive the light that Hercules' bold action has caused to pour upon him. Having hemmed in the monster with unexpected light (*insperata . . . luce*, 247), Hercules bears down upon him (250). With flight cut off, Cacus resorts to sending forth smoke from his jaws to hide himself and confuse Hercules. Virgil expresses this plainly when he states that Cacus takes away the view from Hercules' eyes (*prospectum eripiens oculis*, 254), filling the house with a smoke that is *caeca* (253), an adjective that offers a play on Cacus' name, beyond the obvious association with κακός.[86] Virgil's use of this adjective demonstrates aptly the tension between the darkness that Cacus represents and the power that sight and light wield. In a "bravura of high-flown rhetoric,"[87] Virgil continues the contrast of light and darkness by explaining that fire, typically bright and searching, here acts as a weapon to obscure vision.

Despite the thick smoke, Hercules leaps straight through the flames (256–257) and grasps fire-breathing Cacus:

'hic Cacum in tenebris incendia uana uomentem
corripit in nodum complexus, et angit inhaerens
elisos oculos et siccum sanguine guttur.' *Aen.* 8.259–261

["And here, as Cacus vomits useless fires
within that black mist, Hercules grips him
as in a knot and, clinging, squeezes out
his strangled eyes, his throat run dry of blood." (M. 8.338–341)]

The issue of Cacus' mouth attempts to obscure Hercules' vision. Hercules appropriately cuts off the source of the fire by squeezing Cacus' throat dry until, in Virgil's "extremely bold" description, Cacus' eyes bulge from their sockets.[88] The loss of Cacus' eyes symbolically parallels the darkness associated with him in life and the blindness that his name suggests. Hercules thus takes away from his antagonist any potential for vision. Hercules' vision of light triumphs over the dark and even "blind" false vision of the monster, whose attempt to use smoke to obscure Hercules' vision has failed. Having been transformed from the "evil one" (Greek, κακός) to the "blind one" (*caecus*), Cacus has now become the Shade that he imitated in life.

After Hercules' victory, Evander portrays him with the conquered Cacus amidst a crowd of onlookers who gaze on the victor and his prey:

'panditur extemplo foribus domus atra reuulsis
abstractaeque boues abiurataeque rapinae
caelo ostenduntur, pedibusque informe cadauer
protrahitur. nequeunt expleri corda tuendo
terribilis oculos, uultum uillosaque saetis
pectora semiferi atque exstinctos faucibus ignis.' *Aen.* 8.262–267

["At once the house of darkness is thrown open,
the doors torn off—the stolen oxen and
the perjured plunder plain before the heavens.

The shapeless corpse is dragged out by the feet.
We cannot get enough of watching Cacus:
his terrifying eyes, his face, the shaggy
and bristling chest of that half-beast, his jaws
with their extinguished fires." (M. 8.342–349)]

Virgil's description is comparable to graphic representations of exhausted victors and fallen prey that would have been readily available in the Roman world. An example of this type can be seen in a fresco of Theseus from the House of Gavius Rufus in Pompeii[89] (Figure 5.1). The onlookers in the fresco, much like Hercules' audience, simply cannot be sated with gazing upon the defeated monster (265). In Evander's account, the audience is particularly captivated by the beast's eyes, face and chest (266–267). As in the wall painting, only the monster's torso commands the foreground and the attention of the audience. The remainder of the beast is symbolically obfuscated by the shadows in the background. Theseus, by contrast, stands out as a victor in clear light symbolic of the hero's power over the brutal Minotaur.

Virgil's similar use of witnesses to Hercules' victory recapitulates and affirms the role of vision in this episode, for Hercules is *voyant*, one who sees by bringing light and sight to a place entirely devoid of these qualities; the realization that he is also *visible* occurs through the crowd's admiring gaze upon him.[90] Hercules' victory over Cacus is characterized in terms of light and darkness that anticipate the conflict between the power of images to clarify and the power of rhetoric to obfuscate. In this way, Hercules prefigures the Aeneas of the poem's concluding scene, a highly visible person whose final act is beheld by both Rutulians and Trojans.

FAILURE OF RHETORIC (PART 2): THE FUTILITY OF BATTLEFIELD ENTREATY IN BOOKS 10–12

In the first three books of the *Aeneid*, we see several examples of those engaged in combat who fail to obtain what they implore. In this section, I shall examine how Virgil uses the verb *orare* in the battlefield environment. While this verb appears only once in the *Eclogues* and three times in the *Georgics*, the verb occurs forty-seven times in the *Aeneid*, with twenty-six of those occurrences in the second half of the poem. My purpose, however, is not to compile statistics but rather to consider examples of the verb *orare* as used by those pleading mercy from their conquerors. The verb's treatment in such scenes obviously differs, for example, from embassy scenes in which ambassadors come to ask for succor, debate terms of treaties, or explain the pres-

Figure 5.1. *Theseus Having Slain the Minotaur.* Pompeian Fresco. Museo Archeologico Nazionale, Naples.

ence of a group of people in a particular place at a particular time. While oral supplication fails in the poem's last three books, vision of the protagonists prompts action.

The futility of battlefield appeals is connected to the failure of ambassadorial rhetoric in the second half of the poem. Disturbingly, a plea for one's life is even less effective than other kinds of requests. The precedent for failure of battlefield entreaty has already been set in Homer. In comparison with the four instances of battlefield supplication in the *Iliad*, spread out between Books 6 and 21, the appeals to Aeneas in Virgil's poem are more clustered, occurring in *Aeneid* 10–12. Only two of those in the *Iliad* are directed at Achilles: that of Tros,[91] who died in the midst of Achilles' rage on the battlefield, and that of Lykaon,[92] whose brutal slaying and the depositing of his body in the Scamander caused that river to rebuke and restrain Achilles.[93] Of the other examples, one is the locus classicus of deception and betrayal, namely, the Doloneia,[94] in which Dolon is killed by Diomedes only after divulging much useful information. The other instance of battlefield supplication is interesting, for Menelaus shows that it is possible for an epic warrior to consider sparing a suppliant;[95] were it not for Agamemnon's intervention, Adrestos would have lived.[96]

The situation in the *Aeneid*, however, is different. Those who appeal to Aeneas on the battlefield do so to no avail, for they encounter him only after he is kindled with anger because of Pallas' death. There is no situation like that of Menelaus and Adrestos before the poem's final scene. Rather, those who pray are unsuccessful, and their appeals are in vain. The verbs these unsuccessful suppliants employ are *rogare*, *precari* or, more often, *orare*. The last is the root source of the word *orator*, which signifies "ambassador" in the *Aeneid* but also signals the notion of rhetoric. Now let us consider those who seek mercy in battle, noting that their petitions, like those of the embassies, do not achieve a high degree of success.

Magus

The first instance of failure of a battlefield suppliant begging for mercy before meeting death at the hands of his conqueror occurs near the middle of Book 10. Shortly after Pallas' death—again, before Pallas' death there are no examples of Aeneas failing to spare suppliants—an irate Aeneas sees visions of Pallas and Evander that prompt him to brutal action:

> Pallas, Euander, *in ipsis*
> *omnia sunt oculis*, mensae quas aduena primas
> tunc adiit, dextraeque datae. Sulmone creatos
> quattuor hic iuuenes, totidem quos educat Vfens,
> uiuentis rapit, inferias quos immolet umbris
> captiuoque rogi perfundat sanguine flammas. *Aen.* 10.515–520

> [Pallas . . .
> Evander . . . all are now before his eyes . . .
> the tables he first came to as a stranger,
> the pledged right hands. He grabs four youths alive,
> four sons of Sulmo, then four raised by Ufens,
> to offer up as victims to the Shade
> of Pallas, to pour out as captive blood
> upon the funeral pyre. (M. 10.710–717)]

It is difficult to justify Aeneas' brutality at this moment. Virgil does, however, include a vital detail that helps to explain Aeneas' actions: the poet notes that visions of the past animate Aeneas' actions in the present. This is not merely a point of detail; Aeneas here shows that he reacts to the visions that he sees (*in ipsis / omnia sunt oculis,* 515–516). The four youths that must die represent retribution for Pallas' death.

The visions that Aeneas sees are scenes specifically from his past, the faces of those who were especially important to him, Pallas and Evander, and he sees with them the symbols of the closeness of their relationship (tables and pledged hands). As in Book 2, where he encountered Creusa and Hector, here again in Book 10, images of Aeneas' past prompt him to act.

Following the sacrifice of the youths, Aeneas continues his violent acts of retribution. Virgil soon depicts how Magus acts as a suppliant before he faces the lance of Aeneas:[97]

inde Mago procul infensam contenderat hastam:
ille astu subit, at tremibunda superuolat hasta,
et genua amplectens effatur talia supplex:
'per patrios manis et spes surgentis Iuli
te precor, hanc animam serues gnatoque patrique.'   *Aen.* 10.521–525

> [Next from far
> Aeneas casts his hostile lance at Magus;
> but Magus is adroit enough to stoop,
> and quivering, the lance flies over him.
> He grips Aeneas' knees and, suppliant,
> he begs him: "By your Father's Shade and
> your hopes in rising Iülus, I entreat,
> do spare this life for my own son and father." (M. 10.717–724)]

Magus's appeal in 524 is couched not in the visible and present but by the past (*patrios manis*) and the future (*spes . . . Iuli*). But Aeneas's focus is on Magus himself, a character otherwise unknown, whose name is an adaptation of the Greek μάγος, meaning "charlatan" or "magician."[98] His words, however, fail to charm,[99] and Magus falls to Aeneas:[100]

sic fatus galeam *laeua* tenet atque reflexa
ceruice orantis *capulo tenus* applicat *ensem.*   *Aen.* 10.535–536

[With this he grips the Latin's helmet crest
in his left hand; his right drives on the sword
hilt-high into that bent, beseeching neck. (M. 10.736–738)]

Aeneas' killing of Magus recalls Diomedes' killing of Dolon in *Iliad* 10:

Ἦ, καὶ ὁ μέν μιν ἔμελλε γενείου χειρὶ παχείῃ
ἁψάμενος λίσσεσθαι, ὁ δ' αὐχένα μέσσον ἔλασσε
φασγάνῳ ἀΐξας, ἀπὸ δ' ἄμφω κέρσε τένοντε·
φθεγγομένου δ' ἄρα τοῦ γε κάρη κονίῃσιν ἐμίχθη.   *Iliad* 10.454–457

[He spoke, and the man was trying to reach his chin with his strong
    hand
and cling, and supplicate him, but he struck the middle of his neck
with a sweep of the sword, and slashed clean through both tendons,
and Dolon's head still speaking dropped in the dust.]

In the *Iliad*, Diomedes severs Dolon's head even while Dolon continues to
speak (457). Diomedes' imperviousness to Dolon's supplication provides a
model for Aeneas, for Virgil's description of Aeneas' death stroke interrupt-
ing Magus's extended appeal for mercy echoes Homer's description. In both
accounts, the suppliant beseeches the epic warrior even unto the moment
of death.

The sequence of killing, which began with the sacrifice of the four inno-
cent youths and is now directed toward Magus, was precipitated by the appearance of the images of Pallas and Evander "before the eyes" of Aeneas.[101]
By an allusion to one of the most violent scenes in the poem, Virgil further emphasizes that Aeneas will not respond to verbal supplication.[102] This
scene, from Book 2, records Aeneas' description of Priam's brutal murder. In
it, Aeneas offers details about the death stroke itself:

> . . . altaria ad ipsa trementem
> traxit et in multo lapsantem sanguine nati,
> implicuitque *comam laeua*, dextraque coruscum
> extulit ac lateri *capulo tenus* abdidit *ensem*.   *Aen.* 2.550–553

[. . . he dragged him to the very altar stone,
with Priam shuddering and slipping in
the blood that streamed from his own son. And Pyrrhus
with his left hand clutched tight the hair of Priam;
his right hand drew his glistening blade, and then
he buried it hilt-high in the king's side. (M. 2.738–743)]

The phrase *capulo tenus . . . ensem*, with *laeua* in the position of a penthe-
mimeral caesura in the previous line, only occurs in the passages from

Aeneid 2 and *Aeneid* 10. This internal allusion links Aeneas to Pyrrhus' brutality in a clearly negative manner; Aeneas is, by association, also capable of ignoring the pleas of a suppliant. Magus' death is thus connected to one of the most merciless deaths in the *Aeneid* and, not surprisingly, Magus' words, posture, and attempts to buy his freedom do not avail (*iacent pernitus defossa talenta / caelati argenti,* 10.526–527).[103] Magus, then, is the first of those in *Aeneid* 10–12 whose pleas for mercy fail on the battlefield.

Tarquitus

The next victim to beg for mercy is Tarquitus, who bears a name strikingly similar to the Etruscan king of Rome. Aeneas, described as a true child of Troy (*Dardanides,* 10.545), kills Tarquitus as Tarquitus leaps before him in battle:

> Tarquitus exsultans contra fulgentibus armis,
> siluicolae Fauno Dryope quem nympha crearat,
> obuius ardenti sese obtulit. ille reducta
> loricam clipeique ingens onus impedit hasta,
> tum caput *orantis* nequiquam et multa parantis
> dicere deturbat terrae, truncumque tepentem
> prouoluens super haec inimico pectore fatur. . . .   *Aen.* 10.550–556

> [. . . came Tarquitus, who swaggered in bright armor—
> he was the son of Dryope, the nymph,
> and Faunus, who was keeper of the forests.
> Aeneas draws his lance, pins Tarquitus'
> cuirass and ponderous shield; as Tarquitus
> prays helplessly, wanting to say so much,
> Aeneas strikes his head to earth and kicks
> the warm trunk over, cries with hating heart. . . . (M. 10.760–767)]

Like Magus, Tarquitus clearly has not yet finished speaking, for Aeneas dashes Tarquitus' head to the ground even as he vainly begs. The ineffectiveness of Tarquitus' entreaty is emphasized in this case by the adverb *nequiquam,* and Virgil indicates that Tarquitus was preparing to add more words. Again, this description is comparable to the death of Dolon at Diomedes' hands (*Il.* 10.457). While supplication entirely suits the epic genre, Virgil emphasizes the remarkable lack of pity on Aeneas' part, as reflected in his merciless vaunting over Tarquitus' corpse (*Aen.* 10.557–560). Aeneas again shows no regard for entreaty (554).

Liger

This pattern of failed entreaty recurs yet again within a few lines. After Lucagus has already met death at Aeneas' hands, Lucagus' brother, Liger, also encounters Aeneas. Aeneas quickly dispatches Liger, despite his vain attempt at supplication:[104]

> . . . frater tendebat inertis
> infelix palmas curru delapsus eodem:
> 'per te, per qui te talem genuere parentes,
> uir Troiane, sine hanc animam et miserere precantis.'
> pluribus *oranti* Aeneas: 'haud talia dudum
> dicta dabas. morere et fratrem ne desere frater.'   *Aen.* 10.595–600

> [Tumbling down
> from that same chariot, the luckless brother,
> Liger, stretched out his helpless hands and pleaded:
> "O Trojan hero, by yourself and by
> the parents who have brought to birth so great
> a son, spare me my life; with pity hear
> my prayer." There had been more; Aeneas cut
> him off: "These words were not your words before.
> Die; do not leave your brother all alone." (M. 10.817–825)]

As Harrison points out, "The appeal to his [Liger's] parents should have some effect on *pius Aeneas*, but Vergil makes him follow the Iliadic Achilles in ignoring it in his passion for revenge" (220).[105] Harrison aptly compares Aeneas' passion to *Iliad* 22.338, where Hector entreats Achilles, by Achilles' parents, to spare him. Instead of recalling his parents (597), Aeneas orders Liger to show his own family loyalty by joining Lucagus in the Underworld. Although Aeneas' wrath in *Aeneid* 10–12 is directly attributable to Pallas having become for Aeneas like a member of his own family, Aeneas exhibits contempt for family connections in his interaction with Liger. With the statement, *haud . . . dicta dabas*, Aeneas expresses his disdain for words that Liger had previously uttered:

> 'non Diomedis equos nec currum cernis Achilli
> aut Phrygiae campos: nunc belli finis et aeui
> his dabitur terris.' uesano talia late

dicta uolant Ligeri. sed non et Troius heros
dicta parat contra. . . .   *Aen.* 10.581–585

["This is not Achilles' chariot
nor Diomedes' horses that you see,
and not the plain of Phrygia; now and here,
upon our land, you end your life and warfare."
Mad Liger scatters words like these. And yet
the Trojan hero does not ready words
against his enemy. . . . (M. 10.798–804)]

Liger refers directly to Aeneas' encounter with Diomedes at *Iliad* 5.297–298
and 20.273–274. He also calls attention to vision; in stating that Aeneas does
not "see" the chariot of Achilles (581), Liger implies that he rather sees a different chariot, one that will bring death to Aeneas. Aeneas offers none of his
own words in response to Liger's predictions, and, in line 599, Aeneas will
be similarly unwilling to hear Liger's plea.

FAILURE OF RHETORIC (PART 3):
SIGHT MAKES RIGHT AND THE *AENEID*'S FINALE

Other characters also fail to respond to suppliants elsewhere in the second half of the *Aeneid*. Camilla ignores Orsilochus' plea in Book 11,[106] bru-
tally doubling his wounds, while Messapus kills the suppliant Aulestes in
Book 12.[107] Similarly, near the end of Book 11, in a manner that recalls
Aeneas' prayer of *Aeneid* 1 (*ante ora patrum*, 94), the Rutulians are routed
before the city walls (*exclusi ante oculos lacrimantumque ora parentum*,
11.887)[108] and beg to be allowed inside (*nec sociis aperire uiam nec moenibus
audent / accipere orantis*, 11.885–886).[109] Yet their appeal fails, and, in light
of that failure, comes a somber fulfillment of the pronouncement made by
Aeneas during the sea storm of the first book (1.94–95).

Beyond these various examples of the failure of appeals, there are four
battlefield exchanges, linked together through the themes of vision and the
failure of rhetoric, that deserve detailed consideration. The first of these, Pallas' death at the hands of Turnus, will provoke the final act in the poem.
Pallas' death is also linked to Lausus' demise through Virgil's manipulation
of vision, particularly in his description of the interaction between Aeneas
and Mezentius. Moreover, Virgil uses visual clues in Mezentius' death scene
to foreshadow the death of Turnus, the last of the four exchanges.

The Death of Pallas

Turnus engages in extended prayers in Book 9 (24), yet he fails to request the gods' help when he encounters Pallas in the next book. By contrast, Pallas does pray to Hercules during the battle, though without immediate effect:

> 'per patris hospitium et mensas, quas aduena adisti,
> te precor, Alcide, coeptis ingentibus adsis.
> *cernat* semineci sibi me rapere arma cruenta
> uictoremque ferant *morientia lumina* Turni.'   *Aen.* 10.460–463

> ["Hercules,
> I pray you by my father's welcome to you,
> the board that you, a stranger, shared with him,
> to help my great attempt! Let dying Turnus
> see me strip off his bloody weapons, let
> his dying eyes see me a conqueror." (M. 10.638–643)]

Pallas' prayer poignantly calls attention to Turnus' vision, in particular, for he wishes Turnus to pass from this life with a clear picture of his defeat (462–463). To portray this, Pallas uses a verb of sight (*cernat*, 462). He elaborates by referring specifically to the imagined "half-dead"[110] status of Turnus (462) and to his "dying eyes" (463). Though Hercules wishes to respond, he cannot (464–465).[111]

Pallas' prayer responds to the address that Turnus gives his comrades as he prepares to face Pallas. Turnus' words frame a macabre wish that Evander were present to see Pallas die:

> ut uidit socios: 'tempus desistere pugnae;
> solus ego in Pallanta feror, soli mihi Pallas
> debetur; *cuperem ipse parens spectator adesset.*'
> haec ait, et socii cesserunt aequore iusso.   *Aen.* 10.441–444

> [And when he sees his comrades, Turnus shouts:
> "You have had enough of battle. I alone
> meet Pallas; he is owed to me, my own;
> I could have wished his father here to watch."
> This said, his comrades left the field as ordered. (M. 10.612–616)]

This description of a battle with a spectator clearly evokes the image of a public spectacle.[112] By it, Virgil also alludes poignantly to Aeneas' initial statement that those who die *ante ora patrum* are especially blessed (1.95). In the mouth of Turnus, however, the prayer that Aeneas had once uttered in desperation in the face of imminent disaster has been transformed into the overweening pride of a brutal assailant.

In the lines that follow, Pallas himself speaks in a manner that suggests he has prior knowledge of Turnus' boastful prayer:

at Rutulum abscessu iuuenis tum iussa superba
miratus stupet in Turno corpusque per ingens
lumina uoluit obitque truci procul omnia *uisu*,
talibus et dictis it contra dicta tyranni:
'aut spoliis ego iam raptis laudabor opimis
aut leto insigni: sorti pater aequus utrique est.
tolle minas.'   *Aen.* 10.445–451

[But when they have gone off, the youth, amazed
at Turnus' arrogance, admires him;
he runs his eyes across that giant frame
and from a distance, grim, scans everything,
then casts these words against the prince's words:
"Soon I shall win my glory, either by
the spoils I carry off from a commander
or by a splendid death. My father can
stand up to either fate. Enough of threats." (M. 10.617–625)]

Pallas' reference to his father's readiness for any outcome and his command for Turnus to cease threatening shows that Pallas is responding to some of Turnus' actions and words. Vision, too, has a significant presence in the encounter of these two warriors. From Turnus' callous desire for Evander to behold Pallas' death, to the gladiatorial atmosphere that permeates the scene,[113] to Pallas' visual perusal of Turnus' huge body, vision continually provides information about this battle. Pallas' gaze (*lumina uoluit*, 10.447) anticipates the *uoluens oculos*[114] of Aeneas at the epic's close, prior to his killing of Turnus. Harrison notes that the use of *uoluere* for eyes is apparently a Virgilian innovation,[115] and Virgil himself does not use it in this manner before the *Aeneid*.[116]

Turnus responds to Pallas in similarly visual terms: '*aspice num mage sit nostrum penetrabile telum'* (10.481).[117] Before Turnus responds to Pallas' attack, he addresses the young man as if he has overheard the visual aspects of Pallas' earlier petition for Turnus to witness his own demise (462–463), for Turnus commands Pallas to "behold" his weapon's power to penetrate armor (481). Later in the poem, Turnus refers to the vision of others in his attempt to plead for his life (12.936–937).

Such taunts ultimately arise from Virgil's normal modus operandi of alluding to and reusing Homeric topoi such as those of *Iliad* 22, where Hector commands Achilles to receive a blow from his spear[118] (νῦν αὖτ' ἐμὸν ἔγχος ἄλευαι / χάλκεον· ὡς δή μιν σῷ ἐν χροϊ πᾶν κομίσαιο [*Il.* 22.285–286]).[119] Virgil's conversation between warriors, however, differs from Homer's depiction. Nowhere in Hector's speech (*Il.* 22.279–288) or in the preceding speech of Achilles (*Il.* 22.261–272) do the characters themselves mention vision specifically.[120] Conversely, in Virgil, vision is a point of discussion, for Turnus commands Pallas to look upon the spear that will kill him. Likewise, Lausus' sight of Mezentius' death prompts him to act (10.790), a passage to which we shall now turn.

The Death of Lausus

Pallas' death is rightly compared to the death of Lausus that occurs in the same book.[121] Lausus' death is not an act of vengeance on Aeneas' part, nor does he relish the killing. In contrast to Turnus,[122] Aeneas does not specifically seek to engage a younger, weaker opponent; he acts only when Lausus interferes with the battle between Aeneas and Mezentius:

> ingemuit cari grauiter genitoris amore,
> *ut uidit,* Lausus, lacrimaeque per ora uolutae—
> hic mortis durae casum tuaque optima facta,
> si qua fidem tanto est operi latura uetustas,
> non equidem nec te, iuuenis memorande, silebo—
> ille pedem referens et inutilis inque ligatus
> cedebat clipeoque inimicum hastile trahebat.   *Aen.* 10.789–795

> [But Lausus, for the love of his dear father,
> groaned deep as he saw this; his tears were many.
> And here I shall not leave untold—
> for such a deed can be more readily
> believed because it was done long ago—
> the trial of your harsh death and gallant acts

and you yourself, young man to be remembered.
Mezentius—helpless, hampered—lumbered off;
the bitter lance trailed from his shield. (M. 10.1085–1093)]

Lausus' entrance into the "evil chance"[123] that will bring about his death is
marked by the temporal clause, *ut uidit*. The son comes to his father's aid,
weeping at the sight of his father's situation (790). Virgil subjectively comments on the narrative by speaking of Lausus' bravery in the first person.

Aeneas directly addresses Lausus before their encounter:

. . . sustinet et Lausum increpitat Lausoque minatur:
'quo moriture ruis maioraque uiribus audes?
fallit te incautum pietas tua.'   *Aen.* 10.810–812

[. . . and he taunts Lausus, menacing:
"Why are you rushing to sure death? Why dare
things that are past your strength? Your loyalty
has tricked you into recklessness." (M. 10.1112–1115)]

Although Aeneas' words seem somewhat "taunting," they also serve as "a
genuine warning to a younger and weaker opponent to abandon the duel."[124]
While in no way can Aeneas be entirely exonerated from his disregard of
the prayers of numerous suppliants in *Aeneid* 10–12, Aeneas clearly has no
desire to kill this juvenile.

To heighten the pathos, Virgil adds details pertaining to Lausus' family:

nec minus ille
exsultat demens, saeuae iamque altius irae
Dardanio surgunt ductori, extremaque Lauso
Parcae fila legunt. ualidum namque exigit ensem
per medium Aeneas iuuenem totumque recondit;
transiit et parmam mucro, leuia arma minacis,
et tunicam molli mater quam neuerat auro,
impleuitque sinum sanguis; tum uita per auras
concessit maesta ad Manis corpusque reliquit.   *Aen.* 10.812–820

[And yet
the youth is wild and will not stop; at this,
harsh anger rises in the Dardan chief;
the Fates draw the last thread of Lausus' life.

Right through the belly of the youth Aeneas
now plunges his tough sword until it hides
hilt-high. The blade passed through the shield, too thin
for one who was so threatening, and through
the tunic Lausus' mother spun for him
of supple gold. His chest was filled with blood;
across the air his melancholy life
passed on into the Shades and left his body. (M. 10.1115–1126)]

Aeneas' death blow transfixes the tunic that, Virgil tells us, was woven by Lausus' mother. The tunic's golden weave indicates the worth of the wearer as well as the intrinsic worth of the garment. The conjunction of Lausus' blood and the golden material offers a striking visual detail within the death scene.[125] When looking upon the dying Lausus, Aeneas is moved to pity and picks up the body:

> At uero *ut uultum uidit* morientis et ora,
> ora modis Anchisiades pallentia miris,
> ingemuit miserans grauiter dextramque tetendit,
> et mentem patriae subiit pietatis imago.   *Aen.* 10.821–824

[But when he saw the look and face of dying
Lausus—he was mysteriously pale—
Anchises' son sighed heavily with pity
and stretched out his right hand; the image of
his love for his own father touched his mind. (M. 10.1127–1131)]

The phrase *ut uultum uidit* (821) is not only a "strong temporal marker"[126] but also the close of the visual frame of Lausus' death scene that began with Lausus' vision of his doomed father (*ut uidit*, 10.790).[127] Now, based on his vision of the dying boy, Aeneas is motivated by thoughts of his relationship with his own father.[128] Commentators have rightly noted that Virgil's application of the patronymic to Aeneas here evokes Aeneas' filial *pietas*.[129]

While Lausus never begs Aeneas for mercy, Lausus' prayers uttered to Hercules earlier in this book are of no avail (460–461).[130] Lausus ignores Aeneas' warning that Lausus' *pietas* has deceived him (811–812). Aeneas responds to his sight of the dead youth with touching words:

> 'quid tibi nunc, miserande puer, pro laudibus istis,
> quid pius Aeneas tanta dabit indole dignum?

'arma, quibus laetatus, habe tua; teque parentum
manibus et cineri, si qua est ea cura, remitto.
hoc tamen infelix miseram solabere mortem:
Aeneae magni dextra cadis.' increpat ultro
cunctantis socios et terra subleuat ipsum
sanguine turpantem comptos de more capillos.   *Aen.* 10.825–832

["Poor boy, for such an act what can the pious
Aeneas give to match so bright a nature?
Keep as your own the arms that made you glad;
and to the Shades and ashes of your parents
I give you back—if Shades still care for that.
But, luckless, you can be consoled by this:
You fall beneath the hand of great Aeneas."
He even calls the hesitating comrades
of Lausus, and he lifts the body off
the ground, where blood defiled the handsome hair. (M. 10.1132–1141)]

As Aeneas lifts up the broken body to return it to its own household, his
vision of Lausus causes him to recall his own sense of family values. Aeneas'
compassion starkly contrasts with the disposition of Turnus, who strips Pallas' lifeless body of its spoils (10.490–500). In the Lausus tale, vision twice
prompts action: first, the valiant intervention of a son for a father (790) and
second, the honorable return of the son to the father.[131] These episodes frame
the narrative and suggest that vision causes a direct emotional response
through deeds and not merely through words.

The Death of Mezentius

Aeneas encounters Lausus' father at the end of Book 10, and their battle
offers a telling comparison with the poem's finale. Aeneas draws his sword
and speaks to Mezentius:

> . . . 'ubi nunc Mezentius acer et illa
> effera uis animi?' contra Tyrrhenus, ut auras
> *suspiciens hausit caelum* mentemque recepit. . . .   *Aen.* 10.897–899

[. . . "Where now is brave Mezentius, and where is
his ruthless force of mind?" The Tuscan drank
the air and watched the sky and came to life. . . . (M. 10.1232–1234)]

These words resonate closely with the *Aeneid*'s closing scene. Mezentius gazes upwards and *hausit caelum*,[132] an action prototypical of Aeneas' own gazing and, in particular, of his "quaffing" of the *saeui monimenta doloris* with his eyes (12.945).

In contrast to the *Aeneid*'s closing, where he emphasizes the victor's vision, Virgil is more concerned here with his description of the vision of the suppliant Mezentius. Mezentius' wish reveals him to be of noble character:

'unum hoc per si qua est uictis uenia hostibus *oro:*
corpus humo patiare tegi. scio acerba meorum
circumstare odia: hunc, *oro,* defende furorem
et me consortem nati concede sepulcro.'
haec loquitur, iuguloque haud inscius accipit ensem
undantique animam diffundit in arma cruore.   *Aen.* 10.903–908

["I ask you only this: if any grace
is given to the vanquished, let my body
be laid in earth. I know my people's harsh
hatred that hems me in. I beg of you
to save me from their fury, let me be
companion to my son within the tomb."
So says Mezentius; then, with full awareness,
he gives his throat up to the sword and pours
his life in waves of blood across his armor. (M. 10.1240–1248)]

As Harrison points out, the general tone and swift brutality of Mezentius' death anticipate the final victory of Aeneas over Turnus. Mezentius' plea stands in stark contrast to the appeal of Turnus, for Mezentius does not ask to be spared.[133] Rather, he begs simply for burial with his family. To reinforce this, he uses the verb *orare* twice in close proximity (903, 905). We never specifically learn, in Mezentius' case, whether Aeneas grants this plea; Aeneas chooses not to respond as he kills Mezentius with the sword. Aeneas' lack of response to Mezentius, however, contrasts with Aeneas' specific denial of Turnus' request for burial.

We have seen that suppliants of Aeneas who employ the verb *orare* fail to achieve their desired goals. Even in Mezentius' case, Aeneas' silence does not permit Mezentius to die with peace about his burial. Mezentius is connected to Turnus not only through Aeneas' pitiless act but also through the fact that both Mezentius' and Turnus' appeals stand out as the centerpieces of their respective death scenes.[134]

Aeneas and Turnus

When Aeneas brandishes his spear in the poem's final moments, he jeers at Turnus for retreating (889). Turnus responds that Aeneas' words do not frighten him and that only the gods give reason to fear (894–895). He pursues Aeneas with a large stone but fails to hit him:

> sed neque currentem se nec cognoscit euntem
> tollentemue manus saxumue immane mouentem;
> genua labant, gelidus concreuit frigore sanguis.
> tum lapis ipse uiri uacuum per inane uolutus
> nec spatium euasit totum neque pertulit ictum.   *Aen.* 12.903–907

> [But Turnus does not know if it is he
> himself who runs or goes or throws
> that massive rock; his knees are weak; his blood
> congeals with cold. The stone itself whirls through
> the empty void but does not cross all of
> the space between; it does not strike a blow. (M. 12.1203–1208)]

The ineffectiveness of Turnus' throw demonstrates not merely his panicked flight but also a catastrophic failure of strength (905). Turnus' throw proves to be essential for understanding the tension between vision and rhetoric in the poem's final scene. His failure to strike Aeneas with the rock introduces a simile that alludes to a passage from the *Iliad*,[135] sheds light on Turnus' state of mind, and, more importantly, suggests that Turnus' rhetorical skills are about to fail him. Virgil explains this failure with a description of a dreaming person:

> ac uelut in somnis, oculos ubi languida pressit
> nocte quies, nequiquam auidos extendere cursus
> uelle uidemur et in mediis conatibus aegri
> succidimus; *non lingua ualet,* non corpore notae
> sufficiunt uires *nec uox aut uerba sequuntur:*
> sic Turno, quacumque uiam uirtute petiuit,
> successum dea dira negat.   *Aen.* 12.908–914

> [Just as in dreams of night, when languid rest
> has closed our eyes, we seem in vain to wish
> to press on down a path, but as we strain,
> we falter, weak; our tongues can say nothing,

the body loses its familiar force,
no voice, no word, can follow: so whatever
courage he calls upon to find a way,
the cursed goddess keeps success from Turnus. (M. 12.1209–1216)]

Virgil involves the reader at this critical juncture in the text. The dream that Virgil portrays is one that we—note the first-person plural reference at 910—might experience when we are weak. In this dream, our tongues cannot move (911), and our voices have stopped functioning. Turnus, as if in a dream (903), will soon vainly seek escape; his command of rhetoric begins to fail him (*nec uox aut uerba sequuntur*, 912), as does his strength (912).[136] Many years ago, Hunt noted that "the most terrifying aspect of the simile applied to Turnus is the absolute soundlessness, as though . . . he were enveloped in a deathly silence, unable to make any sound himself."[137] This dream anticipates Turnus' loss of the rhetorical power we have seen him wield in the past.[138]

For the moment, however, Virgil focuses on the *sensus . . . uarii* (914–915) that course through Turnus' heart:

> . . . Rutulos *aspectat* et urbem
> cunctaturque metu letumque instare tremescit,
> nec quo se eripiat, nec qua ui tendat in hostem,
> nec currus usquam *uidet* aurigamue sororem.
>   Cunctanti telum Aeneas fatale coruscat,
> sortitus fortunam *oculis*, et corpore toto
> eminus intorquet.   *Aen.* 12.915–921

[. . . he looks in longing at the Latin ranks
and at the city, and he hesitates,
afraid; he trembles at the coming spear.
He does not know how he can save himself,
what power he has to charge his enemy;
he cannot see his chariot anywhere;
he cannot see the charioteer, his sister.
In Turnus' wavering Aeneas sees
his fortune; he holds high the fatal shaft;
he hurls it far with all his body's force. (M. 12.1218–1227)]

In these lines, Turnus is recorded as twice hesitating and twice looking as he anticipates his own impending death, rather freely interpreted by Mandelbaum as "the coming spear" (M. 12.1220). These hesitations alternate with

Turnus' glances at his people and his city. He looks for his absent chariot and then hesitates as Aeneas comes upon him. Throughout the episode, Turnus' vision does not prompt decisive action.

Soon, however, Virgil shifts to Aeneas' perspective. Virgil notes that, unlike the hesitating Turnus, Aeneas takes hold of his opportunity with his eyes (*sortitus fortunam oculis*, 920). Virgil's depiction of Aeneas as one who sees and utilizes opportunities is indebted to the duel between Hector and Achilles in *Iliad* 22, where Achilles looks upon the fair skin of his adversary (εἰσορόων χρόα καλόν, ὅπῃ εἴξειε μάλιστα, 22.321) prior to delivering the death blow. The placement of Virgil's allusion to Homer is significant because the allusion comes just after the description of Turnus' hesitating glances.[139]

Achilles carefully avoids the windpipe to allow the wounded Hector to respond (*Il.* 22.328–329). The prolonging of dialogue as a form of retribution plays a role in Achilles' vengeance. Like Achilles, Aeneas does not kill his enemy immediately but allows for a final exchange.[140] Aeneas strikes Turnus in the thigh, causing his knees to buckle (926–927), and the spectators rise up with a groan. Turnus, now fallen to the position of a suppliant, speaks to Aeneas:

> ille humilis supplex *oculos* dextramque precantem
> protendens 'equidem merui nec deprecor' inquit;
> 'utere sorte tua. miseri te si qua parentis
> tangere cura potest, *oro* (fuit et tibi talis
> Anchises genitor) Dauni miserere senectae
> et me, seu corpus spoliatum lumine mauis,
> redde meis.'   *Aen.* 12.930–936

> [Then humble, suppliant, he lifts his eyes
> and, stretching out his hand, entreating, cries:
> "I have indeed deserved this; I do not
> appeal against it; use your chance. But if
> there is a thought of a dear parent's grief
> that now can touch you, then I beg you, pity
> old Daunus—in Anchises you had such
> a father—send me back or, if you wish,
> send back my lifeless body to my kin." (M. 12.1240–1248)]

With Turnus' appeal for Aeneas to pity the old age of Daunus, Virgil clearly alludes to Homer's description of Priam's appeal to Achilles to pity him based on the memory of Peleus (*Il.* 24.503–504).[141] On that occasion, Priam's plea was successful, for Achilles wept, recalling his father and Patroclus (αὐτὰρ Ἀχιλλεὺς κλαῖεν ἑὸν πατέρ', ἄλλοτε δ' αὖτε / Πάτροκλον, *Il.* 24.511–512).[142] Barchiesi links these scenes further by comparing Turnus' gesture of his outstretched hand (930–931) to Achilles' offering of his hand to Priam to kiss (*Il.* 24.506).[143] In that scene, Homer had also stressed the vision that Achilles has of Priam: ὡς Ἀχιλλεὺς θάμβησεν ἰδὼν Πρίαμον θεοειδέα (*Il.* 24.483).[144]

Turnus' invocation of the memory of Daunus and Anchises also recalls the prominent father and son relationship of Lausus and Mezentius in which vision plays a role.[145] This rhetorical use of *commiseratio* is strengthened by Turnus' ocular gesture (930–931).[146] Although, in the past, vision provided a stimulus for heroic acts such as Lausus' intervention for Mezentius, Turnus now hopes to use his own vision to prevent Aeneas from the harshest possible action at the climax of the narrative.

Putnam comments on the way that Virgil calls attention to vision in these lines.[147] Having referred to Aeneas' eyes earlier in this passage (920), Virgil mentions Turnus' eyes. As he gazes at Aeneas, Turnus shows his supplicating attitude (930). The vision of Turnus defeated was the very thing for which Pallas had prayed (10.463). To a certain extent, Aeneas now fulfills Pallas' prayer, though Turnus sees Aeneas, not Pallas, as victor.[148]

As Virgil goes on to describe Turnus in this final scene, he places emphasis on Turnus' words.[149] Turnus tenders, in his final breaths, the last occurrence of *orare* in the poem (933). The oral supplication that characterizes Turnus' final moments is the very sort of supplication that characterized Turnus from the moment he was introduced in his confrontation with Allecto in Book 7 (*iuueni oranti*, 446). Turnus also weighed down heaven with prayers at the ninth book's opening (9.24) and played the orator in the assembly with Drances, on which occasion he used the verb *orare* to indicate his wish to confront Aeneas in battle (11.442). That wish has now been granted, and Turnus reverts to supplication, his familiar pattern of behavior in dire moments.[150] Now, in the midst of his last appeal, Turnus seeks to manipulate the visual aspects of their final encounter. Turnus attempts to convince Aeneas that it is sufficient that the crowd has seen him conquered:

> 'uicisti et uictum tendere palmas
> Ausonii *uidere*; tua est Lauinia coniunx,
> ulterius ne tende odiis.' stetit acer in armis
> Aeneas *uoluens oculos* dextramque repressit;

et iam iamque magis cunctantem flectere sermo
coeperat, infelix umero cum apparuit alto
balteus et notis fulserunt cingula bullis
Pallantis pueri, uictum quem uulnere Turnus
strauerat atque umeris inimicum insigne gerebat.　　*Aen.* 12.936-944

["For you have won, and the Ausonians
have seen me, beaten, stretch my hands; Lavinia
is yours; then do not press your hatred further."
Aeneas stood, ferocious in his armor;
his eyes were restless and he stayed his hand;
and as he hesitated, Turnus' words
began to move him more and more—until
high on the Latin's shoulder he made out
the luckless belt of Pallas, of the boy
whom Turnus had defeated, wounded, stretched
upon the battlefield, from whom he took
this fatal sign to wear upon his back,
this girdle glittering with familiar studs. (M. 12.1249-1261)]

The vision of the crowd is deemed by Turnus to be ample punishment. One should contrast Turnus' view with the first sentiments of Aeneas, who once proclaimed the blessedness of those who had died in the sight of their fathers.[151] When Turnus mentions his father, however, it is with a view to being spared (12.932-936). Accordingly, it is interesting that Turnus encompasses both the mention of spectators (*Ausonii uidere*, 937) that had been an aspect of Aeneas' opening speech (*ante ora patrum*, 1.95) and the sense of suffering that a son's mortal combat can bring to a father. But, instead of citing the nobility and honor of dying in the sight of one's parent, Turnus attempts to use his rhetorical ability to gain freedom by employing the notions of vision and fathers to form a pretext of mercy.[152] Turnus' rhetoric begins to take hold, and Aeneas, as once the Homeric Menelaus did for Adrestos (*Il.* 6.45-50), considers sparing Turnus.[153] Putnam observes, "For a moment at least, words appear to triumph over deeds."[154]

It is not, however, a contrast between words and deeds that Virgil posits in the final lines, but between words that fail to persuade and vision that *produces* deeds. Through Turnus' last attempt to employ rhetorical persuasion, the hesitation that had first belonged to Turnus briefly comes upon Aeneas (940), as Turnus' appeal begins for a moment, to achieve its goal.

Denis Feeney reduces Highet's *Speeches* to the formula "poetry good, rhetoric bad."[155] Feeney cautions against adopting such a facile posture and then states,

> What does emerge from the *Aeneid* is a mistrust of powerful language . . . : powerful language distorts reality, or the truth, in its single-minded pursuit of its particular aim; and it exploits ungovernably the emotions of speaker and audience. The power of words in a private and a public context is thus suspect in analogous ways.[156]

Feeney then adds, "High rhetoric does not admit of dubiety: it is concerned in the first and last resort, not with any objective establishment of a truth, but with getting its way."[157]

Through his rhetorical appeal, Turnus nearly does get his way;[158] Aeneas stays his right hand and rolls his eyes,[159] an action that contrasts distinctly with Turnus' extension of his gaze toward Aeneas (930). Aeneas takes note of Turnus' eyes and his gesture: "his pleading right hand . . . dramatizes the total helplessness of the once proud warrior."[160] Conversely, he who was introduced with his hands raised in supplication now must check his right hand (939), which also contrasts to Turnus' brachial posture.[161]

Aeneas' vision tells him what to do. This formulation is important precisely because Aeneas has been regarded as having a moral blindness that allows him to become angry.[162] But Virgil is not stressing inward vision or blindness. Rather he writes of physical, almost "atomic" vision. Aeneas is prompted to act *literally* by what he sees.

When Philodemus writes about anger, he considers it in terms of θεραπεία (therapy) and suggests that, when a person can see his situation clearly, he will seek a remedy (*De Ira* 3.3). In the final moments of the poem, Aeneas sees—physically sees—a token of the past.[163] In this case, the physical object is the *imago* that reminds Aeneas synecdochically both of the retributive justice of the Danaids[164] and, more importantly, that the buckler was worn by Turnus unjustly:

> ille, oculis postquam *saeui monimenta doloris*
> exuuiasque *hausit*, furiis accensus et ira
> terribilis: 'tune hinc spoliis indute meorum
> eripiare mihi? Pallas te hoc uulnere, Pallas
> immolat et poenam scelerato ex sanguine sumit.'
> hoc dicens ferrum aduerso sub pectore condit

feruidus; ast illi soluuntur frigore membra
uitaque cum gemitu fugit indignata sub umbras.   *Aen.* 12.945–952

[And when his eyes drank in this plunder, this
memorial of brutal grief, Aeneas,
aflame with rage—his wrath was terrible—
cried: "How can you who wear the spoils of my
dear comrade now escape me? It is Pallas
who strikes, who sacrifices you, who takes
this payment from your shameless blood." Relentless,
he sinks his sword into the chest of Turnus.
His limbs fell slack with chill; and with a moan
his life, resentful, fled to Shades below. (M. 12.1262–1271)]

The sight of Pallas' buckler evokes the memory of a meaningful past relationship; this recollection parallels the way that Pallas and Evander had appeared before his eyes in Book 10.[165] On that occasion, too, "right hands" were
an aspect of his movement into battle, for Aeneas there recalled the pledges
that were offered in good faith (8.169).[166] Now Aeneas' vision will prompt an
action similar to one that he took in Book 10, just after seeing the vision of
Pallas and Evander.

Just as Hercules brought light into Cacus' darkness,[167] Aeneas kindles like
a flame (946) and prepares to dispatch Turnus to the darkness (*umbras*, 952);
a glittering *balteus* (12.941–942) leads to the deprivation of light that Turnus'
words had foreshadowed (*spoliatum lumine*, 12.935). Knauer pointed out
many years ago that Turnus' departure to the Underworld (951–952) refers
to the *Aeneid* 1 passage in which Aeneas' members loosen with chill and he
groans while extending his hands to heaven (*soluuntur frigore membra / in-
gemit*, 1.92–93) just before he makes his *terque quaterque* pronouncement.[168]
He who was once powerless before the darkness of the storm now exhibits
his power to dispatch his enemy to darkness (952).

Turnus' effort to manipulate vision through rhetoric represents rhetoric's
final attempt in the poem to hold its place in the new world of visual communication. Conversely, Aeneas' action is prompted by what he sees, and
he grasps at least one aspect of the message recorded in Pallas' *balteus* (945).
Aeneas "drinks in" visually not only the item that evokes Pallas' death but
the content that prods him to retributive justice, namely a memorial of the
Danaids.[169] As Michael Putnam once noted, "Aeneas now also absorbs the
symbolism of the scene Turnus has donned and kills in a burst of passion-

ate vengeance" (157).[170] This victory, Harrison points out, is coordinated with the statue group that adorned the portico of Augustus's temple of Palatine Apollo. That statue group clearly represents the barbarous kind of opposition that Augustus had faced at Actium.[171]

The symbolic content of the buckler represents the retribution of one generation on behalf of another. By killing their husband/cousins, the daughters of Danaus avenge their father's banishment. Aeneas retaliates against Turnus on behalf of Pallas, who is likewise of a different generation. Furthermore, like the Danaids who kill their bridegrooms on their wedding night, Aeneas, in slaying Turnus, kills not just any bridegroom but the one who would have otherwise married Lavinia.[172]

There is yet another subtext to the Danaid theme, noted by Gian Biagio Conte, namely, the motif of those who die before their time. The obvious association is with Pallas, whose life was interrupted as were the lives of the sons of Aegyptus. Epigrams in the *Palatine Anthology* and even Roman inscriptions offer numerous examples of the sadness of lives cut short. Thus, Conte notes, the intertext of the tale of the Danaids is necessarily that of Pallas' cruel fate.[173]

The myth of these women, however, presumably also contains an element of mercy, insofar as Hypermestra set herself apart from her sisters by sparing Lynceus. Even if Hypermestra and Lynceus are not at the centerpiece of the portrayal on Pallas' *balteus*, their story is certainly an aspect of that myth. Accordingly, as Aeneas beholds the final artistic image that he will see in the poem, he is confronted with a tale characterized by both retribution and mercy.

The action he takes is prompted by his vision not only of the object itself but also of the image's unforgiving message; that is clearly how Aeneas chooses to interpret its content. By slaying Turnus, Aeneas not only fulfills the teleological expectations of *dum conderet urbem*, for which Turnus' death as rival bridegroom is a necessary prerequisite, but, more importantly, he also shows that the power of the vision of the buckler and its content outweighs the power of Turnus' rhetoric. Turnus' attempt ultimately fails because the power of images triumphs over the power of persuasion. Aeneas' vision will not be obscured by any obfuscating information that pours from Turnus' mouth; one might also recall that Hercules did not yield to the vision-impairing smoke that Cacus poured forth from his jaws (8.252–253).

In the final analysis, vision in the *Aeneid* is causative, prompting action. Ever since Julius Caesar's famous Pontic triumph, vision and victory had been intimately joined in the alliterative "telegraphic"[174] message *ueni, uidi, uici*, which connotes swift action in response to visual appraisal.[175] Moreover, Roman topography also suggested the supremacy of iconography. To enter the Forum of Augustus, one would leave the old forum, characterized by its rostra, curia, comitium, and other elements of its rhetorical Republican past, traverse Caesar's forum, which connected the new senate house with Caesar's personal tribute to the Julian *gens*, and finally come into the visually rich Forum of Augustus, which was being constructed at the very time Virgil was writing the *Aeneid*. Society mirrored the topographical change of the time. Even as a Roman could pass between these fora, Rome was now passing from one means of communication into another.

The final battle of Aeneas and Turnus marks, at the conclusion of Virgil's grand narrative, a similar transition: the telos of Troy's refounding as Rome depends both on Aeneas' dismissal of the rhetorical appeal of Turnus and on Aeneas' response to the visual stimuli that Pallas' buckler encompasses. Rhetorical skill cannot sway Aeneas, for he acts upon what he sees and, as *voyant-visible*, secures vision's victory over rhetoric.[176] The ending's humanity, its glory,[177] however, lies in the *voyant-visible*'s hesitation, his momentary willingness to listen one last time, before embracing the images and their power.

CHAPTER 6

Conclusion

ANTE ORA PARENTUM

❧

During the early to middle Augustan age when Virgil was writing the *Aeneid*, Rome was in the midst of a generally positive period. Civil wars had ended, and the emperor's extensive building program was well underway. Romans were seeing the tangible symbols of a new order, and the sights they beheld underscored the constructive aspects of the *pax Augusta*. The doors of the temple of Janus were closed, old structures were being refurbished while new were being built, and there was an aura of security and optimism. The first emperor used monuments to reach the widest possible audience, for the Augustan settlement was confirmed by what was visible.

The optimism that this visible message generated can be fruitfully considered in the light of Merleau-Ponty's ontology of vision, which gives sight the primary place in humankind's construction of reality. Such primacy of vision contrasts with the negative gaze that in Merleau-Ponty's own time stemmed from his contemporary Sartre, later to be adopted and enhanced by Lacan.[1] Merleau-Ponty's understanding of vision, by contrast, is certainly more positive and perhaps even more natural.

My use of the word "natural" when referring to Merleau-Ponty's views is based on a loose connection between his phenomenological theory and the natural philosophy of the ancient atomists such as Democritus, Philodemus, or Lucretius. Yet this connection is, perhaps, not so tenuous as one might guess, for Merleau-Ponty himself saw it:

One has to admit a sort of truth in the naïve descriptions of perception: εἴδωλα or simulacra, etc. the thing of itself giving perspectives, etc. But all this takes place in an order that is no longer that of objective Being, that is the order of the lived or the phenomenal which is precisely to be justified and rehabilitated as the foundation of the objective order.[2]

Merleau-Ponty wanted to rehabilitate the ancient principles of atomism and to connect them with his own version of a "down-to-earth" phenomenological philosophy. This so-called rehabilitation was the elevation of vision to primary status among the senses, which resulted in his establishment of it as the quintessential means by which to define the human experience:

> Vision is not a certain mode of thought or presence to self; it is the means given me for being absent from myself, for being present at the fission of Being from the inside, the fission at whose termination, and not before, I come back to myself.[3]

Here Merleau-Ponty offers his version of a spiritual transcendence, but not one that goes to the level of the God's-eye view. Rather, it is tied to and confirmed by the reality of what is seen. The confirmation of one's surroundings by vision allows the person who sees "to return to himself," thereby establishing and confirming the person's existence through clear perception of present circumstances. Such perception is Merleau-Ponty's "order of the lived or the phenomenal," which provides "the foundation of the objective order" cited above.

Merleau-Ponty's work offers a general guideline for considering Virgilian characterization: Aeneas, as *voyant-visible*, defines his reality on the authority of what he sees. Merleau-Ponty's ideas also allow us to consider Virgil generally, his text as a whole, and the milieu in which Virgil lived and wrote, for among Merleau-Ponty's many metaphors is that of the painter who, as an artist, uniquely participates in vision. "The painter," Merleau-Ponty writes, "whatever he is, *while he is painting* practices a magical theory of vision." The painter "celebrates . . . visibility" and, with a sense of informed wonder, "lives in fascination" of the world, for "the hand that paints is the same hand that touches worldly things."[4] In my analysis of vision in the *Aeneid*, I have generally regarded Virgil as such a painter, and the *Aeneid* as his canvas.

When Virgil puts the final brushstroke on that canvas, vision emerges as a driving force within the narrative. In killing Turnus before the eyes of the Italians (12.928, 937) Aeneas fulfills the pronouncement he made when we met him in the first book. There he proclaimed those who had died on the plains of Troy to be three and four times blessed, better off than he and his men, who appeared likely to die in obscurity on the sea (1.94). The public fate that in Book 1 Aeneas had preferred to undistinguished death at sea he now imputes to Turnus. Virgil thus brings Aeneas' pronouncement full circle; death comes not to Aeneas but through him when he responds violently to visual stimulus provided by the buckler of Pallas, while Daunus will be consoled only by seeing or soon learning of Turnus' public death.

The theme of visual response to circumstances in the midst of which he himself is an object of others' vision begins and ends Aeneas' public life and work. In the phenomenological terms of Merleau-Ponty, Aeneas is the *voyant-visible* who is seen and who simultaneously perceives, whose visible actions establish Virgil's visual agenda for the poem. Hints about the primacy of vision, particularly in battle scenes, are evident throughout the poem. When, in the second book, Aeneas details the horror of the fall of Troy, he offers a poignant exemplar of death before a father's eyes. He describes the slaughter of Polites, specifically stating that Polites, wounded and hotly pursued by Pyrrhus, had come within the sight of his parents (*ut tandem ante oculos euasit et ora parentum, / concidit ac multo uitam cum sanguine fudit*, 2.531–532).[5] Soon Aeneas will cite this very event to convince his own father to leave Troy:

> . . . iamque aderit multo Priami de sanguine Pyrrhus,
> natum *ante ora patris*, patrem qui obtruncat ad aras.
> hoc erat, alma parens, quod me per tela, per ignis
> eripis, ut mediis hostem in penetralibus utque
> Ascanium patremque meum iuxtaque Creusam
> alterum in alterius mactatos sanguine *cernam?*   *Aen.* 2.662–667

>   [. . . Pyrrhus—
> who massacres the son before his father's
> eyes, and then kills the father at the altars—
> still hot from Priam's blood, will soon be here.
> And was it, then, for this, my gracious mother,
> that you have saved me from the blade, the fire—
> that I might see the enemy within
> the heart of my home, my son Ascanius,
> my father, and Creüsa at their side,
> all butchered in each other's blood? (M. 2.894–903)]

To rouse Anchises from depression and lethargy, Aeneas juxtaposes Priam's vision of Polites with Pyrrhus' subsequent murder of Priam. The rhetorical question he poses to his mother here is likewise dependent upon vision:

Aeneas cites his own perception of the situation, and the massacre to which he refers is that of the entire family at once, all generations cut down together horrifically before his own eyes.

After Creusa's appeal to Aeneas to allow her to accompany him, Virgil puts a similar phrase (*ora parentum*) to more affirming use:

> Talia uociferans gemitu tectum omne replebat,
> cum subitum dictuque oritur mirabile monstrum.
> namque manus inter *maestorumque ora parentum*
> ecce leuis summo de uertice uisus Iuli
> fundere lumen apex, tactuque innoxia mollis
> lambere flamma comas et circum tempora pasci.   *Aen.* 2.679–684

> ["So did Creüsa cry; her wailing filled my father's house. But even then there comes
> a sudden omen—wonderful to tell:
> between the hands, before the faces of
> his grieving parents, over Iülus' head
> there leaps a lithe flametip that seems to shed
> a radiance; the tongue of fire flickers,
> harmless, and plays about his soft hair, grazes
> his temples." (M. 2.920–928)]

Anchises, who also witnesses this spectacle, interprets it correctly to betoken Iulus' and Troy's future hope and, based on a further confirmation of thunder and a shooting star (692–694), agrees to go with Aeneas. Vision confirms the destiny of Aeneas' line, triggering in Anchises a willingness to acquiesce and follow his son.

This thread of visual confirmation charges the text with a sense of purpose throughout, for it is closely connected with one generation's beholding the other, especially in situations involving battle. When, in Book 5, Aeneas witnesses the mock warfare in Sicily, not surprisingly the phrase *ante ora parentum* occurs again. As children enact the *lusus Troiae*, it is clear that a new generation has learned from the previous one that war shall be a part of its way of life:

> incedunt pueri pariterque *ante ora parentum*
> frenatis lucent in equis, quos omnis euntis
> Trinacriae mirata fremit Troiaeque iuuentus.   *Aen.* 5.553–555

[The boys advance high on their bridled horses;
in even ranks, before their parents' eyes,
they glitter; as they pass, the men of Troy
and Sicily admiringly murmur. (M. 5.727–730)]

As Romans later would do at the *lusus Troiae* festival, established as a regular event by Augustus,[6] the Trojan sons and fathers clearly enjoy these games. The spectators take delight not merely in the panoply but in the similarity of sons to their fathers:

excipiunt plausu pauidos gaudentque tuentes
Dardanidae, ueterumque *agnoscunt ora parentum.*
postquam omnem laeti consessum oculosque suorum
lustrauere in equis, signum clamore paratis
Epytides longe dedit insonuitque flagello.   *Aen.* 5.575–579

[The cheering Dardans greet the anxious squadrons
and, watching those young faces, recognizing
the features of their ancestors, are glad.
And when the boys had crossed the whole enclosure,
had ridden happily before their elders,
then Epytides gave the signal shout
from far and cracked his whip. (M. 5.755–761)]

Virgil's twofold inclusion of the phrase *ante ora parentum* suggests that, even amidst the excitement of such games, parents derive satisfaction in seeing one generation succeeding another. Yet the occurrence of the phrase in a mock battle perhaps also offers a reminder that a son may die in battle. The mock battle (580–587) that immediately follows these lines confirms the latter possibility and reinvests the phrase with due solemnity.

This solemnity of theme is sustained when Aeneas enters the Underworld. There he sees youths placed upon pyres before their fathers' faces (*impositique rogis iuuenes ante ora parentum*, 6.308).[7] Such pathos is an important aspect of sight in the *Aeneid*: fathers see sons die, and parents bury their children.

The ineffectiveness of the Rutulians begging before the walls of the Latin capital offers another somber example of this phrase:

. . . nec sociis aperire uiam nec moenibus audent
accipere *orantis*, oriturque miserrima caedes

defendentum armis aditus inque arma ruentum.
exclusi *ante oculos lacrimantumque ora parentum*
pars in praecipitis fossas urgente ruina
uoluitur, immissis pars caeca et concita frenis
arietat in portas et duros obice postis.   *Aen.* 11.884–890

[. . . they do not dare to open them for their
own comrades and are deaf to any prayers.
And then, a wretched butchery: some guard
the gates with swords; their own companions charge
against them. Some, shut out, are rolled headlong
into the trenches, driven by the rout,
before the eyes, the very presence of
their weeping parents; some, with loosened reins,
blind, spur ahead and batter at the gates,
the tough and bolted doors. (M. 11.1171–1180)]

Here the failure of rhetorical appeal of the returning soldiers is contrasted with the vision of those who are watching from within the city. In this passage, vision heightens and invests the narrative with pathos; the visibly pathetic state of the Latins before the walls does not permit their appeals to be successful. Rather, vision informs reality, and, even though the situation of those perishing is dire, the defenders of the city will not hear their plea because they understand that some must perish to save others. In a general way, Virgil's inclusion of this detail of the sacrifice of a smaller band of men for the good of the city resumes the old theme of *unum pro multis* laid out in Book 5 (815), at the close of which book Palinurus fulfills Neptune's prophecy. That same axiom of one being sacrificed for many informs the way that rhetorical appeal fails in the poem's second half, in which the necessity of dealing with visible realities, such as those cited above, proves to be more important than the appeals to a less violent and less obviously sacrificial objective.

The poem's final scene, as we have observed, is the culmination of the development of the idea of vision's primacy. Virgil's hero has been visible throughout the poem. He commanded the center of attention in the storm of Book 1 not merely by what he said during the storm but by the way he was perceived after the storm, when he and the storm's survivors had washed up on the Carthaginian shores. In that first speech after the storm, the image of a confident leader in the midst of a crisis is crucial, and Aeneas is aware of this need. For this very reason he feigns hope with his face and suppresses his own fear (*spem uultu simulat, premit altum corde dolorem*, 1.209 ["he counterfeits hope in his face; his pain / is held within, hidden" (M. 1.291–292)]). Visibility thus provides Aeneas a platform among his men and garners the attention of the gods, of Dido, of the Sibyl, and even of the Underworld's shades. In the poem's second half, visibility gives him credibility and authority on the battlefield. He is visible, and his acts, however violent, are also visible. There is a kind of disclosure to Aeneas' conduct, for one sees this hero at work in a way that is thoroughly different from the behavior of Achilles, who remains withdrawn from the fighting during much of the *Iliad*. Both Aeneas' inner struggle to act upon what he sees and his unwillingness at the poem's close to indulge Turnus reveal that, in the struggle between words and sight, vision has emerged as the victor. Aeneas' final action in the poem confirms vision's primacy. It is to the hero's credit that he acts upon what he sees with a reluctance that befits one who tries to combine both clemency and justice.

This act of killing Turnus is the quintessential act of foundation for the city of Rome, the poem's telos, and it establishes the legacy of the visible empire that Augustus will inherit from his forebear. In short, the final appeal in the poem succumbs to vision. Such a prompt for action is perhaps fitting for the first founder of the city that Augustus would later find brick but leave marble. Rhetoric has lost its strength in the face of the vision that Aeneas allows to motivate him. In the Rome of Augustus, the words and arguments of the old Republic are losing their hold upon the Roman psyche and, in their place, the power of images has begun to take hold. With the *Aeneid*'s final scene, the words of Turnus are silenced, but the image of Aeneas as victor over his enemy endures, as do the monuments of Augustan Rome.

Notes

❧

1. *PROPHAENOMENA AD VERGILIUM*

1. John Keats, "On First Looking into Chapman's Homer." This and all subsequent quotations of John Keats' poetry come from *The Poems of John Keats*, ed. Jack Stillinger (Cambridge, MA, 1978).

2. See Richard Heinze, *Virgils Epische Technik* (Stuttgart, 1972; rpt. of 1915), ch. 4, 169–170; for the contributions of Heinze, Otis, and Anderson, see below, p. 6.

3. William S. Anderson, *The Art of the* Aeneid (Englewood Cliffs, NJ, 1969), 25–26.

4. Brooks Otis, *Virgil: A Study in Civilized Poetry* (Oxford, 1963), 41–96.

5. Otis, *Virgil*, 49.

6. Don Fowler, "Narrate and Describe: The Problem of Ekphrasis," *JRS* 81 (1991): 25–35; Don Fowler, "Deviant Focalization in Vergil's *Aeneid*," *Proceedings of the Cambridge Philological Society* 216 (1990): 42–63. Both are reprinted in Fowler's *Roman Constructions: Readings in Postmodern Latin* (Oxford, 2000).

7. Gérard Genette, *Narrative Discourse: An Essay in Method*, trans. Jane E. Lewin (Ithaca, 1980); translation of *Figures III: Discours du récit* (Paris, 1972).

8. J. Davidson, "The Gaze in Polybius' *Histories*," *JRS* 81 (1991): 10–24.

9. A thorough study is that of Matthew Leigh, *Lucan: Spectacle and Engagement* (Oxford, 1997).

10. Mary Jaeger, *Livy's Written Rome* (Ann Arbor, 1997), esp. 24–27; Andrew Feldherr, *Spectacle and Society in Livy's* History (Berkeley, 1998).

11. R. A. Smith, *Poetic Allusion and Poetic Embrace in Ovid and Virgil* (Ann Arbor, 1997), esp. 141–159.

12. Michael C. J. Putnam, "Pius Aeneas and the Metamorphosis of Lausus," in Putnam, *Virgil's* Aeneid: *Interpretation and Influence* (Chapel Hill, 1995), 134–151.

13. That speech in general is important to the *Aeneid*'s telos is clear

from Jupiter's pronouncements about the Fates in Book 1. See Denis Feeney, *The Gods in Epic* (Oxford, 1991), 139–140.

14. Generally on rhetoric's ineffectiveness, see Gilbert Highet, *The Speeches in Vergil's* Aeneid (Princeton, 1972), 285–289; Denis C. Feeney, "The Taciturnity of Aeneas," *CQ* n.s. 33 (1983): 204–219.

15. Two well-known works describe each kind of power, namely, Paul Zanker, *The Power of Images in the Age of Augustus* (Ann Arbor, 1988), and George Kennedy, *The Art of Rhetoric in the Roman World 300 BC–AD 300* (Princeton, 1972).

16. Zanker, *Power of Images*, 4.

17. Karl Galinsky, *Augustan Culture: An Interpretive Introduction* (Princeton, 1996), 148. For an overview of Galinsky's study, see my review in *BMCR* 97.2.24.

18. Galinsky, *Augustan Culture*, 200.

19. David Castriota, *The Ara Pacis Augustae and the Imagery of Abundance in Later Greek and Early Roman Imperial Art* (Princeton, 1995), 124–144.

20. Philip Hardie, *Virgil's* Aeneid: *Cosmos and Imperium* (Oxford, 1986), 336–375 (on the ecphrasis of the shield of Aeneas in *Aen.* 8); see also his "*Ut pictura poesis?* Horace and the Visual Arts," in *Horace 2000: A Celebration: Essays for the Bimillenium*, ed. Niall Rudd (Ann Arbor, 1993), 120–139; also discussed vis-à-vis Augustan poetry by Peter White, *Promised Verse: Poets in the Society of Augustan Rome* (Cambridge, MA, 1993).

21. Galinsky, *Augustan Culture*, 260–261; Michael C. J. Putnam, *Artifices of Eternity: Horace's Fourth Book of Odes* (Ithaca, 1986), 327–339; R. O. A. M. Lyne, *Horace: Behind the Public Poetry* (New Haven, 1995).

22. Michael C. J. Putnam, *Tibullus: A Commentary* (Norman, OK, 1973), 43–46, 182–195.

23. Barbara Kellum, "Sculptural Programs and Propaganda in Augustan Rome: The Temple of Apollo on the Palatine," in *The Age of Augustus: An Interdisciplinary Conference Held at Brown University April 30–May 2, 1982*, ed. R. Winkes (Louvain, 1985), 169–176. Also Eckard Lefèvre, "Das Bild-Programm des Apollo-Tempels auf dem Palatin," *Gymnasium* 98 (1991): 84–85.

24. Hardie, *Cosmos and Imperium*, 379.

25. Other characters, too, have traits of the *voyant-visible;* while I will comment on these characters as such from time to time, Aeneas will be the primary focus of this study.

26. Roman Ingarden, *Cognition of the Literary Work of Art*, trans. Ruth A. Crowley and Kenneth R. Olsen (Evanston, IL, 1974); Hans-George Gadamer, *Truth and Method*, ed. Joel C. Weinsheimer and Donald G. Marshall (New York, 1993).

27. Gotthold Ephraim Lessing, *Laocoon: An Essay on the Limits of Painting and Poetry*, trans. Edward A. McCormick (Baltimore, 1990); see Ingarden, *Cognition*.

28. For examples of this type of analysis on medieval and Renaissance literature, one might consider Michèle Gally and Michel Jourde, *L'Inscrip-*

tion du Regard: Moyen Âge-Renaissance (Paris, 1995); for Shakespeare's work, see Philip Armstrong, Shakespeare's Visual Regime: Tragedy, Psychoanalysis, and the Gaze (New York, 2001).

29. David Fredrick, ed., The Roman Gaze: Vision, Power, and the Body (Baltimore, 2002).

30. Alison R. Sharrock, "Looking at Looking: Can You Resist a Reading?" in The Roman Gaze, ed. David Fredrick, 276–278.

31. Friedrich Nietzsche, "Beyond Good and Evil," in The Philosophy of Nietzsche, ed. Willard H. Wright, trans. Helen Zimmern (New York, 1954), 449; Martin Jay, Downcast Eyes: The Denigration of Vision in Twentieth-Century French Thought (Berkeley, 1993), 189, 265.

32. Jean-Paul Sartre, The Words, trans. Bernard Frechtman (New York, 1964).

33. "The White Mythology: Metaphor in the Text of Philosophy," in Jacques Derrida, Margins of Philosophy, trans. Alan Bass (Chicago, 1982), 250–251. See Jay, Downcast Eyes, 509–510.

34. Jean-Francois Lyotard, Discours, Figure (Paris, 1985).

35. Jay, Downcast Eyes, esp. 298–328.

36. Generally on Merleau-Ponty's philosophy, see Galen A. Johnson, The Merleau-Ponty Aesthetics Reader: Philosophy and Painting (Evanston, IL, 1993); also Michael B. Smith and Galen A. Johnson, eds., Ontology and Alterity in Merleau Ponty (Evanston, IL, 1990).

37. Maurice Merleau-Ponty, The Visible and the Invisible, trans. Alphonso Lingis (Evanston, IL, 1968), 1–4; cf. Maurice Merleau-Ponty, "Eye and Mind," in The Primacy of Perception and Other Essays on Phenomenological Psychology, the Philosophy of Art, History and Politics, ed. James M. Edie (Evanston, IL, 1964), 168.

38. Merleau-Ponty, "Eye and Mind," 176.

39. Merleau-Ponty, "Eye and Mind," 175.

40. Merleau-Ponty, "Eye and Mind," 168.

41. Merleau-Ponty, "Eye and Mind," 168.

42. Heinze, Virgils Epische Technik, 259–260: "die Wärme des sympathetischen Gefühls, andererseits die Kraft des sittlich-religiösen und nationalen Empfindens, beides zusammen. . . ."; translation of Hazel Harvey, David Harvey, and Fred Robertson, Virgil's Epic Technique by Richard Heinze (Berkeley, 1993), 207–208.

43. Heinze, Virgils Epische Technik, 169–170.

44. Otis, Virgil, 49. See also Gian Biagio Conte, The Rhetoric of Imitation: Genre and Poetic Memory in Virgil and Other Latin Poets, ed. Charles Segal (Ithaca, 1986), esp. 166–172; Heinze, Virgils Epische Technik, 69–70.

45. Anderson, Art of the Aeneid, 25–26. Moreover, Conte, Rhetoric of Imitation, 154–158, et passim, discusses the polycentricity that Virgil's use of multiple points of view allows. While point of view will be, from time to time, an aspect of my argument, my concern is broader, for I consider vision to be a feature of narrative per se, not only to indicate viewpoint. On Virgil's empathetic style, see also Anderson's recent contribution, "Aeneid 11: The Saddest Book," in Reading Vergil's Aeneid, ed. Christine Perkell (Norman,

OK, 1999), 195–209. On literary approaches to point of view, see Conte, *Rhetoric of Imitation*, 154n.

46. Cf. Lucretius' description of *templa serena / despicere unde* (*DRN* 2.8–9), discussed below. Charles Segal, "Art and the Hero: Participation, Detachment, and Narrative Point of View in *Aen.* 1." *Arethusa* 14 (1981): 54, refers to Aeneas' participatory voice.

47. Maurice Merleau-Ponty, "The Metaphysical Man," in *Maurice Merleau-Ponty, Sense and Non-Sense*, trans. Hubert L. Dreyfus and Patricia Allen Dreyfus (Evanston, IL, 1964), 90.

48. Merleau-Ponty, "Metaphysical Man," 134; my emphasis.

49. Merleau-Ponty, "Metaphysical Man," 94: "From the moment I recognize that my experience, precisely insofar as it is my own, makes me accessible to what is not myself, that I am sensitive to the world and to others, all the beings which objective thought placed at a distance draw singularly nearer to me. Or, conversely, I recognize my affinity with them; I am nothing but an ability to echo them, to understand them, to respond to them."

50. Immanuel Levinas, *Totality and Infinity: An Essay on Exteriority*, trans. Alphonso Lingis, Duquesne Studies 24 (Pittsburgh, 1969), 50–51, is critical of Merleau-Ponty's establishment of "the gaze" as an important aspect of his concept of the *voyant-visible*. Levinas goes so far as to regard gaze to be an act of dominating "the other" by confining that person within our own categories. As such, gaze could be seen as a violation of the difference, a stifling of the other's "infinity."

51. On this word, see Martin Heidegger, *The Question Concerning Technology and Other Essays*, ed. W. Lovitt (New York, 1977), 163. See also Jay, *Downcast Eyes*, 269–270; also, Gadamer, *Truth and Method*, 111.

52. Fowler, "Narrate and Describe."

53. Michael C. J. Putnam, *Virgil's Epic Designs: Ekphrasis in the* Aeneid (New Haven, 1998).

54. See also Alessandro Barchiesi, "Virgilian Narrative: Ecphrasis," in *The Cambridge Companion to Vergil*, ed. Charles Martindale (Cambridge, 1997), 271–281; B. W. Boyd, "*Non Enarrabile Textum*: Ecphrastic Trespass and Narrative Ambiguity in the *Aeneid*," *Vergilius* 41 (1995): 71–90; Hardie, *Cosmos and Imperium*, 336–337. I have elsewhere considered examples of Virgilian ecphrasis, *Poetic Allusion*, 26–43, 171–188.

55. Zanker, *Power of Images*, 24.

56. For this, generally see Zanker, *Power of Images*, 210–215; Galinsky, *Augustan Culture*.

57. Above, p. 2.

58. On the importance of the concept of telos to the *Aeneid* and how, from early on in the poem, Virgil uses the Latin term *finis* to reflect this concept, see Feeney, *Gods in Epic*, 137–138.

59. See *OED*, s.v. vision; Martin Jay has an excellent presentation of visual words (*Downcast Eyes*, 1).

60. See *OLD*, s.v. *uideo*; also Lewis and Short, s.v. *uideo*.

61. [. . .] s.v. *spic-* and *uid-*. Also [. . .], s.v. *aspicio, uideo*. Alois Walde and Julius Pokorny, *Vergleichendes Wörterbuch der Indogermanischen Sprachen*

(Berlin, 1927–1932). Johann Hofmann and Alois Walde, *Lateinsches etymologisches Wörterbuch* (Heidelberg, 1938–1956).

62. Netta Berlin, "War and Remembrance: *Aeneid* 12.554–60 and Aeneas' Memory of Troy." *AJP* 119 (1998): 13–14.

63. On the connection between images and memory, see Ellen J. Esrock, *The Reader's Eye: Visual Imaging as Reader Response* (Baltimore, 1994), 188–190.

64. Elizabeth Block, *The Effects of Divine Manifestation on the Reader's Perspective in Vergil's* Aeneid (New York, 1981), 122.

65. Block, *Effects of Divine Manifestation*, 120.

66. A. J. Boyle, "The Canonic Text: Virgil's *Aeneid*," in *Roman Epic*, ed. A. J. Boyle (London, 1993), 101, takes the poem itself to be an *imago*. While one need not expect the word to have had so broad an interpretation in antiquity, clearly this particular term suggests a wide range of possibilities.

67. See Harriet I. Flower, *Ancestor Masks and Aristocratic Power in Roman Culture* (Oxford, 1996), 109–114, 209–211.

68. "If the fortresses / of Carthage and the vision of a city / in Libya can hold you, who are Phoenician, / why, then, begrudge the Trojans' settling on / Ausonian soil?" (M. 4.471–475).

69. Maurice Merleau-Ponty, "Primacy of Perception and Its Philosophical Consequences," in *The Primacy of Perception and Other Essays on Phenomenological Psychology, the Philosophy of Art, History and Politics*, ed. James M. Edie (Evanston, IL, 1964), 13.

70. On this relationship, see *Vergil, Philodemus, and the Augustans*, ed. David Armstrong, Jeffrey Fish, Marilyn B. Skinner, and Patricia Johnston (Austin, 2004).

71. "Es ist weiter auffallig, wie atomistiche sozusagen die Menschenweld des virgilischen Epos geschilderd ist!" (Heinze, *Virgils Epische Technik*, 411) ["Moreover it is remarkable how 'atomistic', so to speak, is the world of men which Virgil depicts in his epic" (translation of Harvey, Harvey, and Robertson, *Vergil's Epic Technique*, 319)].

72. H. Diels and W. Kranz, *Fragmente der Vorsokratiker*, 6th ed. (Berlin, 1952) = *DK*, 21A86 (= Theophrastus, *De sensu* 7); see Cyril Bailey, ed., *Titi Lucreti Cari: De Rerum Natura Libri Sex*, vol. 3 (Oxford, 1947), 1180.

73. Fragment cited from G. S. Kirk and J. E. Raven, *The Presocratic Philosophers: A Critical History with a Selection of Texts*, 2nd ed. (Cambridge, 1983), 428.

74. Translation of Kirk and Raven, *Presocratic Philosophers*, 428.

75. In his customary way of linking opposites, Alcmaeon posits that from the water that surrounds the eye afire "flashes forth when it's struck" (*DK*, 14A5. Cf. Aristotle, *De sensu* 437a24; see also W. K. C. Guthrie, *Greek Philosophers, from Thales to Aristotle* [New York, 1960], 348).

76. Kirk and Raven, *Presocratic Philosophers*, 428–429.

77. Further on the cave and Plato's use of images generally, see W. J. T. Mitchell, *Iconology: Image, Text, Ideology* (Chicago, 1986), 91–93.

78. English translation by Hippocrates G. Apostle, *Aristotle's Metaphysics* (Grinnell, IA, 1979). Greek text of W. Jaeger, ed., *Aristotelis Meta-*

physica, 980a22–25 (Oxford, 1957): καὶ μάλιστα τῶν ἄλλων ἡ διὰ τῶν ὀμμάτων. οὐ γὰρ μόνον ἵνα πρ ἄττωμεν ἀλλὰ καὶ μηθὲν μέλλοντες πράττειν τὸ ὁρᾶν αἰρούμεθα ἀν τι πάντων ὡς εἰπεῖν τῶν ἄλλων.

79. The Orphic concept of vision seems to have been an empathetic process; see F. M. Cornford, *From Religion to Philosophy: A Study in the Origins of Western Speculation* (New York, 1957), 198–199; Aristotle, fr. 45 1483a19. See Jay, *Downcast Eyes,* 30 n. 33, who notes that the Pythagoreans did not regard vision as having particularly emotional aspects.

80. For that reason, Lucretius advises his reader to flee the *simulacra* of the object of love: *nam si abest quod ames, praesto simulacra tamen sunt / illius et nomen dulce obuersatur ad auris. / sed fugitare decet simulacra . . .* (4.1061–1063) ["For if the object of your love is absent, yet images of her are at hand, her loved name is present to your ears. But it is best to flee those images. . . ."]. Lucretius' language seems to make the seen lover into a mere object. See William A. Merrill, ed., *T. Lucreti Cari De Rerum Natura* (New York, 1907), ad loc., p. 643.

81. *De ira,* fr. 6.

82. E.g., Accius, Ennius, Plautus, Terence, etc.; two stone theaters are built or begun in Rome in the 50s BC (the theater of Pompey and the theater of Marcellus).

83. E.g., the famous statues (all fine Greek imports) that Atticus placed in the Porticus Pompeiana.

84. On the distinction based on stylistic categories, see August Mau, *Pompeii: Its Life and Art,* trans. Francis W. Kelsey (Washington, DC, 1973), 456–457. For a recent reappraisal of these categories and development of the discussion, see John R. Clarke, *Houses of Roman Italy, 100 B.C.–A.D. 250: Ritual, Space and Decoration* (Berkeley, 1991), 31–77; also Eleanor Winsor Leach, "Patrons, Painters, and Patterns: The Anonymity of Romano-Campanian Painting and the Transition from the Second to the Third Style," in *Literary and Artistic Patronage in Ancient Rome,* ed. Barbara K. Gold (Austin, 1982), 135–173.

85. This included gem collections, Pliny tells us, a painting of Ajax and Medea by Timomachus (*HN* 7.126, 35.26, and 136), an infamous statue of Cleopatra (Cass. Dio 51.22.3; Appian, *BellCiv* 2.102), and corselet made of British pearls (Pliny, *HN* 9.116). See L. Richardson, jr, *New Topographical Dictionary of Ancient Rome* (Baltimore, 1992), 167; Galinsky, *Augustan Culture,* 208.

86. Zanker, *Power of Images,* 24.

87. See C. J. Mackie, *The Characterisation of Aeneas* (Edinburgh, 1988), 19–20; Debra Hershkowitz, "The *Aeneid* in *Aeneid* 3," *Vergilius* 37 (1991): 73. Hans-Peter Stahl ("Aeneas—An '(Un)heroic' Hero?," *Arethusa* 14 [1981], 161) regards Aeneas' speech as heroic in the epic tradition.

88. *Iliad* 12.22–23: "and Simoeis, where much ox-hide armour and helmets were tumbled / in the river mud, and many of the race of the half-god mortals" (trans. Richmond Lattimore, *The* Iliad *of Homer* [Chicago, 1951]).

89. Wendell Clausen, "An Interpretation of the *Aeneid,*" in *Virgil: Critical Assessments of Classical Authors,* vol. 4, ed. Philip Hardie (London,

1999), 66, notes that Aeneas is simply not the adventurer that Odysseus is and that Aeneas has none of Odysseus' resilience or lightheartedness.

90. All text of the *Odyssey* is taken from Thomas W. Allen, ed. *Homeri Opera*, vols. 3–4, 2nd ed. (Oxford, 1975).

91. All translations of the *Odyssey* are from Richmond Lattimore, trans. *The Odyssey of Homer* (New York, 1975).

92. For a different understanding of this passage, see Joseph Farrell, "*Aeneid* 5: Poetry and Parenthood," in *Reading Vergil's Aeneid: An Interpretive Guide*, ed. Christine Perkell (Norman, OK, 1999), 104.

93. R. O. A. M. Lyne (*Further Voices in Vergil's* Aeneid [Oxford, 1987]) notes that "heroes like Odysseus may and do indulge the vast, passionate and superb egoism which is their natural prerogative. . . . Odysseus indulges despair, rage, and revenge. . . . And Aeneas? He too is by nature a hero of this stamp. . . . [p. 107] In the storm of Book 1, he despairs and gives vent to that egoistic emotion. But he — and here is the crucial difference — minded to subordinate his emotional impulses to nothing and no one, *must* subordinate them: to Fate and Jupiter's Will" (106). Despite many apt observations in comparing these two passages, Lyne fails to show how, in Aeneas' *terque quaterque* speech, the hero subordinates his emotion to the will of Jupiter.

94. Virgil notably imitates the song of Demodocus with the ecphrasis of *Aeneid* 1.453–493, to which Aeneas also responds tearfully. In that passage, Aeneas sees the visual images that Odysseus only heard.

95. Cf. Horace, *Odes* 4.4.116–117.

96. Charles Segal, "Art and the Hero: Participation, Detachment, and Narrative Point of View in *Aen.* 1," *Arethusa* 14 (1981): 67–83, reprinted in *Virgil: Critical Assessments of Classical Authors*, ed. Philip Hardie, 4 vols. (London, 1999), notes that Aeneas' speech here "is as fully immersed in the participatory voice as it is in the violence of the storm," Segal, in Hardie vol. 4, 44–45.

97. Suggested translation of Lewis and Short, s.v. *incubo* 1.B.3; this seems to me preferable to Mandelbaum's translation of the verb he renders "hangs on" (M. 1.128).

98. Fol. 77r.

99. *Aen.* 1.112. Kenneth Quinn (*Virgil's* Aeneid: *A Critical Description* [Ann Arbor, 1969], 103) has noted, "We watch it [the storm] for a while through Aeneas's eyes . . . before returning to the world of fantasy for the following episode" (124–156).

100. Viktor Pöschl, *The Art of Vergil: Image and Symbol in the* Aeneid, trans. Gerda Seligson (Ann Arbor, 1970), 20–21. Commentators have also posited this connection; see R. G. Austin, ed., *P. Vergili Maronis Aeneidos Liber Primus* (Oxford, 1971), ad 587 and R. D. Williams, ed., *The* Aeneid *of Virgil*, vol. 1, *Books 1–6* (New York, 1972), ad loc.

101. "Perhaps one day you will remember even / these our adversaries with pleasure" (M. 1.283–284).

102. "He counterfeits hope in his face" (M. 1.291).

103. See also Sarah Spence, *Rhetoric of Reason and Desire: Vergil, Augustine, and the Troubadours* (Ithaca, 1988). Spence argues that, in spite of

passages such as this one that affirm oratory's effectiveness, "Vergil himself incorporates elements that question just such a conclusion" (20).

104. Anderson (*Art of the* Aeneid, 25) comments on the statesman simile: "Using anachronism with skill, Vergil evokes a scene of the Roman civil wars—potentially recognizable to every adult in his first audiences. . . . Neptune's activity . . . indicates the goal of peace and political stability toward which Aeneas is groping, then beyond that, points to the achievement of Augustus." See also Spence, *Rhetoric of Reason and Desire*, 11–15.

105. For an alternate view of Aeneas' motivation for hunting the stags, see Gregory A. Staley, "Aeneas' First Act: 1.180–94," in *Why Vergil? A Collection of Interpretations*, ed. Stephanie Quinn (Wauconda, IL, 2000), 52–64.

106. Segal, "Art and the Hero," 390, notes that Aeneas here enjoys "a god-like vista."

107. Harry C. Rutledge, "*Pius Aeneas:* A Study of Vergil's Portrait," *Vergilius* 33 (1987): 15.

108. E.g., Jacques Derrida, *Writing and Difference* (Chicago, 1978), 27–28. Derrida wishes to emancipate his reader from standard phenomenological terminology such as fact (the viewed) and meaning (the mental construction of what is viewed). He recognizes that such emancipation is not possible but suggests that one can resist it.

109. P. DeLacy, "Distant Views: The Imagery of Lucretius 2," *CJ* 60 (1964): 49–55.

110. This and all subsequent texts and translations of the *DRN* are taken from Bailey, *Titi Lucreti Cari*, vol. 1.

111. ["They blow across the earth in a tornado; together . . . [they] attack the sea. . . ." (M. 1.120–123)] This aspect of the parallel is noted in passing by Segal, "Art and the Hero," 46.

112. Thomas Rakoczy, *Böser Blick, Macht des Auges und Neid der Götter: Eine Untersuchung zur Kraft des Blickes in der griechischen Literatur.* Classica Monacensia 13 (Tübingen, 1996).

113. Raymond Prier, *Thauma Idesthai: The Phenomenology of Sight and Appearance in Archaic Greek* (Tallahassee, 1989).

114. See also Galen A. Johnson, *Earth and Sky, History and Philosophy: Island Images Inspired by Husserl and Merleau-Ponty* (New York, 1989).

115. Licinia Ricottilli, *Gesto e Parola nell'Eneide* (Bologna, 2000).

116. J. William Hunt, *Forms of Glory: Structures and Sense in Virgil's Aeneid* (Carbondale, IL, 1973), 8.

117. E.g., Hunt, *Forms of Glory*, 83: "Three vivid pictures of concrete action stand out memorably in the whole expanse of the *Aeneid:* the sword buried in the breast of Dido, the magic shield raised on Aeneas' shoulder, the sword buried in the breast of Turnus."

118. Hunt, *Forms of Glory*, 10.

119. Zanker, *Power of Images*, 3.

120. Galinsky, *Augustan Culture*, 245 et passim.

121. Feeney, *Gods in Epic*, 129–187.

122. See Eleanor Winsor Leach, "Viewing the *Spectacula* of Aeneid 6," in

Reading Vergil's Aeneid, ed. Christine Perkell (Norman, OK, 1999), 111-127, esp. 122.

123. Cf. Highet, Speeches, 285.

2. RUSE AND REVELATION

1. Punctuation is that of Helen Gardner, ed., The New Oxford Book of English Verse (Oxford, 1972), no. 467, p. 486.

2. Both Milton and Jerusalem were published in 1804.

3. As, for example, in his longer Jerusalem, Blake does with such lines as the alliterative "O melancholy Magdalen behold the morning over Malden break" (Jerusalem 65.38).

4. Fundamental studies of the gods' encounters with human beings have already been done. These include Werner Kühn, Götterzenen bei Vergil (Heidelberg, 1971); Elizabeth Block, The Effects of Divine Manifestation on the Reader's Perspective in Vergil's Aeneid (New York, 1981); Denis Feeney, The Gods in Epic (Oxford, 1991), 129-187; Anne Peper Perkins, "Divine Epiphany in Epic: Supernatural Episodes in the 'Iliad,' the 'Odyssey', the 'Aeneid' and 'Paradise Lost'" (Diss., Washington University, 1986), DAI-A 47/08, p. 3028, Feb. 1987; Jacques Perret, "Les Dieux de l'Eneide," AFL Nice 50 (1985): 331-337; E. L. Harrison, "Divine Action in Aeneid Book 2," in Oxford Readings in Vergil's Aeneid, ed. Stephen J. Harrison (Oxford, 1990), 46-59; Agathe Thornton, The Living Universe: Gods and Men in Virgil's Aeneid. Mnemosyne ser. (Lugdunum, 1976); Robert Coleman, "The Gods in the Aeneid," in Virgil, ed. Ian McAuslan and Peter Walcot (Oxford, 1990), 39-64; A. Perotti, "De diis in Aeneide," Latinitas 38 (1990): 10-24.

5. See, on this topic, P. Heuzé, "Miratur: Sur quelques nuances de l'admiration vergilienne," Hommages à la memoire de Ernest Pascal, ed. L. Finette, Cahiers des Études Anciennes 24.2 (1990): 397-403.

6. See Kenneth Reckford, "Recognizing Venus (I): Aeneas Meets His Mother," Arion ser. 3, col. 3 (1995-1996): 1-42. Reckford offers many apt observations on the sexual tension in this passage. Also Antonie Wlosok, Die Göttin Venus in Vergils Aeneis, Bibliothek der Klass. Altertumswissenschaft, NF 2 Reihe 21 (Heidelberg, 1967), 97.

7. Od. 7.19, 13.221.

8. Michelle Wilhelm, "Venus, Diana, Dido, and Camilla in the Aeneid," Vergilius 33 (1987): 45. See also Gail C. Polk, "Vergil's Penelope: The Diana Simile in Aeneid 1.498-502," Vergilius 42 (1996): 40.

9. R. D. Williams, ed., The Aeneid of Virgil: Books 1-6 (New York, 1972), ad loc.

10. Wlosok, Die Göttin Venus, 77.

11. Cf. Turnus with Camilla, Aen. 11.507.

12. R. D. Williams ([1972], ad 382, p. 190) points out that many have noted that Apollo, not Venus, actually aids Aeneas in the third book. Yet, as Williams suggests, Virgil here exploits the irony of the situation.

13. Feeney (Gods in Epic, 183) notes that it is typical of Virgil to allow

human characters to have "difficulty in recognizing the divine at work in the poem."

14. R. G. Austin, ed., *P. Vergili Maronis Aeneidos Liber Primus* (Oxford, 1971), ad 404.

15. Further on divine deception, see James J. O'Hara, *Death and Optimistic Prophecy in Vergil's* Aeneid (Princeton, 1990), 118–122; also Tamar R. M. E. Nelson, "Deception, Gods and Goddesses in Homer's *Iliad,*" *Acta Ant. Hung.* 37 (1996/1997): 181–197.

16. R. D. Williams (1972), ad loc., who so comments on *restitit* (588).

17. Michael von Albrecht ("The Art of Mirroring in Virgil's *Aeneid,*" in *Virgil: Critical Assessments of Classical Authors*, vol. 4, ed. Philip Hardie [London, 1999], 3) has noted that each character sees the other as a divinity in this first encounter. He calls this Virgil's "mirroring technique."

18. See Damien Nelis, *Vergil's* Aeneid *and the* Argonautica *of Apollonius Rhodius.* ARCA Classical and Medieval Texts, Papers and Monographs 39 (Leeds, 2001), 123.

19. Austin (1971), ad 589–593. See also John C. Conington and Henry N. Nettleship, eds., *The Works of Virgil* (Hildesheim, 1979), vol. 2, ad loc.

20. See Peter E. Knox, "A Note on *Aeneid* 1.613," *CP* 79 (1984): 304–305. Nicolas P. Gross (*Amatory Persuasion in Antiquity: Studies in Theory and Practice* [Newark, DE, 1985], 42) notes that Nausicaa's speech reveals her "intense, amatory interest" in Odysseus.

21. "First at the very sight of him . . . / . . . Sidonian Dido / was startled" (M. 1.859–861).

22. "I'll hold her fast / with great love for Aeneas" (M. 1.944–945). Austin (1971), ad loc., understands line 675 to mean either, "just as I love him myself," or "on my side" (also Conington/Nettleship); R. D. Williams (1972), ad loc., also follows Conington/Nettleship, "be kept on my side," to sustain the possible military metaphor of 673. I believe, however, that Venus' "battle plan" is clearly that of love, so she employs Amor to carry out this charge.

23. Feeney (*Gods in Epic*, 133) notes that Virgil manufactures a connection between Juno's name and the verb *iungo*, which makes Juno uniquely suited to pronounce that a couple be joined in wedlock.

24. On the tension between Venus and Juno and how it differs from Virgil's models of Apollonius and Homer, see Nelis, *Vergil's* Aeneid, 146–148.

25. "I shall unite the two in certain marriage / And seal her as Aeneas' very own; / And this shall be their wedding" (M. 4.167–169).

26. So R. D. Williams (1972), ad loc.

27. Gross (*Amatory Persuasion in Antiquity*, 106) suggests that Dido is easily captured by Cupid because she was childless.

28. Ellen Oliensis, "Freud's *Aeneid,*" *Vergilius* 47 (2001): 52; Stavros Frangolidis, "Duplicity and Gift-Offerings in Vergil's *Aeneid* 1 and 2," *Vergilius* 38 (1992): 33; for a highly erotically suggestive reading, see Akbar Kahn, "The Boy at the Banquet: Dido and Amor in Vergil *Aen.* 1," *Athenaeum* 90.1 (2002): 193–195.

29. On erotic connotations of *foueo*, e.g., see J. N. Adams, *The Latin Sexual Vocabulary* (London, 1982), 208.

30. I shall consider the appearance of Mercury to Aeneas below.

31. F. E. Brenk points out that night is consistently associated with Palinurus in "Wind, Waves, and Treachery: Diodorus, Appian, and the Death of Palinurus in Virgil," *Aevum* 62 (1988): 69–80.

32. R. D. Williams, ed., *P. Vergili Maronis Aeneidos Liber Quintus* (Oxford, 1960), ad 843, p. 204. On the genealogy of the Trojan kingship, see William S. Anderson, "Trojan, Dardania, Roman: The Power of Epithets in the *Aeneid*," in *Approaches to Teaching Vergil's* Aeneid, ed. W. S. Anderson and Lorina N. Quartarone (New York, 2002), 56.

33. W. H. Roscher in *Ausführliches Lexikon der Griechischen und Römischen Mythologie*, ed. W. H. Roscher, vol. 1 (Leipzig, 1884–1887), 422–449, s.v. Apollon.

34. On Neptune's role, see R. O. A. M. Lyne, *Words and the Poet: Characteristic Techniques of Style in Vergil's* Aeneid (Oxford, 1989), 176–177. Lyne connects Neptune's desire for this sacrifice with divine cannibalism, based on the etymology of "Saturnus" as deriving from *saturare* and Venus' reference to Juno's having devoured the city of the Phrygians (*Phrygum exedisse . . . / urbem*, 5.785–786). The etymology of Phorbas' name might suggest that there is something to Lyne's views. There has been little shortage of discussion about Virgil's account of Palinurus, or Aeneas' confusion (6.161) as to which corpse needs to be expiated, according to the Sibyl's instructions in *Aeneid* 6.149–153. See R. D. Williams (1972), xxvii–xxviii; Vinzenz Buchheit, *Von der Entstehung der Aeneis*. Nachr. Der Giessner Hochschulgesellschaft 33 (Munich, 1964), 131–143, attempts to reconcile the two traditions preserved in the *Aeneid*, while others, such as T. Beres (*Die Entstehung der Aeneis* [Wiesbaden, 1982], 281–282) suggest that the accounts are incompatible but Virgil would have reconciled them upon revision of the poem. F. E. Brenk ("*Vnum pro multis caput:* Myth, History and Symbolic Imagery in Vergil's Palinurus Incident," *Latomus* 43 [1984]: 776–801) states that Virgil allowed both versions to stand because each has its own attractive features. Brenk (796–781) traces the account's literary ancestry to the anthology tradition of shipwrecked sailors (e.g., *Anth. Pal.* 7.273). See Philip Hardie, *The Epic Successors of Virgil* (Cambridge, 1993), 32; and C. Bandera, "Sacrificial Levels in Virgil's *Aeneid*," *Arethusa* 14 (1981): 223. Julia Dyson (*King of the Wood: The Sacrificial Victor in Virgil's* Aeneid [Norman, OK, 2001], 77–94) regards the conflict in Virgil's text as representing a twofold account of death on land and death by drowning, which is a feature also of the tradition surrounding Aeneas' own death (see esp. 93–94). Further on the etymology of Phorbas' name, see Michael Paschalis, *Virgil's* Aeneid: *Semantic Relations and Proper Names* (Oxford, 1997), 201.

35. ["And you will only have to mourn one Trojan, / one lost within the eddies of the sea; / one life shall be enough instead of many" (M. 5.1075–1077).] On the application of the phrase *unum pro multis* to Palinurus, not to Misenus, see Richard Heinze, *Virgil's Epic Technique*, trans. David Harvey, Hazel Harvey, and Fred Robertson (Berkeley, 1993), 366–367 n. 15 (= [1928] 452 n. 1).

36. It seems possible that such correspondences anticipate the poem's

final scene where, also at a book's end, Aeneas will hesitate (*cunctantem*, 940) while his eyes drink in spoils (*oculis . . . / exuuiasque hausit*, 945–946), before he kills Turnus as a sacrificial victim (*immolat*, 949). The eyes (here of Palinurus) must resist the words (of Phorbas) and, through this resistance, a child of Troy will die. In the final scene, the child of Troy will resist words but prevail.

37. Nicholas Horsfall (*Virgil*, Aeneid 7: *A Commentary* [Leiden, 2000], ad loc.) states that "this is a rare, yet insignificant name."

38. Although the meaning "covering" is rare, the derivative from καλύπτειν is clear. See Pierre Chantraine, *La formation des noms en grec ancien* (Paris, 1932; rpt. 1968), 23, s.v. καλύπτειν; also Hjalmar Frisk, *Griechisches Etymologisches Wörterbuch*, vol. 1. (Heidelberg, 1954–1960), s.v. καλύπτειν, 768–769.

39. See R. D. Williams (1972), ad 421, who explains the legend and how it conflicts internally with the description of peace under Latinus at 7.46.

40. For *transcribi*, the primary meaning is that of the transference of power, and secondarily, as Servius notes, a financial metaphor. See Servius, ad loc., referring to a financial metaphor at Horace, *Sermones*, 2.3.69–76; also R. D. Williams (1972), ad loc.

41. R. D. Williams (1972), ad 7.425–426.

42. "Your task: / to guard the shrines and images of the gods. / Let men run war and peace: war is their work" (M. 7.586–588).

43. All commentators since Servius note the Homeric citation. See Conington/Nettleship, ad loc., vol. 3, pp. 44–45. The comparison between Turnus and Hector contains an aspect of irony in that Hector appears as a champion of the Trojan War, while Turnus appears as a warrior who sleeps while the enemy invades his land.

44. Horsfall, ad loc.

45. See R. D. Williams (1972), ad 456–457.

46. Iarbas specifically asks Jupiter if he sees the events in Carthage (*aspicis haec?* 208).

47. While his words are different from Turnus' final appeal to Aeneas in Book 12, we shall see that Iarbas' general comportment toward Jupiter is not entirely unlike Turnus' attitude toward Aeneas in the poem's closing scene.

48. Monica R. Gale, "Poetry and the Backward Glance in Virgil's *Georgics* and *Aeneid*," TAPA 133 (2003): 334, with n. 33.

49. *et nunc ille Paris cum semiuiro comitatu, / Maeonia mentum mitra crinemque madentem / subnexus, rapto potitur . . .* (4.215–217). ["And now this second Paris, with his crew / of half-men, with his chin and greasy hair / bound up beneath a bonnet of Maeonia, / enjoys his prey. . . ." (M. 4.287–290)].

50. See J. H. Starks, "*Fides Aeneia*: The Transference of Punic Stereotypes in the *Aeneid*," CJ 94 (1999): 255–284.

51. Sara Mack, *Patterns of Time in Vergil* (Hamden, CT, 1978), 62.

52. See Michael C. J. Putnam, "The Hesitation of Aeneas," in *Virgil's Aeneid: Interpretation and Influence*, ed. Michael C. J. Putnam (Chapel Hill,

1995), 152–171. Putnam regards Aeneas' hesitation as the result of Dido's irrationality rather than a reluctance on Aeneas' part to regain his vision of his fated land.

53. See O'Hara, *Death and the Optimistic Prophecy*, 70–71; Walter Moskalew, *Formular Language and Poetic Design in the* Aeneid. *Mnemosyne*, Suppl. 73 (Leiden, 1982), 132; F. J. Worstbrock, *Elemente einer Poetik der Aeneis*. *Orbis Antiquus* (Münster, 1963), 116–117; Viktor Pöschl, *The Art of Vergil: Image and Symbol in the* Aeneid, trans. Gerda Seligson (Ann Arbor, 1962), 96; Georg Nicolaus Knauer, *Die Aeneis und Homer: Studien zur poetischen Technik Vergils, mit Listen der Homerzitate in der Aeneis* (Göttingen, 1964), 275–276; William A. Camps, *An Introduction to Virgil's* Aeneid (Oxford, 1960), 39; Kühn, *Götterzenen bei Vergil*, 124–126.

54. Iris does appear in Book 4 to cut Dido's lock, but this is not a true vision. See W. R. Johnson's discussion, *Darkness Visible* (Berkeley, 1976), 67–68.

55. Lines 607–610. There will be, however, a description of her ascension that O'Hara (*Death and Optimistic Prophecy*, 72) takes as a link between these two scenes. This echo does not necessarily suggest that Iris is deceptive on this occasion. The goddess focuses on the need for Turnus to take swift action because of the removal of Aeneas from the battle.

56. On water and sacred groves, see Ingrid E. M. Edlund, *The Gods and the Place: Location and Function of Sanctuaries in the Countryside of Etruria and Magna Graecia (700–400 B.C.)* (Stockholm, 1987), 54; also O'Hara, *Death and Optimistic Prophecy*, 72.

57. On the location of Turnus by a stream, see Dyson, *King of the Wood*, 113.

58. Philip Hardie, ed., *Virgil* Aeneid *Book IX* (Cambridge, 1994), ad 9.12.

59. Hardie, ad 9.12.

60. Dyson, *King of the Wood*, 163.

61. We recall that Aeneas complied with the god's request by saying, *"sequimur te, sancta deorum, quisquis es"* (4.576–577).

62. R. D. Williams (1972), ad 19–20, p. 279.

63. "his eyes rush in to everything, admiring" (M. 8.801).

64. J. Foster ("Three Passages in Virgil," *SO* 66 [1991]: 109–114) suggests that Virgil's use of the verb *orare* even evidences a bit of arrogance on Turnus' part.

65. Hardie, ad loc.

66. While Turnus' religious washing of his hands certainly follows the proper procedure for a ritual, as Aeneas' own sacral cleansing had in the previous book, Turnus' burdening of the atmosphere with prayers after the revelation stands in stark contrast to Aeneas' promises to respect Tiber and other local deities (8.72–78). Tiber responds to Aeneas' invocation.

67. On nocturnal visions of Aeneas and Turnus in particular, see C. J. Mackie, *"Nox Erat . . . :* Sleep and Visions in the *Aeneid," G&R* 38 (1991): 60–61.

68. Beginning already with Servius, ad loc.; see also Conington/Nettle-

ship: "'Concessere,' have given way, doubtless to milder feelings" (ad loc.); also K. W. Gransden, ed., *Virgil* Aeneid *Book XI* (Cambridge, 1991), ad loc.; R. D. Williams (1972), ad loc.

69. O'Hara, *Death and Optimistic Prophecy*, 32.

70. On this adjective, see Dyson (*King of the Wood*, 60–67), who suggests that the adjective indicates a "menacing tone" (61). While there is no question that some associations with Tiber are more threatening than others (e.g., *Aen.* 8.330–332; cf. Dyson, 67), and Dyson's associations are well reasoned, there is also a descriptive aspect of the word that I believe to be foremost here. At one level, at least, Tiber is greenish blue because such an epithet befits a river, however tawny he may appear to be elsewhere (on *flauus*, see Dyson, 60). I believe, *pace* Dyson, that the association of *caeruleus* with the color blue takes precedence here because, when Virgil has Tiber say in that same line (8.64) that he is *caeruleus Thybris, caelo gratissimus amnis*, Virgil is likely alluding to Ennius' *caeli caerula templa* (*Ann.* 48 Sk.; see Otto Skutsch, ed., *The* Annals *of Q. Ennius* [Oxford, 1985], 281; James J. O'Hara, *True Names: Vergil and the Alexandrian Tradition of Etymological Wordplay* [Ann Arbor, 1996], 51, 138. Also see Philip Hardie, *Virgil's Aeneid: Cosmos and Imperium* [Oxford, 1986], 257). Nevertheless, Dyson's point that Virgil was well aware that Tiber takes his name from the drowning of Aeneas' descendant King Tiberinus is well taken. As in the case of so much of Virgilian narrative, there are voices at work, though here I believe the voice most prominent is the power of the vision itself, a vision that confirms Aeneas' mission and destiny.

71. By having Tiber call attention to the appearance of his own water, Virgil injects into the narrative the visual quality that a first-person account of such an event might have had: just as Aeneas might have described Tiber to engender credence in the hearer (e.g., *ipse deum manifesto in lumine uidi*, 4.358), Tiber describes himself, so that we know some of the details of "what Aeneas saw." Having seen Tiber, Aeneas will see the sow, the sight of which will confirm in yet another way this land to be the land of his destiny. Vision confirms and, indeed, outstrips words.

72. I owe this point to one of the anonymous reviewers at the University of Texas Press.

73. Whether the line is spurious or not, the idea behind *hic locus urbis erit* (46) obtains for this passage.

74. *heu quid agat? quo nunc reginam ambire furentem / audeat adfatu? quae prima exordia sumat?* ["What can he do? With what words dare / he face the frenzied queen? What openings / can he employ?" (M. 4.378–380)].

75. Aeneas leaves orders for the Trojans to guard the camp and not to engage Rutulians in the plain. In these orders one finds a description of the camp as if it were a city, for it has walls (*muros*, 43), turrets (*turribus*, 46), and doors (*portas*, 45). Indeed, in the lines that follow, Virgil tells us that Turnus, accompanied by the advance guard, draws close to the "city" (48). See S. F. Wiltshire, "The Man Who Was Not There," in *Reading Vergil's* Aeneid, ed. Christine Perkell (Norman, OK, 1999), 162–177. Wiltshire aptly characterizes Aeneas' absence as heroic.

76. This is the same person whom Aeneas, in Book 1, had looked for after the storm (1.180–185). In a passage where Aeneas is searching for lost comrades, it is fitting that Aeneas looks for but fails to find "Caicus."

77. *G.* 4.370; see Richard Thomas, ed., *Virgil:* Georgics, 2 vols. (Cambridge, 1988), ad loc., p. 214.

78. Cf. the way that Aeneas reacts before acting when he sees a deity such as Mercury (*attonitus*, 4.282) or a vision such as the white sow (*oculis mirabile monstrum*, 8.83).

79. Turnus is also called "audax" at 7.409, 9.123, and 10.276.

80. Forms of the verb *orare* with Turnus as subject are more frequent than this "frequent" adjective. Cf. 7.446.

81. Lyne (*Words and the Poet*, 186) suggests that *geminas acies* here deviously insinuates the absence of Remus, Romulus' twin.

82. Commentators such as Conington (in Conington/Nettleship, ad 792) have seen a rough analogy between *condet/saecula* and *conderet/urbem*.

83. R. D. Williams (1972), ad 801–802.

84. The lions are notably harnessed by the Dionysiac vines (6.804).

85. This and all translations of the *Georgics* are from L. P. Wilkinson, trans., *Virgil: The* Georgics (Penguin; Middlesex, England, 1982).

86. "In the middle of the shrine, as patron god, I will have Caesar placed."

87. David O. Ross (*Virgil's Elements: Physics and Poetry in the* Georgics [Princeton, 1987], 151) has suggested that the *armenta* approximate *arma* of battle, and Orpheus and Eurydice are obviously a model both for Creusa and Aeneas and for Dido and Aeneas. The Creusa scene contains a reference to the Orpheus-Eurydice passage (in which one should note that, in alternate traditions, another name for Creusa is Eurydice). Virgil is careful at the opening of *Aeneid* 5 to speak of Aeneas as looking back upon smoking Carthage. It is, of course, the looking back of Orpheus that brings about Eurydice's demise. Further, in *Aeneid* 6, Aeneas, as had Orpheus, makes a katabasis and sees Dido in the Underworld.

88. Virgil is also heir to Roman tradition, as the allusion to Ennius shows. On Pindar, see L. P. Wilkinson, *The* Georgics *of Virgil* (Cambridge, 1969; rpt., 1997), 166–171.

89. Karl Galinsky, *Augustan Culture: An Interpretive Introduction* (Princeton, 1996), 223–224, with n. 167; see Andreas Alföldi, *Die Zwei Lorbeerbäume des Augustus* (Bonn, 1973), 55, with pls. V.2–3 and XXI.1; Barbara Kellum, "The City Adorned: Programmatic Display at the *Aedes Concordia Augustae*," in *Between Republic and Empire: Interpretations of Augustus and His Principate*, ed. K. Raaflaub and M. Toher (Berkeley, 1990), 282–283; J. Pollini, "The Acanthus of the Ara Pacis as an Apolline and Dionysiac Symbol of *Anamorphosis, Anakyklosis and umen Mixtum*," in *Von der Bauforschung zur Denkmalpflege: Festschrift für Alois Machatschek*, ed. M. Kubelik and E. Swartz (Vienna, 1993), 182–217, esp. 193–198; J.-B. Giard, *Bibliothèque nationale: Catalogue des monnaies de l'Empire romain I Auguste* (Paris, 1976; rev. 1988), 74–77; Hardie, *Cosmos and Imperium*, 257. Galinsky notes that artistic evidence of the Augustan period reveals Dionysiac motifs often conjoined with the laurel of Apollo. Moreover, Hardie,

Cosmos and Imperium, following an idea of Buchheit (*Von der Entstehung*), also mentions that the comparison of Augustus with Hercules and Dionysus fulfills the requirements of *synkrisis*, the fundamental aim of classical rhetoric's *auxesis* (magnification) in encomium.

90. Horace, too, makes a similar association in the third book of his *Odes: hac arte Pollux et uagus Hercules / enisus arcis attigit igneas, / quos inter Augustus recumbens / purpureo bibet ore nectar, / hac te merentem, Bacche pater, tuae / uexere tigres indocili iugum / collo trahentes, hac Quirinus / Martis equis Acheronta fugit* (*Carm.* 3.3.9–16). ["By such address both Pollux and roving Hercules / aspired to and reached the starry citadels, / reclining with whom Augustus shall/ sip nectar with empurpled lips. / On account of such merit, father Bacchus, / you were conveyed by tigers bearing yokes / on untamed necks; and you, Quirinus, / with Mars's steeds escaped from Acheron"; translation from *Horace: The Complete Odes* and *Epodes with the Centennial Hymn*, trans. W. G. Shepherd (London, 1983).] Augustus is here surrounded by Pollux, Hercules, and even Bacchus, who is the nectar that he sips with *purpureo . . . ore* (14). From this, Horace metonymically glides into an address of Bacchus and describes his train in a manner similar to Anchises' description in *Aeneid* 6. In each passage, Augustus is associated with both Hercules and Bacchus, and Bacchus' visual qualities are described. On the iconographic relationship between Antony and Dionysus, see Christopher Pelling, *Plutarch and History* (Llandysul, Wales, 2002) 197–198, 203–204.

91. Eduard Norden, "Ein Panegyricus auf Augustus in Vergils Aeneis," *RhM* 54 (1899): 466–482, rpt. in *Kleine Schriften zum klassichen Altertum* (Berlin, 1966), 422–436, from which references below are cited.

92. *Suetonius*, trans. J. C. Rolfe (Loeb edition; Cambridge, MA, 1979).

93. Norden (*Kleine Schriften*, 425) once demonstrated that the rhetorician Menander grouped Hercules, Dionysus and Alexander the Great together, and Lucian has Alexander say as much in *Dial. Mort.* 14.6.

94. Moreover, in this tale there is an association of wine with a flame (*quod infuso super altaria mero tantum flammae emicuisset*), the very combination in the middle (*ignis ubi in medio et socii cratera coronant*, 2.528) that presaged, at the close of *Georgics* 2, Caesar "in the middle" at the opening of *Georgics* 3. Perhaps Bacchus, who dominates and civilizes the *oikoumene*, and fearfully demands allegiance, saves those left behind, and because his train is highly visible, perhaps he is a good choice after all for comparison to Augustus. Further on the connection of Octavian/Augustus with Alexander, see Vinzenz Buchheit, *Der Anspruch des Dichters in Vergils Georgika. Impulse der Forschung* 8 (Darmstadt, 1972), 118–147.

95. S.v. oratores, G. Calboli, *Enciclopedia Virgiliana* 3 (Rome, 1987), 869–872; also C. J. Fordyce, ed., *Aeneidos Libri VII–VIII* (Oxford, 1977), ad 153, p. 93.

96. Fordyce, ad loc.

97. Horsfall, ad 170.

98. Horsfall (ad 170) notes that there is a "possibility (given that the previous word too is used in an etymological sense) that Virgil refers to an edi-

fice not only majestic but also the sanctuary of the *gens* itself." Horsfall (ad 171, in reference to the word *regia*) states that "we may want even to think of Augustus' own *domus* on the Palatine" (174).

99. *G.* 4.228, though the Vaticanus lat. 3867 Romanus reads *angustam* ad loc., which reading is adopted by Thomas. For a full and cogent discussion, see Thomas, ad loc.

100. Servius, ad 170; see also R. D. Williams (1972), ad 170–171, and Fordyce, ad 153.

101. The combination *mora festinant* occurs only on one other occasion in Virgil, namely, 6.177, in which they hasten to follow the Sibyl's command to bury Misenus.

102. The shield's description is precisely 100 lines long. Mention of Augustus occurs precisely in the fiftieth line of the description.

103. On the vivid realism of Virgil's depiction, see David A. West ("*Cernere erat:* The Shield of Aeneas," *PVS* 15 [1975–1976]: 1–6), who argues that the narrative could conceivably have been so wrought in metal.

104. Gransden (1991), ad 680–681, pp. 176–177.

105. Augustus is likely to have been so represented in graphic arts as well. One obvious example is the Boscoreale cup, where Augustus is seated in the middle between Venus and Mars. See Ann Kuttner, *Dynasty and Empire in the Age of Augustus: The Case of the Boscoreale Cups* (Berkeley, 1995), 30. Kuttner adds, "The most striking compositional aspect of the central Boscoreale triad is that Mars and Venus are both clearly subordinate in height to Augustus on his throne. Augustus would be no taller standing on their level, yet as he is enthroned, his head is over both of theirs, irresistibly evoking the image of Jupiter, who sits enthroned above the other gods" (34).

3. VISION PAST AND FUTURE

1. On these terms, see Introduction, above, pp. 5–7.

2. Other apparitions in the *Aeneid* often occur at night when the hero is sleeping or when in prayer; cf. Anne Peper Perkins, "Divine Epiphany in Epic: Supernatural Episodes in the 'Iliad,' the 'Odyssey,' the 'Aeneid,' and 'Paradise Lost'" (Diss., Washington University, 1986), esp. 168–200. Following the model of L. Dolezel, *Narrative Modes in Czech Literature* (Toronto, 1973), Perkins makes distinctions between the kinds of viewpoints that Virgil employs for Aeneas' encounter and the posture that Aeneas adopts when he describes his sight of an epiphany (the objective, rhetorical, and subjective modalities). Perkins makes much of the importance of sight in Aeneas' encounters with the divine, considering Virgil's usage of the verb *uidere*, in particular. According to Perkins, the passive use of the verb can suggest possibility or conditionality (186, 189).

3. Ovid may later playfully imitate this passage with reference to Amor when he apparently alludes to this passage in *Ex Ponto* 3.3.16–17.

4. See John C. Conington and Henry N. Nettleship, eds., *The Works of Virgil* (Hildesheim, 1979), ad 159. Conington makes this connection between these "great" gods (cf. 9.258) and their words.

5. My translation. See also L. Richardson, jr, *New Topographical Dictionary of Ancient Rome* (Baltimore, 1992), s.v. *Penates Dei, Aedes*.

6. *Annales* 23, duly noted by all commentators.

7. Heinrich Klausen, *Aeneas und die Penaten*, vol. 1 (Hamburg, 1839), 357.

8. Servius, ad *Aen*. 3.12.

9. See R. D. Williams, ed., *The* Aeneid *of Virgil: Books 1-6* (New York, 1972), ad 167-168.

10. On the connection of Ilus, Iulus, and Ilium, see James J. O'Hara, *True Names: Vergil and the Alexandrian Tradition of Etymological Wordplay* (Ann Arbor, 1996), 121. O'Hara does not, however, treat Ilioneus.

11. Cf. *Aen*. 1.1-7.

12. See Franz Bömer, *Rom und Troia* (Baden-Baden, 1951), 117 n. 14.

13. Brooks Otis, *Virgil: A Study in Civilized Poetry* (Oxford, 1963), 241-242.

14. Philip Hardie, *The Epic Successors of Virgil: A Study in the Dynamics of a Tradition* (Cambridge, 1993), 102. Cf. Elizabeth Block, *The Effects of Divine Manifestation on the Reader's Perspective in Vergil's* Aeneid (New York, 1981), 118.

15. "And I myself / seemed then to weep, to greet him with sad words..." (M. 2.384-385). Cf. Otto Skutsch, ed., *The* Annales *of Quintus Ennius* (Oxford, 1985), 73, fr. 44 (43): *Exim compellare pater me uoce uidetur.* ... ["Then it was father who seemed to lift up his voice and speak to me...."] Translation of E. H. Warmington, *Remains of Old Latin*, vol. 1, *Ennius and Caecilius* (Loeb edition; Cambridge, MA, 1967 [1979]). See also R. G. Austin, ed., *P. Vergili Maronis, Aeneidos Liber Secundus* (Oxford, 1964), ad loc.

16. The translation in brackets has been added to reflect the verb *cerno*, omitted by Mandelbaum's rendering.

17. Austin (1964), ad 282, aptly remarks how dreamlike Aeneas' words are, thus explaining why Aeneas has forgotten Hector's fate.

18. Poulheria Kyriakou, "Aeneas' Dream of Hector," *Hermes* 127 (1999): 321.

19. E. H. Warmington, ed. and trans., *Remains of Old Latin*, vol. 1: *Alexander* (Loeb edition; Cambridge, MA, 1956), 76-79, 244.

20. See Austin (1964), ad 286.

21. See Debra Hershkowitz, "The *Aeneid* in *Aeneid* 3," *Vergilius* 37 (1991): 69.

22. The translation in brackets has been added to reflect the phrase *uisu in medio*, omitted in Mandelbaum's reading.

23. Text of David B. Monro and Thomas W. Allen, eds., *Homeri Opera*, 2 vols., 3rd ed. (Oxford, 1978).

24. This and all subsequent translations of the *Iliad* are from Richmond Lattimore, *The* Iliad *of Homer* (Chicago, 1951).

25. Richard E. Grimm, "Aeneas and Andromache in 'Aeneid' III," *AJP* 88 (1967): 155.

26. Grimm, "Aeneas and Andromache," 155-157.

27. David Quint, "Painful Memories: *Aeneid* 3 and the Problem of the

Past," *CJ* 78 (1982): 33; see also David F. Bright, "Aeneas' Other Nekyia," *Vergilius* 27 (1981): 40-47.

28. Maurizio Bettini, "Ghosts of Exile: Doubles and Nostalgia in Vergil's *parva Troia* (*Aeneid* 3.249ff.)," *CA* 16 (1997): 8-33.

29. Servius, ad 320. ["Rightly so, because she has been admonished about being a concubine" (my translation).]

30. I owe this suggestion to Professor David Quint and other members of the audience for a paper that I read at Yale University, October 2000.

31. With regard to Dido, for example, her downcast gaze follows closely upon Ilioneus' statement that Aeneas, the future hope of Iulus, may not have survived the storm (*sin . . . / nec spes iam restat Iuli . . .* , 1.555-556). When Andromache bends her vision downward, therefore, it is perhaps a display of grief at Aeneas' discomfiting nomenclature *Hectoris Andromache?* and probing question *Pyrrhin conubia seruas?*

32. Grimm, "Aeneas and Andromache," 161-162.

33. On the way the characters and places contrast and are confused by Andromache, see Bettini, "Ghosts of Exile," 12-14, et passim.

34. Julia Dyson, *King of the Wood: The Sacrificial Victor in Virgil's Aeneid* (Norman, OK, 2001), 57.

35. See Julius Pokorny, *Indogermanisches Etymologisches Wörterbuch* (Munich, 1959), s.v. *men-, vol. 1, 726-728.

36. See Mary Jaeger, *Livy's Written Rome* (Ann Arbor, 1997), 15-19.

37. David Quint, *Epic and Empire: Politics and Generic Form from Virgil to Milton* (Princeton, 1993), 59.

38. On this passage, see Block, *Effects of Divine Manifestation*, 120-121. Block, however, regards Creusa as "wifely to the last" (120).

39. Friedrich Klingner, *Virgil: Bucolica, Georgica, Aeneis* (Zürich, 1967), 416.

40. Akbar Kahn, "Exile and the Kingdom: Creusa's Revelations and Aeneas' Departure from Troy," *Latomus* 60 (2001): 907, sees Creusa's words as baffling. While Aeneas clearly does not know specifically where to go, Creusa's words do not seem to mislead Aeneas deliberately. For a more persuasive recent contrast of Creusa's apparition with that of Hector, see Kyriakou, "Aeneas' Dream of Hector," 325-326; also Nicholas Horsfall, "Aeneas the Colonist," *Vergilius* 35 (1989): 11-12.

41. "There days of gladness lie in wait for you: / a kingdom and a royal bride" (M. 2.1056-1057).

42. Conington/Nettleship, vol. 2, ad loc., p. 171.

43. See Monica Gale, "Poetry and the Backward Glance in Virgil's *Georgics* and *Aeneid*," *TAPA* 133.2 (2003): 323-352, esp. 337-339.

44. Accordingly, this departure scene is quite different from the comparable description of Orpheus and Eurydice's departure recorded in *Georgics* 4, where vision spells the doom of the one beheld.

45. Gale ("Poetry," 338) uses the comparable backward glances of Orpheus in *Georgics* 4 and Aeneas in *Aeneid* 2 to contrast Orpheus, a poet who preserves the past by his words, and Aeneas, who secures the future by his actions.

46. ". . . and reached out with his own hands, but could not grasp him; for his spirit departed like smoke beneath the ground, squeaking as it went" [*Virgil:* Georgics, ed. Richard Thomas (Cambridge, 1988), vol. 2, ad 499–502].

47. For more on Anticlea as a model for subsequent literary characters, see Steven Jackson, "Callimachean Istrus and Odysseus' Mother," *WS* 112 (1999): 55–58.

48. Robert J. Edgeworth, "Ascanius' Mother," *Hermes* 129 (2001): 246–250.

49. Kate Mortensen, "Eurydice: Demonic or Devoted Mother," *AHB* 6.4 (1992): 156, considers aspects of Eurydice's motherly role.

50. On Aeneas' first encounter with his mother, see Kenneth Reckford, "Recognizing Venus (I): Aeneas Meets His Mother," *Arion* ser. 3, vol. 3 (1995–1996): 16, where Reckford notes that Venus is a blend of Thetis, Athena, Nausicaa, and the Homeric Aphrodite.

51. 4.471–480.

52. For the details of Palinurus' death, see F. E. Brenk, "*Vnum pro multis caput:* Myth, History and Symbolic Imagery in Vergil's Palinurus Incident," *Latomus* 43 (1984), reviews scholarly opinions, 776–777 and n. 3. See also F. E. Brenk, "Wind and Waves, Sacrifice and Treachery: Diodoros, Appian and the Death of Palinurus in Vergil," *Aevum* 62 (1988): 69–80; more recent, Dyson, *King of the Wood*, 74–94.

53. Reflecting the content of a number of ancient sources, from Pindar (*Ol.* 2.56–62) to Plato (e.g., *Gorgias* 526c and *Phaedo* 114b–c). See Austin (1964), ad 6.637–678; also R. D. Williams (1972), ad 6.637–678.

54. "My father, it was your sad image, / so often come, that urged me to these thresholds" (M. 6.919–920).

55. R. O. A. M. Lyne (*Further Voices in Vergil's* Aeneid [Oxford, 1987], 214) writes: "At this critical moment the hero's gaze is turned from the past to the future, from Troy to Rome."

56. Netta Berlin ("War and Remembrance: *Aeneid* 12.554–60 and Aeneas' Memory of Troy," *AJP* 119 [1998]: 17) suggests that Virgil's use of the word *imago* has "mnemonic force" that causes Aeneas to remember his family.

57. Adam Parry ("The Two Voices of Virgil's *Aeneid*," in *Virgil: A Collection of Critical Essays*, ed. Steele Commager, [Englewood Cliffs, NJ, 1966], 107–123) suggests that Aeneas' inability to embrace the *imago* reflects the mood of sadness and loss, characteristic of the entire epic, further see 112–113. For a similar view, see Wendell Clausen, *Virgil's* Aeneid *and the Tradition of Hellenistic Poetry* (Berkeley, 1987), 83–84.

58. On the significance of *imagines maiorum* in Roman society, see Harriet I. Flower, *Ancestor Masks and Aristocratic Power in Roman Culture* (Oxford, 1996).

59. Paul Zanker, *The Power of Images in the Age of Augustus* (Ann Arbor, 1988), 195.

60. The statues in the Forum of Augustus evoked a collective memory for the viewing Roman. The Roman who came into the Forum of Augustus entered the equivalent of the *ala* of a Roman house, where the wax images of ancestors were frequently housed. These images provoke memories of a past

recognized through vision. Quintilian describes memory as a path one takes through a house (*Inst.* 1). Further on this topic, see Jocelyn Penny Small, *Wax Tablets of the Mind: Cognitive Studies of Memory and Literacy in Classical Antiquity* (London, 1997), 95–116; more recently, Charles Hedrick, *History and Silence: Purge and Rehabilitation of Memory in Late Antiquity* (Austin, 2000), 232–237. On the use of *loci* and *imagines* by Roman orators, see the classic work of Frances A. Yates, *The Art of Memory* (Chicago, 1966), 1–26. Yates, 46, also discusses Augustine's conception of the memory as a series of buildings (*Conf.* 10.8); Georgia Frank, *The Memory of the Eyes: Pilgrims to Living Saints in Christian Late Antiquity* (Berkeley, 2000), 18–21.

61. R. D. Williams (1972), ad loc.; also at *Aeneid* 6.34, Virgil uses *perlegeret* to mean "read" or "scan"; see R. A. Smith, *Poetic Allusion and Poetic Embrace in Ovid and Virgil* (Ann Arbor, 1997), 179–180.

62. Flower, *Ancestor Masks*, 109–114.

63. Denis Feeney, "History and Revelation in Vergil's Underworld," *PCPhS* 212 (1986): 12–15. Cf. Sabine Grebe, *Die vergilische Heldenschau: Tradition und Fortwirken* (Frankfurt am Main, 1989).

64. On the association of Hercules and Bacchus with the emperor, see R. D. Williams (1972), ad. 801, and my discussion in Ch. 2, pp. 52–55.

65. For a view more positive than Feeney's, see Nicholas Horsfall, *A Companion to the Study of Virgil* (Leiden, 2000), 148–149. For a strong assertion of a dark reading, see Richard Thomas, *Virgil and the Augustan Reception* (Cambridge, 2001), 207–213.

66. Austin (1964), ad 824.

67. Austin (1964), ad 845.

68. "Where do you hasten my weary gaze, you Fabii?" writes R. D. Williams (1972), ad 845–846.

69. Sara Mack, *Patterns of Time in Vergil* (Hamden, CT, 1978), 74. In what may be seen as representative of the views of many scholars, Mack regards Anchises' instructions as calling into question the positive aspects of the Augustan peace.

70. Austin (1964), ad 849.

71. R. D. Williams (1972), ad 847–848.

72. Austin (1964), ad loc.

73. Lyne, *Further Voices*, 214–215.

74. See Gilbert Highet, *The Speeches in Vergil's* Aeneid (Princeton, 1972), 284–285.

75. See Eduard Norden, *P. Vergilius Maro: Aeneas Buch VI*, 4th ed. (Darmstadt, 1957), ad 856ff., "mit ennianischen Kolorit" (339). Norden also mentions further Ennian echoes in his note.

76. Norden, 339.

77. "But Rome is as much taller than other cities / As cypress trees than the little viburnums below them." Translation of David Ferry, *The Eclogues of Virgil* (New York, 1999).

78. For a different view of the relationship of Evander and Aeneas, see Charles Lloyd, "The Evander-Anchises Connection: Fathers, Sons, and Homoerotic Desire in Vergil's *Aeneid*," *Vergilius* 45 (1999): 3–21.

79. Lloyd ("The Evander-Anchises Connection," 6 n. 9) calls attention to Evander's recognition based on family resemblance.

80. The Porta Carmentalis was famous in part for its two openings (Livy 2.49). Out of one, the Fabii once made an unsuccessful attempt against the Etruscans (306 BC). Thus, the Porta Carmentalis had one "bad" opening, out of which the Fabii issued (Porta Scelerata).

81. Mack, *Patterns of Time*, writes, "The Roman reader apprehends Evander as the beginning of a chain extending to his own time" (52).

82. There is a clear semantic connection between thought and sight (cf. German *wissen*, "to think" and English "vision"). See Pokorny, *Indogermanisches*, the Indo-European root 2.*u(e)id-*, vol. 1, 1125–1127.

83. Robert Edgeworth, *The Colors of the* Aeneid (New York, 1992), 123.

84. On the precise location, see C. J. Fordyce, ed. *Aeneidos Libri VII–VIII* (Oxford, 1977), ad 342–343.

85. On this connection, see Fordyce, ad 343.

86. See above, p. 92.

87. *uerum tamen neque tam acri memoria fere quisquam est, ut, non dispositis notatisque rebus, ordinem uerborum omnium ut sententiarum complectatur, neque uero tam hebeti, ut nihil hac consuetudine et exercitatione adiuuetur. Vidit enim hoc prudenter siue Simonides siue alius quis inuenit, ea maxime animis effingi nostris, quae essent a sensu tradita atque impressa; acerrimum autem ex omnibus nostris sensibus esse sensum uidendi; qua re facillime animo teneri posse ea, quae perciperentur auribus aut cogitatione, si etiam commendatione oculorum animis traderentur; ut res caecas et ab aspectus iudicio remotas conformatio quaedam et imago et figura ita notaret, ut ea, quae cogitando complecti uix possemus, intuendo quasi teneremus* (De or. 2.87.357). ["though nevertheless hardly anybody exists who has so keen a memory that he can retain the order of all the words or sentences without having arranged and noted his facts, nor yet is anybody so dull-witted that habitual practice in this will not give him some assistance. It has been sagaciously discerned by Simonides or else discovered by some other person, that the most complete pictures are formed in our minds of the things that have been conveyed to them and imprinted on them by the senses, but that the keenest of all our senses is the sense of sight, and that consequently perceptions perceived by the ears or by reflexion can be most easily retained in the mind if they are also conveyed to our mind by the mediation of the eyes, with the result that things not seen and not lying in the field of visual discernment are earmarked by a sort of outline and image and shape so that we keep hold of as it were by an act of sight things that we can scarcely embrace by an act of thought." Translation of E. W. Sutton, *Cicero De Oratore*, 2 vols. (Loeb edition; Cambridge, MA, 1942)], 2.87. See Yates, *Art of Memory*, 1–26.

88. Yates, *Art of Memory*, 4.

89. The problem of Aeneas' departure through the ivory gate has been a subject of debate for generations; for a recent discussion of the topic, see J.-Y. Maleuvre, "Porte d'ivoire et Rameau d'Or: éléments de cacozelie dans

le sixième livre de *l'Énéide,*" *Revue des Études Anciennes* 98 (1996): 91-107; for a somewhat more optimistic reading, see Roland Mayer, "The Ivory Gate Revisited," *Proceedings of the Virgil Society* 21 (1993): 53-63.

90. On Virgilian paronomasia, see O'Hara, *True Names,* 60-63 and esp. 70. O'Hara notes that the play of *cecinit* with the name Carmentis is an example of Vergilian "double etymologizing."

91. Cf. Bettina Bergmann ("The Roman House as Memory Theater: The House of the Tragic Poet in Pompeii." *Art Bulletin* 76 [1994]: 225-256), who considers how wall paintings trigger "memory theater" in a Roman house.

92. The obvious connection of *memento* and *monimenta* scarcely needs to be mentioned in this context.

93. Glenn Most, "Memory and Forgetting in the *Aeneid,*" *Vergilius* 47 (2001): 169.

4. HIC AMOR

1. *Aen.* 4.347-350.

2. *Aen.* 12.70.

3. On different uses of the English word "vision" to refer variously to the physical act of sight as well as to the sense of calling and destiny, see Ch. 1, pp. 9-10.

4. See Damien Nelis, *Vergil's* Aeneid *and the* Argonautica *of Apollonius Rhodius* (Leeds, 2001), 114-115.

5. Servius auctus, ad 1.561: "But by saying 'with downcast gaze,' he [Virgil] has added another kind of *officium*" (my translation).

6. On the notion of there being in this passage a contest of *officia* between Carthaginians and Trojans, see R. K. Gibson, "Aeneas as *Hospes* in Vergil, *Aeneid* 1 and 4," *CQ* 49 (1999): 189.

7. My emphasis here is not on the sequence of favors (i.e., *aliud* versus *alterum*) but on the word *officium*. One might think that *aliud genus* implies another favor, yet that seems to me too strong an interpretation for the seemingly modest expression *uultum demissa*. Rather, I think the "further type of favor" is the possibility of cultural merger, which could possibly also have erotic connotations.

8. Gibson, "Aeneas as *Hospes,*" 196.

9. R. G. Austin, ed., *P. Vergili Maronis Aeneidos Liber Primus* (Oxford, 1971), ad loc.

10. Austin (1971), ad loc.

11. One need only consider how obstinately Dido refuses the advice of Iarbas (4.36, 213-214).

12. Further on the connection of Dido and Diana, see W. W. DeGrummond, "The 'Diana Experience': A Study of the Victims of Diana in Virgil's *Aeneid,*" *Collection Latomus* 239 (1997): 158-194; R. Glei, "Von Probus zu Pöschl: Vergilinterpretation im Wandel," *Gymnasium* 97 (1990): 321-340; Damien Nelis, *Vergil's* Aeneid *and the* Argonautica, 82-86. Wendell Clausen, *Virgil's* Aeneid: *Decorum, Allusion, and Ideology.* Beiträge zur Altertumskunde 162. (Munich, 2002): 29-31.

13. Gordon Williams, *Technique and Ideas in the* Aeneid (New Haven, 1983), 69.

14. G. Williams, *Technique and Ideas,* 69.

15. Gail C. Polk ("Vergil's Penelope: The Diana Simile in *Aeneid* 1.498–502," *Vergilius* 42 [1996]: 42) notes that the verb *gradere* in the *Aeneid* always refers to the movement of distinguished individuals.

16. "She wears a quiver slung across her shoulder; / and as she makes her way, she towers over / all other goddesses" (M. 1.706–708).

17. *Od.* 6.109; *Aen.* 1.502.

18. *Od.* 6.107; *Aen.* 1.501.

19. G. Williams, *Technique and Ideas,* 62.

20. For more on the geography, see Viktor Pöschl, *The Art of Vergil: Image and Symbol in the* Aeneid (Ann Arbor, 1962), 65; also Nelis (*Virgil's* Aeneid *and the* Argonautica, 84), who sees the correspondence between simile and narrative as evidence that Virgil's imitation is "fundamentally Apollonian" rather than Homeric. Certainly some details are indebted to Apollonius, who models his own passage (*Arg.* 3.876–888) on Homer's Nausicaa simile. For this type of "multiple reference" or "conflation," see Richard Thomas, "Virgil's *Georgics* and the Art of Reference," *HSCP* 90 (1986): 194–195.

21. Ovid would exploit Virgil's description of Diana here for his portrayal of her *ipsa dea est colloque tenus supereminet omnis, Met.* 3.182 ["She is that very goddess, and she towers over all as far as her neck" (my translation)].

22. Richard Heinze, *Virgils Epische Technik* (Stuttgart, 1915; rpt. 1972), 138, regards Virgil's use of the phrase *uultum demissa* as a poor choice of words ("Fehlgriff"). See Wendell Clausen, *Virgil's* Aeneid *and the Tradition of Hellenistic Poetry* (Berkeley, 1987), 135 n. 2.

23. Austin (1971), ad loc.

24. Nelis, *Virgil's* Aeneid *and the* Argonautica, 90–91.

25. Brooks Otis (*Virgil: A Study in Civilized Poetry* [Oxford, 1963], 76), in comparing Virgil's treatment of Aeneas and Dido's initial encounter to the treatment of Medea and Jason in Apollonius Rhodius, writes: "*Everything is here seen through Dido:* we empathetically read her mind and share her feelings. The amatory symptoms of Medea are mainly physical: Dido's are far more psychic and intellectual."

26. This and all citations of Apollonius are taken from the Loeb translation of R. C. Seaton, *Apollonius Rhodius: The* Argonautica (Cambridge, 1912; rpt. 1980).

27. So R. D. Williams, ed., *The* Aeneid *of Virgil: Books 1–6* (New York, 1972); John C. Conington and Henry N. Nettleship, eds., *The Works of Virgil* (Hildesheim, 1979); T. I. Papillon and A. E. Haigh, eds., *P. Vergili Maronis Opera,* 2 vols. (Oxford, 1892); Richard C. Monti, *The Dido Episode and the* Aeneid: *Roman Social and Political Values in the Epic. Mnemosyne,* Suppl. 66 (Leiden, 1981), 25–27; Niall Rudd, "Dido's Culpa," in *Oxford Readings in Vergil's* Aeneid, ed. S. J. Harrison (Oxford, 1990), ch. 7.

28. See Nelis, *Virgil's* Aeneid *and the* Argonautica, 82–93, esp. 89–90.

29. Generally on various types of imitation, see A. Reiff, *"Imitatio, aemulatio, interpretatio"* (Diss., Köln, 1958); also David West and A. J. Woodman, *Creative Imitation in Latin Literature* (Cambridge, 1979); specifically on *oppositio in imitando*, see Giuseppe Giangrande, " 'Arte Allusiva' and Alexandrian Poetry," *CQ* n.s. 17 (1967): 85–97, and Thomas, "Virgil's *Georgics."*

30. Nelis, *Virgil's* Aeneid *and the* Argonautica, 8.

31. On the intensity of both Dido's and Medea's passion, see Clausen, *Tradition,* 41.

32. Licinia Ricottilli, *Gesto e Parola nell'*Eneide (Bologna, 2000).

33. "But everything depends upon the expression, and in it itself moreover the power of the eyes is complete." I thank the anonymous reviewer for suggesting this translation.

34. So Austin, ad loc.

35. See Clausen, *Tradition,* 40–41.

36. So Gibson ("Aeneas as *Hospes,"* 196–197) interprets these lines.

37. See Austin (1971), ad 347.

38. Clausen, *Tradition,* 48.

39. Further on *inuidia,* s.v. *inuideo, TLL* 7.2.191; also M. Leumann ("S. 250 Fr.," *Gnomon* 13 [1937]: 33), who confirms that the prefix 'in' is the equivalent of the Greek '*ἐν.*' See also A. Ernout and A. Meillet, *Dictionnaire étymologique de la langue latine: Histoire des mots* (Paris, 1932), XIX, 1108; also T. E. Page, *The* Aeneid *of Virgil: Books VII–XII* (London, 1959), ad 11.337.

40. Tony Woodman and Jonathan Powell, eds., *Author and Audience in Latin Literature* (Cambridge, 1992). Woodman, 183, notes that this is the final speech of Aeneas and Dido in Book 4. This may underscore the bluntness of the words *extera . . . regna* (*Aen.* 4.350), which Woodman suggests evokes the image of Cleopatra.

41. Anne Peper Perkins, "Divine Epiphany in Epic: Supernatural Episodes in the 'Iliad,' the 'Odyssey', the 'Aeneid' and 'Paradise Lost' " (Diss., Washington University, 1986), DAI-A 47/08, p. 3028, Feb. 1987.

42. Charles Lloyd, "The Evander-Anchises Connection: Fathers, Sons, and Homoerotic Desire in Vergil's *Aeneid," Vergilius* 45 (1999): 6–7.

43. Michael C. J. Putnam, *Virgil's* Aeneid: *Interpretation and Influence* (Chapel Hill, 1995), 212–214.

44. Putnam, *Virgil's* Aeneid, 212.

45. Putnam, *Virgil's* Aeneid, 214.

46. On the tricolon with anaphora, see R. D. Williams, "Dido's Reply to Aeneas," in *Vergiliana,* ed. Henry Bardon and Raoul Verdière (Leiden, 1971), 425.

47. Clausen, *Tradition,* 47.

48. "But Aeneas, warned / by Jove, held still his eyes . . ." (M. 4.445–446).

49. See Denis C. Feeney, "The Taciturnity of Aeneas," *CQ* n.s. 33 (1983): 210.

50. E.g., *G.* 1.185–186; *Aen.* 1.430–431.

51. See A. S. Pease, ed., *Publi Vergili Aeneidos Liber Quartus* (Cambridge, MA, 1935), ad 402; also R. D. Williams (1972), ad loc.; Conington/

Nettleship, ad loc.; see also Friedrich Klingner, *Bucolica, Georgica, Aeneis* (Zurich, 1967), 450, compares also Accius' description from a battle scene in *Annales* 26.1.

52. R. A. Smith, *Poetic Allusion and Poetic Embrace in Ovid and Virgil* (Ann Arbor, 1997), 163.

53. Generally on Virgil's subjective style, see Otis, *Virgil,* 41–96; also William S. Anderson, *The Art of the* Aeneid (Englewood Cliffs, NJ, 1969), 25–26; on Dido in particular, see Pöschl, *Art of Vergil,* 60–91.

54. R. D. Williams (1972), ad 408.

55. Matilde Bandini, "Didone, Enea, gli dei e il motivo dell'inganno in Virgilio, *Eneide* IV," *Euphrosyne* 15 (1987): 89–108.

56. Smith, *Poetic Allusion,* 163–164.

57. Above, Ch. 1, pp. 19–20.

58. See Julia Dyson, "Dido the Epicurean," *CA* 15 (1996): 203–221, on Dido's failed attempts to adopt Epicurean principles adequately. G. Williams (*Technique and Ideas,* 189) notes this also: "The address to Dido links her with the viewing reader by the use of the verb (408, *cernenti*), but hers [Dido's] is not a detached viewing."

59. Mandelbaum's rendering of *respice* as "remember" does not fully capture in English the visual coloring of the Latin.

60. Richard F. Moorton, "Love as Death: The Pivoting Metaphor in Vergil's Story of Dido," *CW* 83 (1990): 165–166. See also Maurizio Bettini, "Ghosts of Exile: Doubles and Nostalgia in Vergil's *parva Troia* (*Aeneid* 3.249ff.)," *CA* 16 (1997): 8–33.

61. Laurel Fulkerson, "(Un)sympathetic Magic: A Study of *Heroides* 13," *AJP* 123 (2002): 61–87.

62. For a very different interpretation of this passage, see, e.g., Sara Mack, *Patterns of Time in Vergil* (Hamden, CT, 1978), 63.

63. On Aeneas' lack of deftness as a speaker in the Underworld scene, see Feeney, "The Taciturnity of Aeneas," 211.

64. E.g., R. D. Williams (1972), ad loc.

65. E. Kraggerud, "Caeneus und der Heroinenkatalog, Aeneis VI 440 ff.," *SO* 40 (1965): 66–71; M. Owen Lee, "Seven Suffering Heroines and Seven Surrogate Sons," in *The Two Worlds of the Poet: New Perspectives on Vergil,* ed. Alexander McKay, R. M. Wilhelm, and H. Jones (Detroit, 1992), 82–91. Eduard Norden, *P. Vergilius Maro, Aeneis Buch VI* (Darmstadt, 1957), ad 445ff., esp. 251.

66. E.g., Jacques Perret, "Les compagnes de Didon aux Enfers," *REL* 42 (1964): 247–261; Grace Starry West, "The Significance of Vergil's Eriphyle (*Aeneid* 6.445–446)," *Vergilius* 26 (1980): 52–54; Grace Starry West, "Caeneus and Dido," *TAPA* 110 (1980): 315–324.

67. Lee, "Seven Suffering Heroines," 83–84.

68. W. R. Johnson, *Darkness Visible* (Berkeley, 1976), 83.

69. DeGrummond, "The 'Diana Experience,'" 158–194, esp. 193. Also see Polk, "Vergil's Penelope," 38–49.

70. My translation.

71. On how important the notion of the hunt is for Virgil throughout the epic, see Gregory A. Staley, "Aeneas' First Act, 1.180–94," *CW* 84 (1990): 25–29 [reprinted in *Why Vergil?*].

72. DeGrummond, "The 'Diana Experience,'" 189.

73. *tandem progreditur magna stipante caterva / Sidoniam picto chlamydem circumdata limbo; / cui pharetra ex auro* ["At last the queen appears / among the mighty crowd; upon her shoulders / she wears a robe of Sidon with embroidered / borders. Her quiver is of gold. . . ." (M. 4.181–184)].

74. *hinc atque hinc glomerantur Oreades; illa pharetram / fert umero* ["her followers, / a thousand mountain nymphs, press in behind her, / she wears a quiver slung across her shoulder. . . ." (M. 1.704–706)].

75. First, if only briefly, discussed by Roger A. Hornsby, "The Vergilian Simile as Means of Judgment," in *Why Vergil?: A Collection of Interpretations*, ed. Stephanie Quinn (Wauconda, IL, 2000), 88; see also G. S. Duclos, "Dido as '*Triformis*' Diana," *Vergilius* 15 (1969): 33–41; further, DeGrummond, "The 'Diana Experience,'" 194.

76. Gordon Williams (*Tradition and Originality in Roman Poetry* [Oxford, 1968], 734) notes the power of vision in this passage: "The simile conveys a series of new impressions: of the darkness of the place where Dido now was and the difficulty for human sight, but also of the beauty of the woman and the eagerness of the man to see. The doubt, too, has a new and special point here: 'sees—or thinks he has seen . . . ,' the man cannot believe his eyes."

77. Marilyn Skinner, "The Last Encounter of Dido and Aeneas: *Aen.* 6.450–476," *Vergilius* 29 (1983): 12–13.

78. Observed and discussed by Skinner, "The Last Encounter," 16.

79. Norden, ad loc., pp. 256–257.

80. Feeney, "The Taciturnity of Aeneas," 211.

81. See Patricia Johnston, "Dido, Berenice and Arsinoe: *Aeneid* 6.460," *AJP* 108 (1987): 649–654; Susan Skulsky, "'*Invitus, Regina . . .*': Aeneas and the Love of Rome," *AJP* 106 (1985): 447–455; James Tatum, "Allusion and Interpretation in *Aeneid* 6.440–76," *AJP* 105 (1984): 434–452; Gian Biagio Conte, *The Rhetoric of Imitation: Genre and Poetic Memory in Virgil and Other Latin Poets*, ed. Charles Segal (Ithaca, 1986), 88–90; Skinner, "The Last Encounter," 18 n. 12; R. A. Smith, "A Lock and a Promise: Myth and Allusion in Aeneas' Farewell to Dido in *Aen.* 6," *Phoenix* 47 (1993): 305–312; more recently, Jeffrey Wills, "Divided Allusion: Virgil and the *Coma Berenices*," *HSCP* 98 (1998): 277–305.

82. Michael von Albrecht, "The Art of Mirroring in Virgil's *Aeneid*," in *Virgil: Critical Assessments of Classical Authors*, vol. 4, ed. Philip Hardie (London, 1999), 3.

83. "The goddess / averts her face, her eyes fast to the ground" (M. 1.681–682).

84. See also my discussion, *Poetic Allusion*, 39–40, with n. 33.

85. On the introspection of Medea, see Mary Beard and John Henderson, *Classical Art from Greece to Rome* (Oxford, 2001), 29–31.

86. Beard and Henderson, *Classical Art*, 43.

87. Andrew Feldherr, "Putting Dido on the Map: Genre and Geography in Vergil's Underworld," *Arethusa* 32 (1999): 114.

88. Michael C. J. Putnam, "Wrathful Aeneas and the Tactics of *Pietas* in Virgil, Ovid, and Lucan," in *Virgil's* Aeneid: *Interpretation and Influence,* ed. Michael C. J. Putnam (Chapel Hill, 1995), 214.

89. Feldherr, "Putting Dido on the Map," 115.

90. Feeney notes "speech is not available as a palliative or a private bond in the *Aeneid*" ("The Taciturnity of Aeneas," 216).

91. Julia Dyson, "Lilies and Violence: Lavinia's Blush in the Song of Orpheus," *CP* 94 (1999): 281–288.

92. Ruth N. Todd ("Lavinia Blushed," *Vergilius* 26 [1980]: 28) sees Lavinia as a "functional image."

93. Todd ("Lavinia Blushed," 30) writes, "Lavinia is a symbol, passive instrument and keystone of destiny."

94. *ecce leuis summo de uertice uisus Iuli / fundere lumen apex, tactuque innoxia mollis / lambere flamma comas et circum tempora pasci* ["Over Iülus' head / there leaps a lithe flametip that seems to shed / a radiance: the tongue of fire flickers, / harmless, and plays about his soft hair, grazes his temples." (M. 2.924–928)]. See also R. D. Williams (1972), note ad 7.71–72.

95. *inuitus, regina, tuo de litore cessi,* 6.460; cf. Catullus 66.39–42, the most recent treatment of which is that of Wills, "Divided Allusion."

96. Francis Cairns, *Virgil's Augustan Epic* (Cambridge, 1989), esp. 1–28; on connection with Augustus, 61–64.

97. Mandelbaum's translation does not fully render the visual force of *uisu.* A more accurate rendering might be: "as horrible and amazing to see."

98. On Virgil's indebtedness to the Greek lyric tradition for his description of Lavinia's eyes and other features, see Cairns, *Virgil's Augustan Epic,* 151–176; see also Philippe Heuzé, *L'image du corps dans l'oeuvre de Virgile* (Rome, 1985), 544.

99. Bettina Bergmann, "The Roman House as Memory Theater: The House of the Tragic Poet in Pompeii," *Art Bulletin* 76 (1994): 225–256. The other women depicted are Juno and Briseis.

100. In the Helen portrait, Paris was originally depicted in the ship to the right of the fresco. A man to the right of Helen assists her as she steps onto the gangplank of Paris' ship (Lilly Kahil, s.v. Helen, *LIMC* 4.1, 532). She wears a peplos with a himation wrapped high around her waist in the manner of a cummerbund. An attendant seems concerned, perhaps looking at her feet to make sure that she does not trip as she steps onto the gangway. A child, most likely her daughter Hermione, is visible to the far left of the portrait. Behind Helen, one can see the face and the towering helmet of a soldier who watches her board the ship.

101. Raymond Prier, Thauma Idesthai: *The Phenomenology of Sight and Appearance in Archaic Greek* (Tallahassee, 1989).

102. Nancy Worman, "The Body as Argument: Helen in Four Greek Texts," *CA* 16 (1997): 167.

103. *LIMC*, s.v. Helen 152; cf. also *LIMC*, s.v. Helen 177, 178.

104. Robert Edgeworth, *The Colors of the* Aeneid, American University Studies: Series 17, Classical Languages and Literature, vol. 12 (New York, 1992), 32, refers to this passage as the "most beautiful color passage in the *Aeneid*"; cf. also Todd, "Lavinia Blushed," 27–33; see also Cairns, *Virgil's Augustan Epic*, 162, 175. Dyson, "Lilies and Violence," 281–288.

105. See R. D. Williams (1972), ad 67–69.

106. *Il.* 6.486–487.

107. *Aen.* 4.347–350.

5. *VIDI, VICI*

1. "In the Pontic triumph one of the decorated wagons, instead of a stage-set representing scenes from the war, like the rest, carried a simple three-word inscription: I CAME, I SAW, I CONQUERED!" (Suetonius, *The Twelve Caesars*, trans. Robert Graves [New York, 1989]).

2. Carole Elizabeth Newlands (*Playing with Time: Ovid and the* Fasti [Ithaca, 1995], 92), following *Res Gestae* 21, writes, "Unlike the Ara Pacis, the temple was particularly Augustus' responsibility, for it was built on Augustus' property and was financed from the spoils of war." See also Paul Zanker, *The Power of Images in the Age of Augustus*, trans. Alan Shapiro (Ann Arbor, 1988), 195.

3. L. Richardson, jr, *Topographical Dictionary of Ancient Rome* (Baltimore, 1992), 160–161.

4. Suetonius, *Vita Divi Iulii* 29.1 states that its dedication (12 BC) was rushed and that the temple was not yet finished.

5. Pliny the Elder, *HN* 36.102.

6. Diane Favro, *The Urban Image of Augustan Rome* (Cambridge, MA, 1996), 96–97.

7. Zanker, *Power of Images*, 195; on the *Aeneid*'s influence on art and architecture generally, 208.

8. The statues in the Forum Augustum did have *elogia*, of which we have some extant examples. Nevertheless, the power of the forum lay not in the description of each *elogium* but in the dramatic effect of the two colonnades bearing statue upon statue, even as the saints mounted atop Bernini's colonnades in St. Peter's square are impressive, not individually, but because the sum of them offers an impressive display.

9. Text and translation taken from Sir James George Frazer, *Fasti*, rev. G. P. Goold, Loeb edition (Cambridge, MA, 1989).

10. Zanker, *Power of Images*, 113, with pl. 150.

11. Zanker, *Power of Images*, 209; about the symbolic value of the monument, Zanker writes, "Through didactic arrangements and constant repetition and combination of the limited number of new symbols, along with the dramatic highlighting of facades, statues and paintings, even the uneducated viewer was indoctrinated in the new visual program" (112).

12. Ov., *Ars Am.* 1.79–80.

13. Newlands, *Playing with Time*, 92.

14. G. Karl Galinsky, "The Hercules-Cacus Episode in *Aeneid* VIII," *AJP* 87 (1966): 18–51.

15. As Turnus himself says: *corpus spoliatum lumine*, 12.935 ("my body despoiled of light," my translation).

16. See my discussion, above, Ch. 1, pp. 16–18; Denis Feeney, *The Gods in Epic* (Oxford, 1991), 137.

17. Suetonius describes Augustus calming an unruly crowd by visible actions (*Vita Divi Augusti* 43.5): *nepotum quoque suorum munere cum consternatum ruinae metu populum retinere et confirmare nullo modo posset. transiit e loco suo atque in ea parte consedit, quae suspecta maxime erat.* ["A panic started in the Theatre during a public performance in honour of Gaius and Lucius; the audience feared that the walls might collapse. Augustus, finding that he could do nothing else to pacify or reassure them, left his own box and sat in what seemed to be the most threatened part of the auditorium" (trans. Graves)].

18. Treated above, Ch. 4, p. 100.

19. J. P. Lynch, "Laocoön and Sinon: Virgil, *Aeneid* 2.40–198," in *Virgil: Critical Assessments of Classical Authors*, vol. 4, ed. Philip Hardie (London, 1999): 77.

20. Kenneth Quinn, *Virgil's Aeneid: A Critical Description* (Ann Arbor, 1969), 338–339.

21. Gilbert Highet, *The Speeches in Vergil's Aeneid* (Princeton, 1972), 285; he also notes on the same page, "That Vergil distrusted oratory is shown by another curious fact. In formal speeches and in persuasions and other times of emotional discourse almost all his speakers distort the truth." Highet adds, a few pages later, "Vergil, it seems, held that powerful oratory was incompatible with pure truth, and that every speaker presented his or her own case by misrepresenting the facts" (289). Nicholas Horsfall (*A Companion to the Study of Virgil* [Leiden, 2000], 186) concedes that "some of [Virgil's] characters are copious and compulsive liars," but concludes that this is "incidental," for Virgil's "skilled use of rhetoric . . . makes his speeches such a delight to an audience attuned to the highest standards of late republican oratory." However true this may be, it does not obviate the fact that Virgil seems to problematize rhetorical persuasion in the poem.

22. James O'Hara, *Death and the Optimistic Prophecy in Vergil's Aeneid* (Princeton, 1990), 118.

23. Denis Feeney, "The Taciturnity of Aeneas," *CQ* 33(i) (1983): 204–219, esp. 217.

24. Sarah Spence, *Rhetoric of Reason and Desire: Vergil, Augustine, and the Troubadours* (Ithaca, 1988), 51.

25. Gualtiero Calboli, "oratores," *Enciclopedia Virgiliana* 3 (Rome, 1987), 869–872.

26. Walter Neuhauser, *Patronus und Orator* (Innsbruck, 1958); cf. Otto Skutsch, ed., *The Annals of Q. Ennius*, ad 202.

27. The orator's use of "ambassador" was for Virgil an archaism, which might suggest that in and of itself, oratory, at least as it pertained to embassies, was outdated.

28. Neuhauser, *Patronus und Orator*, 143–151.

29. Austin ([1971], ad loc.) notes that the Trojans are, "in effect, an embassy" seeking "indulgence." See my discussion above in Ch. 4, p. 100.

30. So Calboli, "oratores," 870; see also K. Billmayer, "Rhetorische Studien zu den Reden in Vergils *Aeneis*" (Diss., Würtzburg, 1932), 23; and Highet, *Speeches*, 55.

31. Francis Cairns, *Virgil's Augustan Epic* (Cambridge, 1989), 68.

32. [king], my addition.

33. R. D. Williams, ed. (*The* Aeneid *of Virgil*, 2 vols. [New York, 1972], ad 8.17) writes that this is "a piece of formal language for the envoys to get their tongues round."

34. " 'but no Italian can command so proud / a nation; choose a stranger as your leader' " (M. 8.652–653).

35. "Aeneas is the leader of both Trojans and Italians: the unity towards which the poem, and history, move, is here adumbrated. The mixture of races . . . which will produce the Romans . . . is foretold in Jupiter's final speech, 12.830ff. . . ." K. W. Gransden, ed., *Virgil* Aeneid *Book VIII* (Cambridge, 1976), ad 8.511–513.

36. "take up your way: most brave / chieftain of both Trojans and Italians" (M. 8.668–669).

37. K. W. Gransden, ed. *Virgil* Aeneid *Book XI* ([Cambridge, 1991], ad 11.108–119) rightly calls attention to the sorrowful tenor of Aeneas' speech here, comparing it to the tone of Diomedes' response to Venulus.

38. See Gransden ([1991], ad 11.110–111), who notes the "great emphasis" given to *pacem* here, "sustained by the alliteration with *peremptis*."

39. ". . . Latium / . . . must sue / the Trojan chief for peace" (M. 11.300–302).

40. A number befitting an epic, as C. J. Fordyce notes ad 7.153 (*Aeneidos Libri VII–VIII* [Oxford, 1977]). For the particulars of this embassy, see the next section of this chapter, in which I consider the debate between Drances and Turnus.

41. On Drances as an orator, see R. D. Williams (1972), ad 11.124–125; also Gransden, *Virgil* Aeneid *Book XI*, "Introduction," 14; Elaine Fantham, "Fighting Words: Turnus at Bay in the Latin Council (*Aen.* 11.234–446)," *AJP* 120 (1999): 263–270.

42. On the ambiguous nature of Drances' character, see Gransden (1991), 15. Fantham ("Fighting Words," 270) notes that Virgil's readers "no more share Drances' version of truth and justice than they share those of Juno in her display of tirades in Books 1 and 7."

43. A portion of Aeneas' words (108–111) is cited in the previous section, above, p. 137.

44. Cf. Llewelyn Morgan, *Patterns of Redemption in Virgil's* Georgics (New York, 1999), 118–119.

45. "Drances, who was lavish with wealth and even more with words (his hands too cold for war)" (M. 11.446–448).

46. So Tacitus *Dialogus* 18.2: *Sic Catoni seni comparatus C. Gracchus plenior et uberior, sic Graccho politior et ornatior Crassus, sic utroque dis-*

tinctior et urbanior et altior Cicero, Cicerone mitior Corvinus et dulcior et in uerbis magis elaboratus. ["Thus Gaius Gracchus, as compared with old Cato, has greater fullness and wealth of diction, Crassus is more highly finished and more ornate than Gracchus, while Cicero is more luminous, more refined, more impassioned than either the one or the other. Corvinus again is mellower than Cicero, more engaging, and more careful in his choice of words"; trans. Sir William Peterson, *The Dialogus of Publius Cornelius Tacitus*, ed. T. E. Page (Loeb edition: Cambridge, MA, 1932)]. For a comparison of Drances and Cicero, see William C. McDermott, "Drances/Cicero," *Vergilius* 26 (1980): 34–38. Gransden (1991) points out that Virgil's treatment of Drances is characteristically ambiguous and that Virgil drew generally upon polemical language.

47. Fantham ("Fighting Words," 268) notes that Drances could not have chosen a worse technique if his true goal was to cause Turnus to yield to him.

48. See Gransden (1991), ad loc.

49. Ilioneus also appeals to vision as a component of his explanation of Trojan misfortune (1.526).

50. Gransden ([1991], ad 356) notes that Virgil alludes to Homer's description of Helen as war booty (*Il.* 7.350–353); also Georg Knauer, *Die Aeneis und Homer: Studien zur poetischen Technik Vergils, mit Listen der Homerzitate in der Aeneis* (Göttingen, 1964), 284–285.

51. Servius, ad 11.358; see also Gransden (1991), ad loc.

52. Cairns (*Virgil's Augustan Epic*, 96) sees this as an allusion to the civil war between Pompey and Caesar.

53. My translation of *En supplex uenio* (365).

54. Translation of R. D. Williams (1972), ad 373–374.

55. Highet, *Speeches*, 282. Despite Drances' skill, Gilbert Highet regards Drances as less effective than Turnus, whose speech immediately follows (283–284).

56. Hermagoras had expanded the quadripartite division inherited from Aristotle (*Rhetoric* 3.13.4–5 [1414b]; see D. A. Russell and M. Winterbottom, *Ancient Literary Criticism: The Principal Texts in New Translations* [Oxford, 1972], 158) (προοίμιον, πρόθεσις, πίστις, ἐπίλογος) to six parts, namely, introduction (Aristotle's προοίμιον), narration (Aristotle's πρόθεσις), partition, confirmation (Aristotle's πίστις), refutation, and conclusion (Aristotle's ἐπίλογος). See George Kennedy, *The Art of Rhetoric in the Roman World 300 B.C.–A.D. 300* (Princeton, 1972), 100.

57. Servius, ad 358: *per inrisionem in illum* ("Through derision against that man," my translation).

58. Gransden (1991), introductory note, ad 377–444.

59. Gransden (1991), ad 392–395, follows T. E. Page in noting that the future tense here is "curious" (*The* Aeneid *of Virgil: Books VII–XII* [London, 1956], ad loc.). Gransden takes it as attraction with *arguet.*

60. Commentators (e.g., R. D. Williams) generally follow Page in suggesting that Turnus means "will see, if one cares to look." There seems, however, no reason not to believe that *uidebit* (394) could refer to the present reality of

the loss of Pallas and at the same time predict future victories to be achieved by Turnus.

61. So Achilles fills the Scamander with blood, *Iliad* 21.120-124. Cf. also Catullus 64.357-360.

62. Highet (*Speeches*, 283) believes that Turnus' "emotional energy . . . and youthful earnestness" makes his speech even more effective than that of Drances; see also Fantham, "Fighting Words," 271, 274.

63. *De Sublimitate* 15.1; see Russell and Winterbottom, *Ancient Literary Criticism*, 477-478.

64. Longinus (*de Sublimitate*, 15.9) cites Demosthenes 24.208, an example of visualization in the third person.

65. *quod tamen dixit, conferens se ad alias personas et laudans eos quibus contigit perire, ne ista conspicerent*, ad 415 ("Nevertheless he said this, comparing himself to other characters and praising those to whose lot it fell to perish, that they might not see such things," my translation).

66. Cf. *Aen.* 12.931-933.

67. Servius, ad 414.

68. "'They say/ Aeneas calls on me alone; I pray/ that he may call'" (M. 11.586-588).

69. See my discussion of 7.446 above, in Ch. 2, p. 38; of 9.24 above, in Ch. 2, p. 47.

70. Cf. Aeneas, who uses the verb only when speaking to the Sibyl (6.76, 106).

71. Ever since the regal period of Roman history, the name Turnus had been associated with oratory used against a king (Livy 1.50). Further on Turnus' name, see Cairns, *Virgil's Augustan Epic*, 67; James J. O'Hara, *True Names: Vergil and the Alexandrian Tradition of Etymological Wordplay* (Ann Arbor, 1996), 185-186.

72. Galinsky, "Hercules-Cacus Episode," 18-51.

73. R. O. A. M. Lyne, *Further Voices in Vergil's Aeneid* (Oxford, 1987), 28-35.

74. Lyne, *Further Voices*, 31.

75. "Aeneas stopped. But while he spoke, Evander / for long had scanned his face, his eyes, and all / his body" (M. 8.198-200).

76. "Anchises was the tallest of them all" (M. 8.213).

77. Servius, ad 194.

78. Richard Thomas, *Virgil and The Augustan Reception* (Cambridge, 2001), closely follows Daniel Gillis, *Eros and Death in the Aeneid* (Rome, 1983), 141-144, who sees in Augustus' *superbis / postibus* (8.721-722) an internal allusion to the dwelling of Cacus (*foribusque . . . superbis*, 8.196). Thomas admits the argument of A. Traina ("Suberbia," *Enciclopedia Virgiliana* 4 [Rome, 1988], 1073), who argues that the two passages present a contrast between Cacus and Augustus, but Thomas regards Gillis' interpretation to be more persuasive. Thomas then goes on to argue (207) that "as he makes an attempt on the Trojan camp (*Aen.* 9.672-818), Turnus looks more like Hercules than any other character in the poem." My objection

to Thomas is twofold. First, when Aeneas arrives at the site of the future city of Rome, Evander invites him to take the seat of honor fit for Hercules himself (8.175–178). Karl Galinsky (*The Herakles Theme: The Adaptations of the Hero in Literature from Homer to the Twentieth Century* [Totowa, NJ, 1972], 133–144) offers a detailed comparison of Aeneas and Hercules. Surely no character parallels Hercules quite so clearly as Aeneas. Second, Turnus explicitly identifies himself in the *Aen.* 9 passage not as another Hercules but as another Achilles (8.742). At no point is there an explicit or implicit identification of Turnus with Hercules.

79. Lyne, *Further Voices*, 27–29, here associates *uomens*, as well as other forms of *uomo* applied to Cacus, with the description of Augustus (8.681) on Aeneas' shield, in which Augustus' temples belch forth flames. Certainly the repeated use of *uomo* (27) to describe Cacus' belching of smoke and fire is striking, but *uomo* is a relatively widely used verb in the *Aeneid* and elsewhere in Virgil's poetry, and its meaning can range from "vomit" to "pour forth." While Lyne's argument is clever and introduces suggestive possibilities, it seems to press the text rather tightly to associate Aeneas, Augustus, and Cacus on the basis of this verb. Lyne also concedes (28) that Aeneas should be viewed as a Hercules figure. The description of him elsewhere in Book 8 clearly suggests as much (. . . *quem fulua leonis / pellis obit totum praefulgens unguinibus aureis,* 8.552–553).

80. "Those black fires / that Cacus belched" (M. 8.262–263).

81. "Now all—Rutulians, Trojans, and Italians—/ turned eagerly to look" (M. 12.936–937).

82. Galinsky ("Hercules-Cacus Episode," 48) regards Hercules as a prototype for Aeneas (and Augustus).

83. Gordon Williams, *Technique and Ideas in the* Aeneid (New Haven, 1983), 64.

84. R. D. Williams (1972), ad 243–244.

85. R. D. Williams (1972), ad 245, "from above."

86. So Gransden (1991), ad 253.

87. R. D. Williams (1972), ad 254–255.

88. So Page, ad 8.260.

89. Sam Woodford, *LIMC* 6.1 (68), s.v. Minotauros, p. 579.

90. So the first emperor was both *voyant* and *visible* in Rome. The well-known anecdote of Suetonius, *Vita Divi Augusti* 43.5 (cited above, n. 17), offers a good example.

91. *Il.* 20.463–472.

92. *Il.* 21.71–96.

93. *Il.* 21.214–292.

94. *Il.* 10.377–381.

95. *Il.* 6.46–50.

96. Further on battlefield supplication in the *Iliad*, see Donna Wilson, *Ransom, Revenge, and Heroic Identity in the* Iliad (Cambridge, 2002), 28–29. See also Bernard Fenik, *Typical Battle Scenes in the* Iliad: *Studies in the Narrative Techniques of Homeric Battle Description* (Wiesbaden, 1968), 83.

Fenik mistakenly interprets *Iliad* 6.330 to be an instance of battlefield entreaty.

97. The Homeric model for this passage is Achilles' slaying of Lycaon (*Il.* 21.134–135). See Gordon Williams, *Technique and Ideas,* 101–102.

98. So Stephen J. Harrison, ed. and trans., *Vergil:* Aeneid *10* (Oxford, 1991), ad 521.

99. Michael C. J. Putnam, "Pius Aeneas and the Metamorphosis of Lausus," in his *Virgil's* Aeneid: *Interpretation and Influence* (Chapel Hill, 1995), 139.

100. Julia Dyson (*King of the Wood: The Sacrificial Victor in Virgil's* Aeneid [Norman, OK, 2001], 155–156) sees Magus, Haemonides, Anxur, and Tarquitus as comparable to Hippolytus (*Aen.* 7.778–780) and, by extension, to Aeneas himself. In this scene, Dyson suggests that Aeneas perhaps kills a series of "doubles" of himself.

101. Putnam, "Pius Aeneas" (in his *Virgil's* Aeneid) notes that, in Book 2, Pyrrhus kills Polites "before the eyes of his parents" (142).

102. Harrison, ad loc.

103. "There, hidden deep, / are many talents of chased silver" (M. 10.725–726).

104. On extending hands in supplication see F. A. Sullivan, "*Tendere Manus:* Gestures in the *Aeneid,*" *CJ* 63.8 (1967–1968): 358–362, esp. 361.

105. Harrison, ad 597.

106. 11.697.

107. 12.294.

108. "driven by the rout, / before the eyes, the very presence of / their weeping parents" (M. 11.1176–1178).

109. "They do not dare to open them for their / own comrades and are deaf to any prayers" (M. 11.1171–1172).

110. Harrison (ad loc.) correctly observes that *semineci* is best rendered "dying"; I have rendered it "half-dead" merely to distinguish it from *morientia* in the following line.

111. Alessandro Barchiesi ("Representations of Suffering and Interpretation in the *Aeneid,*" in *Virgil: Critical Assessments of Classical Authors,* ed. Philip Hardie [London, 1999], 326) notes that Hercules acts in this tale as "silent interlocutor."

112. Stephen J. Harrison, "The Sword-Belt of Pallas (*Aeneid* 10.495–505): Moral Symbolism and Poetical Ideology," in *Virgil's* Aeneid: *Augustan Epic and Political Context,* ed. Hans-Peter Stahl (London, 1998), 228–229.

113. See Harrison's excellent note, ad 442–443.

114. *Aen.* 12.939.

115. Harrison, ad 446–447.

116. *OLD,* s.v. *uoluo,* 8.

117. " 'Now see if my shaft pierces more' " (M. 10.665).

118. See Harrison, ad 481; Knauer, *Die Aeneis und Homer,* 293.

119. "and now look out for my brazen spear. I wish it might be taken full length in your body" (trans. Lattimore).

120. Homer merely refers to the way that Achilles looks at Hector with an angry glance (*Il.* 22.260).

121. See M. Owen Lee, *Fathers and Sons in Virgil's* Aeneid: *Tum Genitor Natum* (Albany, 1979), 82.

122. So Harrison (ad 442–443), who, comparing Turnus' vaunt against Pallas with Sarpedon's similar stance against Patroclus at *Iliad* 16.423–425, asserts that Turnus' desire for single combat against Pallas is heroic. Harrison rightly adds, "but the reader also senses that Turnus is keen to seek the easy glory of killing a young and inexperienced hero" (ad loc.).

123. See Harrison's note, ad 791.

124. Harrison, ad 811–812.

125. Robert Edgeworth, *The Colors of the* Aeneid (New York, 1992), 104.

126. Harrison, ad 821–822.

127. Putnam, "Pius Aeneas" (in his *Virgil's* Aeneid, 136–137), adroitly discusses how the sound of the text mimics Aeneas' vision (137).

128. Alessandro Barchiesi, *La traccia del modello: Effetti omerici nella narrazione Virgiliana* (Pisa, 1984), 12.

129. Barchiesi, *Traccia del modello*, 13.

130. Feeney, *Gods in Epic*, 156.

131. For more on this passage, see Lee, *Fathers and Sons*, 89–93.

132. Best rendered "draws air or breath," according to R. D. Williams (1971), ad 899; and Harrison, ad 898–899.

133. Mezentius' twofold appeal represents the eighth and ninth times that the verb *orare* occurs in Book 10, more than in any other book in the poem.

134. Harrison, ad 908.

135. *Il.* 12.447–449, where Hector takes up a stone to wield against the Greeks, and *Il.* 21.403–405, where Athena takes up a stone to fight with Aeneas.

136. Robin Schlunk (*The Homeric Scholia and the* Aeneid: *A Study of the Influence of Ancient Homeric Literary Criticism on Vergil* [Ann Arbor, 1974], 140–146) notes that Virgil has adapted Homer's simile describing the frustration of both Hector and Achilles to explain Turnus' desperation. It is significant, however, that Virgil applies this simile exclusively to Turnus (through the first-person plural reference) and that Virgil's emphasis is not on the failure of one who runs but on the loss of that person's ability to speak.

137. J. William Hunt, *Forms of Glory: Structure and Sense in Virgil's* Aeneid (Carbondale, IL, 1973), 94.

138. Highet, *Speeches*, 283, affirms that Turnus had outspoken even the Rutulians' best speaker, Drances.

139. Cf. *sortitus . . . oculis*, 920, with the weaker Homeric participle εἰσορόων (*Il.* 22.321), which merely reveals Achilles' search for a chink in Hector's armor.

140. Horsfall, *A Companion to the Study of Virgil*, 203.

141. See William S. Anderson, "The Suppliant Voice and Gesture in Ver-

gil and Ovid's *Metamorphoses*." *ICS* 18 (1993): 163–168; see also Jeanne Dion, *Les passions dans l'oeuvre de Virgile* (Nancy, 1993), 78–80.

142. "Achilles wept now for his own father, now again / for Patroklos" (trans. Lattimore).

143. Barchiesi, *Traccia del modello*, 114.

144. "so Achilles wondered as he looked on Priam, a godlike / man" (trans. Lattimore).

145. Lee, *Fathers and Sons*, 89.

146. It has little bearing on my reading here whether or not *humilis* agrees with Turnus or his eyes. See R. D. Williams (1972), ad loc., who discusses the variant in the manuscript tradition (*supplex* or *supplexque*).

147. Michael C. J. Putnam, "Virgil's *Aeneid:* The Final Lines," in *Poets and Critics Read Virgil*, ed. Sarah Spence (New Haven, 2001), 89.

148. He also sees Augustus, in the center of Aeneas' shield, as the victor at Actium. See my discussion above, Ch. 2, pp. 57–58.

149. His gestures, too, would have been perfectly clear to Aeneas; so Putnam, "Pius Aeneas" (in his *Virgil's* Aeneid), 145. See also Barchiesi, *Traccia del modello*, 114.

150. Michael C. J. Putnam, "The Hesitation of Aeneas" (in *Virgil's* Aeneid: *Interpretation and Influence*, ed. Michael C. J. Putnam [Chapel Hill, 1995]), 161, notes that the sight of the belt of Pallas affects Aeneas as would one of Allecto's snakes. In "Pius Aeneas," Putnam views Aeneas as an "elemental power" (146) under the influence of Jupiter's *Dira*.

151. Hans-Peter Stahl, "Aeneas—An 'Unheroic' Hero?" *Arethusa* 14 (1981): 165, connects Aeneas' *ante ora patrum* with Aeneas' drive toward martial glory.

152. Barchiesi, *Traccia del modello*, 114–115, with nn. 27 and 28.

153. See Wilson, *Ransom, Revenge, and Heroic Identity*, 166, on the sparing of Adrestos.

154. Putnam, "The Final Lines," in Spence, *Poets and Critics*, 98.

155. Feeney, "The Taciturnity of Aeneas," 216.

156. Feeney, "The Taciturnity of Aeneas," 216.

157. Feeney, "The Taciturnity of Aeneas," 217.

158. Glenn Most, "Memory and Forgetting in the *Aeneid*," *Vergilius* 72 (2001): 151.

159. Putnam ("Wrathful Aeneas and the Tactics of *Pietas* in Virgil, Ovid, and Lucan," in *Virgil's* Aeneid: *Interpretation and Influence*, ed. Michael C. J. Putnam [Chapel Hill, 1995], 214) suggests that the rolling eyes indicate uncontrolled rage.

160. Anderson, "The Suppliant Voice," 170.

161. Michael C. J. Putnam, "Anger, Blindness, and Insight in Virgil's *Aeneid*." In *Virgil's* Aeneid: *Interpretation and Influence*, ed. Michael C. J. Putnam (Chapel Hill, 1995), 185.

162. Putnam, "Anger, Blindness," 183–186 et passim.

163. For an Epicurean like Philodemus or Lucretius, the act of seeing encompasses the quasi-tactile notion of *simulacra* that would stream from the

object and physically touch the viewer's eye. Cf. *DRN* 4.29–468. Aeneas might therefore be considered to be "touched" by this recollection of the past in a way that supersedes the memory that visual reminder elicits.

164. For a full discussion of the various ways that the Danaid theme is apropos of Pallas' buckler, see S. J. Harrison, "The Sword-Belt of Pallas," 223–242.

165. *Pallas, Euander, in ipsis / omnia sunt oculis; mensae quas aduena primas / tunc adiit, dextraeque datae* ["Pallas . . . / Evander . . . all are now before his eyes . . . / the tables he first came to as a stranger, / the pledged right hands" (M. 10.710–713)].

166. *ergo et quam petitis iuncta est mihi foedere dextra* [" 'Therefore, my right hand, / for which you ask, is joined in league with you' " (M. 8.220–221)]. See Harrison, ad 516–517.

167. See Galinsky, "Hercules-Cacus Episode," 280–281; Llewelyn Morgan, "Assimilation and Civil War: Hercules and Cacus (Aen. 8.185–287)," in *Vergil's Aeneid: Augustan Epic and Political Context*, ed. Hans-Peter Stahl (London, 1998), 175–177.

168. Knauer, *Die Aeneis und Homer*, 320; see also Putnam, "Unity in Closure," in Perkell, *Reading Vergil's Aeneid*, 226.

169. The Danaid theme would have been one that any visitor to the Palatine could easily have seen, as it was depicted in the statue group adorning the library of the newly built temple of Apollo Palatinus. See Eckard Lefèvre, *Das Bild-Programm des Apollo-Temples auf dem Palatin*. Konstanzer Althistorische Vorträge und Forschungen, vol. 24, ed. Wolfgang Schuller (Konstanz, 1989). See also Harrison, "The Sword-Belt of Pallas," 227.

170. Putnam, "The Hesitation of Aeneas"; also Putnam, "The Final Lines," 99; Most, "Memory and Forgetting," 154, aptly states: "In Virgil . . . Aeneas' recognition of the dead Pallas' armor will in the end fulfill an emotional function, changing Aeneas' mood from pity to anger and ensuring Turnus' death."

171. Harrison, *Sword-Belt of Pallas*, 240–241. Kellum has pointed out that one of the Danaids was named "Cleopatra"; Barbara Kellum, "Sculptural Programs and Propaganda in Augustan Rome: The Temple of Apollo on the Palatine," in *The Age of Augustus: An Interdisciplinary Conference Held at Brown University April 30–May 2, 1982*, ed. Rudolf Winkes (Archaeologia Transatlantica, 1985), 174. Paul Zanker, "Der Apollotempel auf dem Palatin. Ausstattung und politische Sinnbezüge nach der Schlacht von Actium," in *Città e architettura nella Roma imperiale*. Analecta Romana Instituti Danici, Supplementum 10 (1983): 21–40.

172. Sarah Spence, "Clinching the Text: The Danaids and the End of the *Aeneid*," *Vergilius* 37 (1991): 13. Spence suggests the statue group in the Palatine complex reflected the victory of Actium over Antony and Cleopatra (15). Aeneas' victory over Turnus is justifiable because Turnus represents Antony (16). Yet a victor also implies, as Spence notes, a loser, and no victory is without loss (19). Further see Harrison, "The Sword-Belt of Pallas," 226–227. William S. Anderson's comment still echoes: "Killing Turnus is a

victory for the cause, but not for Aeneas" (*The Art of the* Aeneid [Englewood Cliffs, NJ, 1969], 100).

173. Gian Biagio Conte, *The Rhetoric of Imitation: Genre and Poetic Memory in Virgil and Other Latin Poets*, ed. Charles Segal (Ithaca, 1986), 188–192.

174. M. Cary and H. H. Scullard, *A History of Rome down to the Age of Constantine*, 3rd ed. (London, 1979), 274.

175. Suetonius writes about the phrase, *non acta belli significantem sicut ceteris, sed celeriter confecti notam* ["This referred not to events of the war, like the other inscriptions, but to the speed with which it had been won" (trans. Graves)].

176. The legacy of rhetoric's waning influence is commemorated a little over a century later when Tacitus writes in his *Dialogus* 41.4: *Quid enim opus est longis in senatu sententiis, cum optimi cito consentiant? Quid multis apud populum contionibus, cum de re publica non imperiti et multi deliberent, sed sapientissimus et unus?* ["What is the use of long arguments in the senate, when good citizens agree so quickly? What is the use of one harangue after another on public platforms, when it is not the ignorant multitude that decides a political issue, but a monarch who is the incarnation of wisdom?" (trans. Peterson)].

177. Adam Parry ("The Two Voices of Virgil's *Aeneid*," in *Virgil: A Collection of Critical Essays*, ed. Steele Commager [Englewood Cliffs, NJ, 1966]) once commented that Jupiter "insists on the terrible price one must pay for this glory. More than blood, sweat and tears, something more precious is continually being lost by the necessary process" (120). Karl Galinsky, "Anger of Aeneas," in *Virgil: Critical Assessments of Classical Authors*, ed. Philip Hardie (London, 1999), 449, states it concisely: "Plainly, the corresponding scene in the *Aeneid* could not be more different. Aeneas listens to Turnus' plea, and it makes him hesitate. Humane sensibility and concern are not an ephemeral affair in the *Aeneid*—in contrast to the end of the *Iliad*, for example—but an ongoing characteristic of both the epic and its hero."

6. CONCLUSION: *ANTE ORA PARENTUM*

1. See, e.g., Jacques Lacan, "On a Question Preliminary to Any Possible Treatment of Psychosis," *Écrits, A Selection*, trans. Alan Sheridan (New York, 1977). In this essay, Lacan interprets gaze to be the result of the desire to fill up what is "lacking" in one's mother's physiology (198).

2. From the notes made by Merleau-Ponty in the last few months of his life, published in *The Visible and the Invisible*, trans. Alphonso Lingis (Evanston, IL, 1968), 209.

3. "Eye and Mind," in *Primacy of Perception and Other Essays on Phenomenological Psychology, the Philosophy of Art, History, and Politics*, ed. James M. Edie (Evanston, IL, 1964), 186.

4. Merleau-Ponty, "Eye and Mind," 166.

5. "until at last / Polites falls before his parents' eyes, / within their presence: he pours out his life / in streams of blood" (M. 2.713–716).

6. Suetonius, *Augustus* 43.

7. "and young men set upon / the pyre of death before their fathers' eyes" (M. 6.405–406).

Bibliography

Adams, J. N. *The Latin Sexual Vocabulary*. London, 1982.

Albrecht, Michael von. "The Art of Mirroring in Virgil's *Aeneid*." In vol. 4 of Hardie, *Critical Assessments*, 1-12.

Alföldi, Andreas. *Die Zwei Lorbeerbäume des Augustus*. Bonn, 1973.

Allen, Thomas W., ed. *Homeri Opera*. Vols. 3-4. 2nd ed. Oxford, 1975.

Anderson, William S. "*Aeneid* 11: The Saddest Book." In Perkell, *Reading Vergil's* Aeneid, 195-209.

———. *The Art of the* Aeneid. Englewood Cliffs, NJ, 1969.

———. "The Suppliant Voice and Gesture in Vergil and Ovid's *Metamorphoses*." *ICS* 18 (1993): 163-177.

———. "Trojan, Dardania, Roman: The Power of Epithets in the *Aeneid*." In Anderson and Quartarone, *Approaches*, 53-59.

Anderson, W. S., and Lorina N. Quartarone, eds. *Approaches to Teaching Vergil's* Aeneid. New York, 2002.

Apostle, Hippocrates G. *Aristotle's* Metaphysics. Grinnell, IA, 1979.

Armstrong, David, Jeffrey Fish, Marilyn B. Skinner, and Patricia Johnston, eds. *Vergil, Philodemus, and the Augustans*. Austin, 2004.

Armstrong, Philip. *Shakespeare's Visual Regime: Tragedy, Psychoanalysis, and the Gaze*. New York, 2001.

Austin, R. G., ed. *P. Vergili Maronis Aeneidos Liber Primus*. Oxford, 1971.

———, ed. *P. Vergili Maronis Aeneidos Liber Quartus*. Oxford, 1955.

———, ed. *P. Vergili Maronis Aeneidos Liber Secundus*. Oxford, 1964.

———, ed. *P. Vergili Maronis Aeneidos Liber Sextus*. Oxford, 1977.

Bailey, Cyril, ed. *Titi Lucreti Cari: De Rerum Natura Libri Sex*. Oxford, 1947.

Bandera, C. "Sacrificial Levels in Virgil's *Aeneid*." *Arethusa* 14 (1981): 217-239.

Bandini, Matilde. "Didone, Enea, gli dei e il motivo dell'inganno in Virgilio, *Eneide* IV." *Euphrosyne* 15 (1987): 89-108.

Barchiesi, Alessandro. "Representations of Suffering and Interpretation in the *Aeneid*." In vol. 3 of Hardie, *Critical Assessments*, 324-344.

————. *La traccia del modello: Effetti omerici nella narrazione Virgiliana.* Pisa, 1984.

————. "Virgilian Narrative: Ecphrasis." In Martindale, *Cambridge Companion to Vergil,* 271–281.

Bardon, Henry, and Raoul Verdière, eds. *Vergiliana.* Leiden, 1971.

Beard, Mary, and John Henderson. *Classical Art from Greece to Rome.* Oxford, 2001.

Beres, T. *Die Entstehung der Aeneis.* Wiesbaden, 1982.

Bergmann, Bettina. "The Roman House as Memory Theater: The House of the Tragic Poet in Pompeii." *Art Bulletin* 76 (1994): 225–256.

Berlin, Netta. "War and Remembrance: *Aeneid* 12.554–60 and Aeneas' Memory of Troy." *AJP* 119 (1998): 11–41.

Bettini, Maurizio. "Ghosts of Exile: Doubles and Nostalgia in Vergil's *parva Troia* (*Aeneid* 3.249ff.)." *CA* 16 (1997): 8–33.

Billmayer, K. "Rhetorische Studien zu den Reden in Vergils *Aeneis.*" Diss., Würtzburg, 1932.

Block, Elizabeth. *The Effects of Divine Manifestation on the Reader's Perspective in Vergil's* Aeneid. New York, 1981.

Bömer, Franz. *Rom und Troia.* Baden-Baden, 1951.

Boyd, B. W. "*Non Enarrabile Textum:* Ecphrastic Trespass and Narrative Ambiguity in the *Aeneid.*" *Vergilius* 41 (1995): 71–90.

Boyle, A. J. "The Canonic Text: Virgil's *Aeneid.*" In Boyle, *Roman Epic,* 79–107.

————, ed. *Roman Epic.* London, 1993.

Brenk, F. E. "*Vnum pro multis caput:* Myth, History and Symbolic Imagery in Vergil's Palinurus Incident." *Latomus* 43 (1984): 776–801.

————. "Wind, Waves, Sacrifice, and Treachery: Diodorus, Appian, and the Death of Palinurus in Virgil." *Aevum* 62 (1988): 69–80.

Bright, David F. "Aeneas' Other Nekyia." *Vergilius* 27 (1981): 40–47.

Buchheit, Vinzenz. *Der Anspruch des Dichters in Vergils Georgika.* Impulse der Forschung 8. Darmstadt, 1972.

————. *Von der Entstehung der Aeneis.* Nachr. Der Giessner Hochschulgesellschaft 33. Munich, 1964.

Cairns, Francis. *Virgil's Augustan Epic.* Cambridge, 1989.

Calboli, G. *Enciclopedia Virgiliana* 3. Rome, 1987.

Campbell, David A., ed. and trans. *Greek Lyric.* Vol. 1, *Sappho Alcaeus.* Loeb edition. Cambridge, MA, 1992.

Camps, Anthony. "Lettura del primo libro dell'*Eneide.*" In Gigante, *Lecturae Vergilianae,* 15–30.

Camps, William A. *An Introduction to Virgil's* Aeneid. Oxford, 1960.

Cary, M., and H. H. Scullard. *A History of Rome down to the Age of Constantine.* 3rd ed. London, 1979.

Castriota, David. *The Ara Pacis Augustae and the Imagery of Abundance in Later Greek and Early Roman Imperial Art.* Princeton, 1995.

Chantraine, Pierre. *Dictionnaire étymologique de la langue grecque. Histoire des mots.* Paris, 1968–1974.

————. *La formation des noms en grec ancien.* Paris, 1932; rpt. 1968.

Clark, Raymond, J. "The Reality of Hector's Ghost in Aeneas' Dream." *Latomus* 57.4 (1998): 832–841.

Clarke, John R. *Houses of Roman Italy, 100 B.C.–A.D. 250: Ritual, Space and Decoration.* Berkeley, 1991.

Clausen, Wendell. "An Interpretation of the *Aeneid*." In vol. 4 of Hardie, *Critical Assessments,* 65–73.

————. *Virgil's* Aeneid *and the Tradition of Hellenistic Poetry.* Berkeley, 1987.

————. *Virgil's* Aeneid: *Decorum, Allusion, and Ideology.* Beiträge zur Altertumskunde 162 (Munich, 2002).

Clayton, Barbara. "Lucretius' Erotic Mother: Maternity as a Poetic Device in *De Rerum Natura*." *Helios* 26.1 (1999): 69–84.

Coleman, Robert. "The Gods in the *Aeneid*." In McAuslan and Walcot, *Virgil,* 39–64.

Commager, Steele, ed. *Virgil: A Collection of Critical Essays.* Englewood Cliffs, NJ, 1966.

Conington, John C., and Henry N. Nettleship, eds. *The Works of Virgil.* Hildesheim, 1979.

Conte, Gian Biagio. *The Rhetoric of Imitation: Genre and Poetic Memory in Virgil and Other Latin Poets.* Ed. Charles Segal. Ithaca, NY, 1986.

Cornford, F. M. *From Religion to Philosophy: A Study in the Origins of Western Speculation.* New York, 1957.

Davidson, J. "The Gaze in Polybius' *Histories*." *JRS* 81 (1991): 10–24.

DeGrummond, W. W. "The 'Diana Experience': A Study of the Victims of Diana in Virgil's *Aeneid*." *Collection Latomus* 239 (1997): 158–194.

DeLacy, P. "Distant Views: The Imagery of Lucretius 2." *CJ* 60 (1964): 49–55.

Derrida, Jacques. *Margins of Philosophy.* Trans. Alan Bass. Chicago, 1982.

————. *Writing and Difference.* Chicago, 1978.

Diels, H., and W. Kranz, *Fragmente der Vorsokratiker,* 6th ed. Berlin, 1952.

Dion, Jeanne. *Les passions dans l'oeuvre de Virgile.* Nancy, 1993.

Dolezel, L. *Narrative Modes in Czech Literature.* Toronto, 1973.

Duclos, G. S. "Dido as 'Triformis' Diana." *Vergilius* 15 (1969): 33–41.

Dyson, Julia. "Dido the Epicurean." *CA* 15 (1996): 203–221.

————. *King of the Wood: The Sacrificial Victor in Virgil's* Aeneid. Norman, OK, 2001.

————. "Lilies and Violence: Lavinia's Blush in the Song of Orpheus." *CP* 94 (1999): 281–288.

Edgeworth, Robert J. "Ascanius' Mother." *Hermes* 129 (2001): 246–250.

————. *The Colors of the* Aeneid. American University Studies, Series 17. Classical Languages and Literature. Vol. 12. New York, 1992.

Edie, James M., ed. *The Primacy of Perception and Other Essays on Phenomenological Psychology, the Philosophy of Art, History and Politics.* Evanston, IL, 1964.

Edlund, Ingrid E. M. *The Gods and the Place: Location and Function of Sanctuaries in the Countryside of Etruria and Magna Graecia (700–400 B.C.)* Stockholm, 1987.

Ernout, A., and A. Meillet. *Dictionnaire étymologique de la langue latine: Histoire des mots.* Paris, 1932.

Esrock, Ellen J. *The Reader's Eye: Visual Imaging as Reader Response.* Baltimore, 1994.

Fantham, Elaine. "Fighting Words: Turnus at Bay in the Latin Council (*Aen.* 11.234–446)." *AJP* 120 (1999): 259–280.

Farrell, Joseph. "*Aeneid* 5: Poetry and Parenthood." In Perkell, *Reading Vergil's* Aeneid, 96–110.

———. *Vergil's* Georgics *and the Traditions of Ancient Epic: The Art of Allusion in Literary History.* New York, 1991.

Favro, Diane. *The Urban Image of Augustan Rome.* Cambridge, MA, 1996.

Feeney, Denis C. *The Gods in Epic.* Oxford, 1991.

———. "The Taciturnity of Aeneas." *CQ* n.s. 33 (1983): 204–219.

———. "History and Revelation in Vergil's Underworld." *PCPhS* 212 (1986): 1–24.

Feldherr, Andrew. "Putting Dido on the Map: Genre and Geography in Vergil's Underworld." *Arethusa* 32 (1999): 85–122.

———. "Spectacle and Society in Livy's History." Diss., University of California, Berkeley, 1991 [1998].

Fenik, Bernard. *Typical Battle Scenes in the* Iliad: *Studies in the Narrative Techniques of Homeric Battle Description.* Hermes: Zeitschrift für Klassische Philologie. Ed. Karl Büchner, Hermann Gundert, Herbert Nesselhauf. Einzelschriften 21. Wiesbaden, 1968.

Ferry, David, trans. *The* Eclogues *of Virgil.* New York, 1999.

Finette, L. ed. *Hommages à la memoire de Ernest Pascal.* Cahiers des Etudes Anciennes 24.2 (Montreal, 1990).

Flower, Harriet I. *Ancestor Masks and Aristocratic Power in Roman Culture.* Oxford, 1996.

Fordyce, C. J., ed. *Aeneidos Libri VII–VIII.* Oxford, 1977.

Foster, J. "Three Passages in Virgil." *SO* 66 (1991): 109–114.

Fowler, Don. "Deviant Focalization in Vergil's *Aeneid*." *Proceedings of the Cambridge Philological Society* 216 (1990): 42–63. Rpt. in Fowler, *Roman Constructions*, 40–63.

———. "Narrate and Describe: The Problem of Ekphrasis." *JRS* 81 (1991): 25–35. Rpt. in Fowler, *Roman Constructions*, 64–85.

———. *Roman Constructions: Readings in Postmodern Latin.* Oxford, 2000.

Frangoulidis, Stavros. "Duplicity and Gift-Offerings in Vergil's *Aeneid* 1 and 2." *Vergilius* 38 (1992): 26–37.

Frank, Georgia. *The Memory of the Eyes: Pilgrims to Living Saints in Christian Late Antiquity.* Berkeley, 2000.

Frazer, Sir James George, trans. *Fasti*, rev. G. P. Goold. Loeb edition. Cambridge, MA, 1989.

Fredrick, David, ed. *The Roman Gaze: Vision, Power, and the Body.* Baltimore, 2002.

Frisk, Hjalmar. *Griechisches Etymologisches Wörterbuch.* Vol. 1, Heidelberg, 1954–1960; Vol. 2, Heidelberg, 1961–1970.

Fulkerson, Laurel. "(Un)sympathetic Magic: A Study of *Heroides* 13." *AJP* 123 (2002): 61–87.

Gadamer, Hans-George. *Truth and Method*. Ed. Joel C. Weinsheimer and Donald G. Marshall. New York, 1993.

Gale, Monica R. "Poetry and the Backward Glance in Virgil's *Georgics* and *Aeneid*." *TAPA* 133 (2003): 323–352.

———. *Virgil on the Nature of Things: The* Georgics, Lucretius *and the Didactic Tradition*. Cambridge, 2000.

Galinsky, G. Karl. "The Anger of Aeneas." In Hardie, *Critical Assessments*, 434–457.

———. *Augustan Culture: An Interpretive Introduction*. Princeton, 1996.

———. "The Hercules-Cacus Episode in *Aeneid* VIII." *AJP* 87 (1966): 18–51.

———. *The Herakles Theme: The Adaptations of the Hero in Literature from Homer to the Twentieth Century*. Totowa, NJ, 1972.

Gally, Michèle, and Michel Jourde. *L'Inscription du Regard: Moyen Âge-Renaissance*. Paris, 1995.

Gardner, Helen, ed. *The New Oxford Book of English Verse*. Oxford, 1972.

Genette, Gérard. *Narrative Discourse: An Essay in Method*. Trans. Jane E. Lewin. Ithaca, NY, 1980. Translation of *Figures III: Discours du récit*. Paris, 1972.

Giangrande, Giuseppe. " 'Arte Allusiva' and Alexandrian Poetry." *CQ* n.s. 17 (1967): 85–97.

Giard, J. B. *Bibliothèque nationale: Catalogue des monnaies de l'Empire romain I Auguste*. Paris, 1976; rev. 1988.

Gibson, R. K. "Aeneas as *Hospes* in Vergil, *Aeneid* 1 and 4." *CQ* 49 (1999): 184–202.

Gigante, Marcello, ed. *Lecturae Vergilianae*. Vol. 3, *L'Eneide*. Naples, 1983.

Gillis, Daniel. *Eros and Death in the* Aeneid. Rome, 1983.

Glei, R. "Von Probus zu Pöschl: Vergilinterpretation im Wandel." *Gymnasium* 97 (1990): 321–340.

Gold, Barbara K., ed. *Literary and Artistic Patronage in Ancient Rome*. Austin, TX, 1982.

Gransden, K. W., ed. *Virgil* Aeneid *Book VIII*. Cambridge, 1976.

———. *Virgil* Aeneid *Book XI*. Cambridge, 1991.

Graves, Robert, trans. *Gaius Suetonius Tranquillus, The Twelve Caesars*. New York, 1989.

Grebe, Sabine. *Die vergilische Heldenschau: Tradition und Fortwirken*. Frankfurt am Main, 1989.

Grimm, Richard E. "Aeneas and Andromache in 'Aeneid' III." *AJP* 88 (1967): 151–162.

Gross, Nicolas P. *Amatory Persuasion in Antiquity: Studies in Theory and Practice* (Newark, DE, 1985).

Guthrie, W. K. C. *Greek Philosophers, from Thales to Aristotle*. New York, 1960.

Hardie, Philip. *The Epic Successors of Virgil*. Cambridge, 1993.

———. "*Ut pictura poesis?* Horace and the Visual Arts." In Rudd, *Horace* 2000, 120–139.

————, ed. *Virgil* Aeneid *Book IX.* Cambridge, 1994.

————. *Virgil's* Aeneid: *Cosmos and Imperium.* Oxford, 1986.

————, ed. *Virgil: Critical Assessments of Classical Authors.* 4 vols. London, 1999.

Harrison, E. L. "Divine Action in *Aeneid* Book 2." In Harrison, *Oxford Readings,* 46–59.

Harrison, Stephen J., ed. *Oxford Readings in Vergil's* Aeneid. Oxford, 1990.

————. "The Sword-Belt of Pallas: Moral Symbolism and Political Ideology (*Aen.* 10.495–505)." In Stahl, *Vergil's* Aeneid, 223–242.

————, ed. and trans. *Vergil:* Aeneid *10.* Oxford, 1991.

Hedrick, Charles. *History and Silence: Purge and Rehabilitation of Memory in Late Antiquity.* Austin, TX, 2000.

Heidegger, Martin. *The Question Concerning Technology and Other Essays.* Ed. W. Lovitt. New York, 1977.

Heinze, Richard. *Virgil's Epic Technique.* Trans. David Harvey, Hazel Harvey, and Fred Robertson. Berkeley, 1993.

————. *Virgils Epische Technik.* Stuttgart, 1915; rpt. 1972.

Hershkowitz, Debra. "The *Aeneid* in *Aeneid* 3." *Vergilius* 37 (1991): 69–76.

Heuzé, Philippe. *L'image du corps dans l'oeuvre de Virgile.* Rome, 1985.

————. "*Miratur:* Sur quelques nuances de l'admiration vergilienne." In Finette, *Hommages,* 397–403.

Highet, Gilbert. *The Speeches in Vergil's* Aeneid. Princeton, 1972.

Hofmann, Johann, and Alois Walde. *Lateinisches etymologisches Wörterbuch.* Heidelberg, 1938–1956.

Hornsby, Roger A. "The Vergilian Simile as Means of Judgment." In Quinn, *Why Vergil?,* 80–89.

Horsfall, Nicholas. "Aeneas the Colonist." *Vergilius* 35 (1989): 8–26.

————. *A Companion to the Study of Virgil.* Leiden, 2000.

————. *Virgil,* Aeneid *7: A Commentary.* Leiden, 2000.

Hunt, J. William. *Forms of Glory: Structure and Sense in Virgil's* Aeneid. Carbondale, IL, 1973.

Ingarden, Roman. *Cognition of the Literary Work of Art.* Trans. Ruth A. Crowley and Kenneth R. Olsen. Evanston, IL, 1974.

Jackson, Steven. "Callimachean Istrus and Odysseus' Mother." *WS* 112 (1999): 55–58.

Jaeger, Mary. *Livy's Written Rome.* Ann Arbor, 1997.

Jaeger, W., ed. *Aristotelis Metaphysica,* 980a22–25. Oxford, 1957.

Jay, Martin. *Downcast Eyes: The Denigration of Vision in Twentieth-Century French Thought.* Berkeley, 1993.

Johnson, Galen A. *Earth and Sky, History and Philosophy: Island Images Inspired by Husserl and Merleau-Ponty.* New York, 1989.

————. *The Merleau-Ponty Aesthetics Reader: Philosophy and Painting.* Evanston, IL, 1993.

Johnson, W. R. *Darkness Visible.* Berkeley, 1976.

Johnston, Patricia. "Dido, Berenice and Arsinoe: *Aeneid* 6.460." *AJP* 108 (1987): 649–654.

Kahil, Lilly. "Helen." *LIMC* 4.1, 532. Zurich, 1981–1997.

Kahn, Akbar. "The Boy at the Banquet: Dido and Amor in Vergil *Aen.* 1." *Athenaeum* 90 (2002): 187–205.

———. "Exile and the Kingdom: Creusa's Revelations and Aeneas' Departure from Troy." *Latomus* 60 (2001): 906–915.

Keats, John. *The Poems of John Keats*, ed. Jack Stillinger. Cambridge, MA, 1978.

Kellum, Barbara. "The City Adorned: Programmatic Display at the Aedes Concordia Augustae." In Raaflaub and Toher, *Between Republic and Empire*, 276–307.

———. "Sculptural Programs and Propaganda in Augustan Rome: The Temple of Apollo on the Palatine." In Winkes, *Age of Augustus*, 159–176.

Kennedy, George. *The Art of Rhetoric in the Roman World 300 BC–AD 300.* Princeton, 1972.

Kirk, G. S., and J. E. Raven. *The Presocratic Philosophers: A Critical History with a Selection of Texts.* Cambridge, 1957 [2nd ed., 1983].

Klausen, Heinrich. *Aeneas und die Penaten.* 2 vols. Hamburg, 1839.

Klingner, Friedrich. *Virgil: Bucolica, Georgica, Aeneis.* Zurich, 1967.

Knauer, Georg Nicolaus. *Die Aeneis und Homer: Studien zur poetischen Technik Vergils, mit Listen der Homerzitate in der Aeneis.* Göttingen, 1964.

Knox, Peter E. "A Note on *Aeneid* 1.613." *CP* 79 (1984): 304–305.

Kraggerud, E. "Caeneus und der Heroinenkatalog, Aeneis VI 440 ff." *SO* 40 (1965): 66–71.

Kubelik, M., and E. Swartz, eds. *Von der Bauforschung zur Denkmalpflege: Festschrift für Alois Machatschek.* Vienna, 1993.

Kühn, Werner. *Götterzenen bei Vergil.* Bibliothek der klass. Altertumswissenschaft NF 2 Reihe 41. Heidelberg, 1971.

Kuttner, Ann. *Dynasty and Empire in the Age of Augustus: The Case of the Boscoreale Cups.* Berkeley, 1995.

Kyriakou, Poulheria. "Aeneas' Dream of Hector." *Hermes* 127 (1999): 317–327.

Lacan, Jacques. *Écrits, A Selection.* Trans. Alan Sheridan. New York, 1977.

Lattimore, Richmond, trans. *Homer the* Odyssey. New York, 1975.

———, trans. *The* Iliad *of Homer.* Chicago, 1951.

Leach, Eleanor Winsor. "Patrons, Painters, and Patterns: The Anonymity of Romano-Campanian Painting and the Transition from the Second to the Third Style." In Gold, *Literary and Artistic Patronage*, 135–173.

———. "Viewing the *Spectacula* of Aeneid 6." In Perkell, *Reading Vergil's* Aeneid, 111–127.

Lee, M. Owen, S. J. *Fathers and Sons in Virgil's* Aeneid: *Tum Genitor Natum.* Albany, 1979.

———. "Seven Suffering Heroines and Seven Surrogate Sons." In McKay, Wilhelm, and Jones, *Two Worlds of the Poet*, 82–91.

Lefèvre, Eckard. *Das Bild-Programm des Apollo-Temples auf dem Palatin.* Konstanzer Althistorische Vorträge und Forschungen. Ed. Wolfgang Schuller. Vol. 24. Konstanz, 1989.

————. "Das Bild-Programm des Apollo-Tempels auf dem Palatin." *Gymnasium* 98 (1991): 84–85.

Leigh, Matthew. *Lucan: Spectacle and Engagement.* Oxford, 1997.

Lessing, Gotthold Ephraim. *Laocoon: An Essay on the Limits of Painting and Poetry.* Trans. Edward A. McCormick. Baltimore, 1990.

Leumann, Manu. "S. 250 Fr." *Gnomon* 13 (1937): 33.

Levinas, Immanuel. *Totality and Infinity: An Essay on Exteriority.* Trans. Alphonso Lingis. Duquesne Studies 24. Pittsburgh, 1969.

Ling, Roger. *Roman Painting.* Cambridge, MA, 1991.

Lloyd, Charles. "The Evander-Anchises Connection: Fathers, Sons, and Homoerotic Desire in Vergil's *Aeneid.*" *Vergilius* 45 (1999): 3–21.

Lynch, J. P. "Laocoön and Sinon: Virgil, *Aeneid* 2.40–198." In Hardie, *Critical Assessments*, 76–84.

Lyne, R. O. A. M. *Further Voices in Vergil's* Aeneid. Oxford, 1987.

————. *Horace: Behind the Public Poetry.* New Haven, CT, 1995.

————. *Words and the Poet: Characteristic Techniques of Style in Vergil's* Aeneid. Oxford, 1989.

Lyotard, Jean-Francois. *Discours, Figure.* Paris, 1985.

Mack, Sara. *Patterns of Time in Vergil.* Hamden, CT, 1978.

Mackie, C. J. "*Nox Erat* . . . : Sleep and Visions in the *Aeneid.*" *G&R* 38 (1991): 59–61.

————. *The Characterisation of Aeneas.* Edinburgh, 1988.

Maleuvre, J.-Y. "Porte d'ivoire et Rameau d'Or: éléments de cacozelie dans le sixième livre de *l'Énéide.*" *Revue des Études Anciennes* 98 (1996): 91–107.

Martindale, Charles, ed. *The Cambridge Companion to Vergil.* Cambridge, 1997.

Mau, August. *Pompeii: Its Life and Art.* Trans. Francis W. Kelsey. Washington, DC, 1973.

Mayer, Roland. "The Ivory Gate Revisited." *Proceedings of the Virgil Society* 21 (1993): 53–63.

McAuslan, Ian, and Peter Walcot, eds. *Virgil.* Oxford, 1990.

McDermott, William C. "Drances/Cicero." *Vergilius* 26 (1980): 34–38.

McKay, Alexander Gordon, Robert M. Wilhelm, and Howard Jones, eds. *Two Worlds of the Poet: New Perspectives on Vergil.* Detroit, 1992.

Merleau-Ponty, Maurice. "Eye and Mind." In Edie, *Primacy of Perception,* 159–190.

————. "The Metaphysical Man." In Merleau-Ponty, *Sense and Non-sense,* 83–98.

————. "Primacy of Perception and Its Philosophical Consequences." In Edie, *Primacy of Perception,* 12–42.

————. *Sense and Non-sense.* Trans. Hubert L. Dreyfus and Patricia Allen Dreyfus. Evanston, IL, 1964.

————. *Signs.* Trans. Richard C. McCleary. Evanston, IL, 1964.

————. *The Structure of Behavior.* Trans. Alden L. Fisher. Boston, 1963.

————. *The Visible and the Invisible.* Trans. Alphonso Lingis. Evanston, IL, 1968.

Merrill, William A., ed. *T. Lucreti Cari De Rerum Natura.* New York, 1907.

Mitchell, W. T. J. *Iconology: Image, Text, Ideology.* Chicago, 1986.

Monro, David B., and Thomas W. Allen, eds. *Homeri Opera.* 4 vols. 3rd ed. Oxford, 1978.

Monti, Richard C. *The Dido Episode and the* Aeneid: *Roman Social and Political Values in the Epic. Mnemosyne.* Suppl. 66. Leiden, 1981.

Moorton, Richard F. "Love as Death: The Pivoting Metaphor in Vergil's Story of Dido." *CW* 83 (1990): 153–166.

Morgan, Llewelyn. "Assimilation and Civil War: Hercules and Cacus (*Aen.* 8.185-267)." In Stahl, *Vergil's* Aeneid, 175-197.

———. *Patterns of Redemption in Virgil's* Georgics. New York, 1999.

Mortensen, Kate. "Eurydice: Demonic or Devoted Mother." *AHB* 6.4 (1992): 156.

Moskalew, Walter. *Formular Language and Poetic Design in the* Aeneid. *Mnemosyne,* Suppl. 73. Leiden, 1982.

Most, Glenn. "Memory and Forgetting in the *Aeneid.*" *Vergilius* 47 (2001): 148-170.

Nelis, Damien. *Vergil's* Aeneid *and the* Argonautica *of Apollonius Rhodius.* ARCA Classical and Medieval Texts, Papers and Monographs 39. Leeds, 2001.

Nelson, Tamar R. M. E. "Deception, Gods and Goddesses in Homer's *Iliad.*" *Acta Ant. Hung.* 37 (1996/1997): 181-197.

Neuhauser, Walter. *Patronus und Orator.* Innsbruck, 1958.

Newlands, Carole Elizabeth. *Playing with Time: Ovid and the* Fasti. Ithaca, NY, 1995.

Nietzsche, Friedrich. "Beyond Good and Evil." In Wright, *Philosophy of Nietzsche,* 369-616.

Norden, Eduard. *P. Vergilius Maro: Aeneas Buch VI,* 4th ed. Darmstadt, 1957.

———. "Ein Panegyricus auf Augustus in Vergils Aeneis." *RhM* 54 (1899): 466-482. Rpt. in *Kleine Schriften zum klassichen Altertum.* Berlin, 1966.

O'Hara, James J. *Death and the Optimistic Prophecy in Vergil's* Aeneid. Princeton, 1990.

———. *True Names: Vergil and the Alexandrian Tradition of Etymological Wordplay.* Ann Arbor, 1996.

Oliensis, Ellen. "Freud's *Aeneid.*" *Vergilius* 47 (2001): 39-63.

Otis, Brooks. *Virgil: A Study in Civilized Poetry.* Oxford, 1963.

Page, T. E. *The* Aeneid *of Virgil: Books VII-XII.* London, 1900; rpt. 1959.

Papillon, T. I., and A. E. Haigh, eds. *P. Vergili Maronis Opera.* 2 vols. Oxford, 1892.

Parry, Adam. "The Two Voices of Virgil's *Aeneid.*" In Commager, *Virgil,* 107-123.

Paschalis, Michael. *Virgil's* Aeneid: *Semantic Relations and Proper Names.* Oxford, 1997.

Pease, Arthur S., ed. *Publi Vergili Aeneidos Liber Quartus.* Cambridge, MA, 1935.

Pelling, Christopher. *Plutarch and History.* Llandysul, Wales, 2002.

Perkell, Christine, ed. *Reading Vergil's* Aeneid: *An Interpretive Guide.* Norman, OK, 1999.

Perkins, Anne Peper. "Divine Epiphany in Epic: Supernatural Episodes in the 'Iliad,' the 'Odyssey,' the 'Aeneid,' and 'Paradise Lost.'" Diss., Washington University, 1986.

Perotti, A. "De diis in *Aeneide*." *Latinitas* 38 (1990): 10–24.

Perret, Jacques. "Les compagnes de Didon aux Enfers." *REL* 42 (1964): 247–261.

———. "Les Dieux de l'*Eneide*." *AFL Nice* 50 (1985): 331–337.

Peterson, Sir William. *The Dialogus of Publius Cornelius*. Ed. T. E. Page. Loeb edition. Cambridge, MA, 1932.

Pokorny, Julius. *Indogermanisches Etymologisches Wörterbuch*. 2 vols. Munich, 1959.

Polk, Gail Cecilia. "Vergil's Penelope: The Diana Simile in *Aeneid* 1.498–502." *Vergilius* 42 (1996): 38–49.

Pollini, J. "The Acanthus of the Ara Pacis as an Apolline and Dionysiac Symbol of *Anamorphosis, Anakyklosis and umen Mixtum*." In Kubelik and Swartz, *Von der Bauforschung zur Denkmalpflege*, 182–217.

Pöschl, Viktor. *The Art of Vergil: Image and Symbol in the* Aeneid. Trans. Gerda Seligson. Ann Arbor, 1962.

Prier, Raymond A. Thauma Idesthai: *The Phenomenology of Sight and Appearance in Archaic Greek*. Tallahassee, FL, 1989.

Putnam, Michael C. J. "*Aeneid* 12: Unity and Closure." In Perkell, *Reading Vergil's* Aeneid, 210–230.

———. "Anger, Blindness, and Insight in Virgil's *Aeneid*." In Putnam, *Virgil's* Aeneid, 170–200.

———. *Artifices of Eternity: Horace's Fourth Book of Odes*. Ithaca, NY, 1986.

———. "The Hesitation of Aeneas." In Putnam, *Virgil's* Aeneid, 152–171.

———. "Pius Aeneas and the Metamorphosis of Lausus." In Putnam, *Virgil's* Aeneid, 134–151.

———. *Tibullus: A Commentary*. Norman, OK, 1973.

———. *Virgil's* Aeneid: *Interpretation and Influence*. Chapel Hill, 1995.

———. "Virgil's *Aeneid:* The Final Lines." In Spence, *Poets and Critics*, 86–104.

———. *Virgil's Epic Designs: Ekphrasis in the* Aeneid. New Haven, CT, 1998.

———. "Wrathful Aeneas and the Tactics of *Pietas* in Virgil, Ovid, and Lucan." In Putnam, *Virgil's* Aeneid, 201–245.

Quinn, Kenneth. *Virgil's* Aeneid: *A Critical Description*. Ann Arbor, 1969.

Quinn, Stephanie, ed. *Why Vergil? A Collection of Interpretations*. Wauconda, IL, 2000.

Quint, David. *Epic and Empire: Politics and Generic Form from Virgil to Milton*. Princeton, 1993.

———. "Painful Memories: *Aeneid* 3 and the Problem of the Past." *CJ* 78 (1982): 30–38.

Raaflaub, K., and M. Toher, eds. *Between Republic and Empire: Interpretations of Augustus and His Principate*. Berkeley, 1993.

Rakoczy, Thomas. *Böser Blick, Macht des Auges und Neid der Götter: Eine Untersuchung zur Kraft des Blickes in der griechischen Literatur*. Classica Monacensia 13. Tübingen, 1996.

Reckford, Kenneth. "Recognizing Venus (I): Aeneas Meets His Mother." *Arion* ser. 3, vol. 3 (1995–1996): 1–42.

Reiff, A. *"Imitatio, aemulatio, interpretatio."* Diss., Köln, 1958.

Richardson, L., jr. *New Topographical Dictionary of Ancient Rome.* Baltimore, MD, 1992.

Ricottilli, Licinia. *Gesto e Parola nell'*Eneide. Bologna, 2000.

Rolfe, J. C., trans. *Suetonius.* Loeb edition. Cambridge, MA, 1979.

Roscher, W. H., ed. *Ausführliches Lexikon der Griechischen und Römischen Mythologie.* Leipzig, 1884–1887.

Ross, David O. *Virgil's Elements: Physics and Poetry in the* Georgics. Princeton, 1987.

Rudd, Niall. "Dido's Culpa." In Harrison, *Oxford Readings,* 145–166.

———, ed. *Horace 2000: A Celebration: Essays for the Bimillennium.* Ann Arbor, 1993.

Russell, D. A., and M. Winterbottom, *Ancient Literary Criticism: The Principal Texts in New Translations.* Oxford, 1972.

Rutledge, Harry C. "Pius Aeneas: A Study of Vergil's Portrait." *Vergilius* 33 (1987): 14–20.

Sartre, Jean-Paul. *The Words.* Trans. Bernard Frechtman. New York, 1964.

Schlunk, Robin. *The Homeric Scholia and the* Aeneid: *A Study of the Influence of Ancient Homeric Literary Criticism on Vergil.* Ann Arbor, 1974.

Seaton, R. C., trans. *Apollonius Rhodius: The* Argonautica. Loeb edition. Cambridge, MA, 1912; rpt. 1980.

Segal, Charles. "Art and the Hero: Participation, Detachment, and Narrative Point of View in *Aen.* 1." *Arethusa* 14 (1981): 67–83.

———. "Art and Hero." In Hardie, *Critical Assessments,* 42–57.

Sharrock, Alison R. "Looking at Looking: Can You Resist a Reading?" In Fredrick, *The Roman Gaze,* 265–296.

Shepherd, W. G., trans. *Horace: The Complete Odes and Epodes with the Centennial Hymn.* London, 1983.

Skinner, Marilyn. "The Last Encounter of Dido and Aeneas: *Aen.* 6.450–476." *Vergilius* 29 (1983): 12–18.

Skulsky, Susan. "*'Invitus, Regina . . .'*: Aeneas and the Love of Rome." *AJP* 106 (1985): 447–455.

Skutsch, Otto, ed. *The* Annals *of Q. Ennius.* Oxford, 1985.

Small, Jocelyn Penny. *Wax Tablets of the Mind: Cognitive Studies of Memory and Literacy in Classical Antiquity.* London, 1997.

Smith, Michael B., and Galen A. Johnson, eds. *Ontology and Alterity in Merleau-Ponty.* Evanston, IL, 1990.

Smith, R. A. "A Lock and a Promise: Myth and Allusion in Aeneas' Farewell to Dido in *Aen.* 6." *Phoenix* 47 (1993): 305–312.

———. *Poetic Allusion and Poetic Embrace in Ovid and Virgil.* Ann Arbor, 1997.

———. Review of Galinsky, *Augustan Culture. BMCR* 97.2.24.

Spence, Sarah. "Clinching the Text: The Danaids and the End of the *Aeneid.*" *Vergilius* 37 (1991): 11–19.

———, ed. *Poets and Critics Read Virgil.* New Haven, CT, 2001.

———. *Rhetoric of Reason and Desire: Vergil, Augustine, and the Trouba-dours*. Ithaca, NY, 1988.

Stahl, Hans-Peter. "Aeneas—An '(Un)heroic' Hero?" *Arethusa* 14 (1981): 157–177.

———, ed. *Vergil's* Aeneid: *Augustan Epic and Political Context*. London, 1998.

Staley, Gregory A. "Aeneas' First Act, 1.180–94." In Quinn, *Why Vergil?*, 52–64.

Starks, J. H. "*Fides Aeneia:* The Transference of Punic Stereotypes in the *Aeneid.*" *CJ* 94 (1999): 255–284.

Sullivan, F. A. "*Tendere Manus:* Gestures in the *Aeneid.*" *CJ* 63.8 (1967–1968): 358–362.

Sutton, E. W., trans. *Cicero* De Oratore. 2 vols. Loeb edition. Cambridge, MA, 1942.

Tatum, James. "Allusion and Interpretation in *Aeneid* 6.440–76." *AJP* 105 (1984): 434–452.

Thomas, Richard. *Virgil and the Augustan Reception*. Cambridge, 2001.

———, ed. *Virgil:* Georgics. 2 vols. Cambridge, 1988.

———. "Virgil's Ekphrastic Centerpieces." *HSCP* 87 (1983): 175–184.

———. "Virgil's *Georgics* and the Art of Reference." *HSCP* 90 (1986): 171–198.

Thornton, Agathe. *The Living Universe: Gods and Men in Virgil's* Aeneid. *Mnemosyne* ser. Lugdunum, 1976.

Todd, Ruth N. "Lavinia Blushed." *Vergilius* 26 (1980): 27–33.

Traina, A. "Suberbia." *Enciclopedia Virgiliana* 4. Rome, 1988.

Walde, Alois, and Julius Pokorny. *Vergleichendes Wörtbuch der Indogermanischen Sprachen*. Berlin, 1927–1932.

Warmington, E. H., ed. and trans. *Remains of Old Latin*. 4 vols. Loeb edition. Cambridge, MA, 1956; rpt. 1979.

West, David A. "*Cernere erat:* The Shield of Aeneas." *PVS* 15 (1975–1976): 1–6; rpt. in Harrison, *Oxford Readings*, 224–238.

West, David A., and A. J. Woodman. *Creative Imitation in Latin Literature*. Cambridge, 1979.

West, Grace Starry. "Caeneus and Dido." *TAPA* 110 (1980): 315–324.

———. "The Significance of Vergil's Eriphyle (*Aeneid* 6.445–446)." *Vergilius* 26 (1980): 52–54.

White, Peter. *Promised Verse: Poets in the Society of Augustan Rome*. Cambridge, MA, 1993.

Wilhelm, Michelle. "Venus, Diana, Dido, and Camilla in the *Aeneid.*" *Vergilius* 33 (1987): 43–48.

Wilkinson, L. P. *The* Georgics *of Virgil*. Cambridge, 1969; rpt., 1997.

———, trans. *Virgil: The* Georgics. Middlesex, England, 1982.

Williams, Gordon. *Technique and Ideas in the* Aeneid. New Haven, CT, 1983.

———. *Tradition and Originality in Roman Poetry*. Oxford, 1968.

Williams, R. D., ed. *The* Aeneid *of Virgil*. 2 vols. New York, 1972.

———. "Dido's Reply to Aeneas." In Bardon and Verdière, *Vergiliana*, 422–428.

————, ed. *P. Vergili Maronis Aeneidos Liber Quintus.* Oxford, 1960.

Wills, Jeffrey. "Divided Allusion: Virgil and the *Coma Berenices.*" *HSCP* 98 (1998): 277–305.

Wilson, Donna F. *Ransom, Revenge, and Heroic Identity in the* Iliad. Cambridge, 2002.

Wiltshire, S. F. "The Man Who Was Not There." In Perkell, *Reading Vergil's Aeneid,* 162–177.

Winkes, Rudolf, ed. *The Age of Augustus: An Interdisciplinary Conference Held at Brown University, April 30–May 2, 1982.* Archaeologia Transatlantica 5 (1985).

Wlosok, Antonie. *Die Göttin Venus in Vergils Aeneis.* Bibliothek der Klass. Altertumswissenschaft. NF 2 Reihe 21. Heidelberg, 1967.

Woodford, Sam. *LIMC* VI.1 (68), 579, s.v. Minotauros. Zurich, 1981–1997.

Woodman, Tony, and Jonathan Powell, eds. *Author and Audience in Latin Literature.* Cambridge, 1992.

Worman, Nancy. "The Body as Argument: Helen in Four Greek Texts." *CA* 16 (1997): 151–203.

Worstbrock, F. J. *Elemente einer Poetik der Aeneis. Orbis Antiquus.* Münster, 1963.

Wright, Willard H., ed. *The Philosophy of Nietzsche.* Trans. Helen Zimmern. New York, 1954.

Yates, Frances A. *The Art of Memory.* Chicago, 1966.

Zanker, Paul. "Der Apollotempel auf dem Palatin. Ausstattung und politische Sinnbezüge nach der Schlacht von Actium." In *Città e architettura nella Roma imperiale.* Analecta Romana Instituti Danici, Supplementum 10 (1983): 21–40.

————. *The Power of Images in the Age of Augustus.* Ann Arbor, 1988.

Subject Index

Index Locorum